SOBER INTOXICATION OF THE SPIRIT

Sober Intoxication of the Spirit

FILLED WITH THE FULLNESS OF GOD

RANIERO CANTALAMESSA, O.F.M. Cap.

Translated by Marsha Daigle-Williamson, Ph.D.

servant
AN IMPRINT OF
FRANCISCAN MEDIA
Cincinnati, Ohio

Scripture passages have been taken from *New Revised Standard Version Bible,* copyright ©1989 by the Division of Christian Education of the National Council of the Churches of Christ in the U.S.A., and used by permission. All rights reserved.

Cover design by Candle Light Studios
Book design by Phillips Robinette, o.f.m.

Library of Congress Cataloging-in-Publication Data

Cantalamessa, Raniero.
  [Sobria ebbrezza dello Spirito. English]
  Sober intoxication of the Spirit : filled with the fullness of God / by Raniero Cantalamessa ; translated by Marsha Daigle-Williamson.
    p. cm.
  ISBN 0-86716-713-0 (pbk. : alk. paper)
  1. Pentecostalism—Catholic Church—Meditations.   I. Title.
BX2350.57C3613 2005
234'.1—dc22
                                2005015042

ISBN-13: 978-0-86716-713-9
ISBN-10: 0-86716-713-0

Published by Servant, an imprint of Franciscan Media
28 W. Liberty St.
Cincinnati, OH 45202
www.FranciscanMedia.org

CONTENTS

This book is a collection of teachings and meditations given at national and international meetings of the Catholic Charismatic Renewal. The only exception is the last chapter ("We Were All Made to Drink of One Spirit") which was a meditation delivered to Pope John Paul II's Pontifical Household and the Roman Curia.

The chapters relate to different phases of the Catholic Charismatic Renewal from its beginnings to the present, which explains the varying tones and some unavoidable repetitions of the same theme.

I dedicate this book first and foremost to my brothers and sisters in the Catholic Charismatic Renewal because much of it was born of their prayer and their inspiring love for the Word of God. "The charismatic renewal," or, as we say in Italy, "the renewal in the Spirit," describes the special grace diffused in the Catholic Church after the Second Vatican Council. More significantly, it also describes the path of salvation presented in Scripture to the whole Church and to every believer: "He saved us, not because of any works of righteousness that we had done, but according to his mercy, through the water of rebirth and renewal by the Holy Spirit" (Titus 3:5).

Because of that, the reflections in this book are not intended for just one particular ecclesial group but for all those who feel a need to open their lives more fully to the powerful breath of the Spirit which is blowing through the Church today "as in a new Pentecost."

I am grateful to St. Anthony Messenger Press and to Servant Books for the opportunity to share these reflections with my brothers and sisters in the United States and in other English-speaking countries with whom I have shared so many times of deep prayer and joyful proclamation of the gospel. I am also glad to share these reflections because I am indebted to them: it was in the United States—New Jersey, to be precise—that in 1977 I myself received the grace of "the baptism of the Spirit."

CHAPTER ONE

"Let Us Drink the Sober Intoxication of the Spirit with Joy!"

In 1975, the day after Pentecost, at the close of the World Congress of the Catholic Charismatic Renewal, Pope Paul VI delivered an address to the ten thousand participants in St. Peter's Basilica. After reading his official address, the Pope spontaneously added:

> In the fourth-century hymn by St. Ambrose that we read this morning in the breviary, there is a simple phrase that is difficult to translate: *Laeti*, which means "with joy," *bibamus*, which means, "let us drink," *sobriam*, which means "sober"or "temperate," *profusionem Spiritus*, which means "the abundant outpouring of the Spirit." *Laeti bibamus sobriam profusionem Spiritus.* This could be the motto for your movement: its plan as well as a description of the movement itself.[1]

The Church has thus outlined a plan for us through the words of her chief pastor. We cannot ignore one word of this text, and we should seek to deepen our understanding of its meaning as a whole, especially the meaning of the Latin words referring to the "sober outpouring" or "intoxication of the Spirit."

"Sober Intoxication" in the Fathers of the Church

The Pope indicated where he had found this idea: in the writings of Saint Ambrose, one of the Fathers of the Church, that inexhaustible treasure house of the living tradition of the Church. I would like to lead you through that treasury of Tradition to discover what the Fathers of the Church meant when they spoke of "the sober intoxication of the Spirit." Was this the idea of an isolated bishop or something more than that?

In looking for the answer to that question, I made a surprising discovery. There was a time in the life of the Church—for about a century—when all of Christendom was experiencing a spiritual intoxication, an inebriation of the Holy Spirit. Several voices from this chorus of Tradition can help us understand the kind of intoxication the Pope meant in his address.

In 348 the bishop of Jerusalem, Cyril, commenting on the words of Peter at Pentecost—"These are not drunk, as you suppose" (Acts 2:15)—said to the catechumens:

> They are not drunk in the way you might think. They are indeed drunk, but with the sober intoxication (*nephalios methē*) which kills sin and gives life to the

2

heart and which is the opposite of physical drunkenness. Drunkenness makes a person forget what he knows; this kind, instead, brings understanding of things that were not formerly known. They are drunk insofar as they have drunk the wine of that mystical vine which affirms, "I am the vine, you are the branches" (John 15:5).[2]

The inebriation that comes from the Holy Spirit thus purifies of sin, renews the heart in fervor and enlightens the mind by a special knowledge of God—not a rational but an intuitive, experiential knowledge, accompanied by inner joy.

From Jerusalem let's go to Milan. The Pope used a verse from a hymn of Saint Ambrose, but this is not the only time that this bishop of Milan spoke of a sober intoxication of the Spirit. Preaching to neophytes he said:

> Every time you drink, you receive the remission of sins and you become intoxicated with the Spirit. It is in that sense that the Apostle said, "Do not get drunk with wine...but be filled with the Spirit" (Ephesians 5:18). He who becomes intoxicated with wine staggers, but he who becomes intoxicated with the Holy Spirit is rooted in Christ. How truly excellent is this intoxication which produces the sobriety of the soul![3]

The Christians in Milan had the same experience as did those in Jerusalem: The Holy Spirit, when received in the sacraments and especially in the Eucharist, gives the soul a kind of intoxication that has nothing disordered or superficial about it. Rather this intoxication takes the soul beyond its normal experience, beyond its poverty and powerlessness, into a state of grace where there is no room for doubts, regrets or self-absorption but only for joy and thanksgiving. The soul is rooted in Christ.

"The Golden Age of the Church"

Another voice from Tradition, Saint Augustine, counsels Christians newly baptized on Easter:

> The Holy Spirit has come to abide in you; do not make him withdraw; do not exclude him from your heart in any way. He is a good guest; He found you empty and He filled you; He found you hungry and He satisfied you; He found you thirsty and He has intoxicated you. May He truly intoxicate you! The Apostle said, "Do not be drunk with wine which leads to debauchery." Then, as if to clarify what we should be intoxicated with, he adds, "But be filled with the Spirit, addressing one another in psalms and hymns and spiritual songs, singing and making melody to the Lord with all your heart" (see Ephesians 5:18ff). Doesn't a person who rejoices in the Lord and sings to Him exuberantly seem like a person who is drunk? I like this kind of intoxication. The Spirit of God is both drink and light.[4]

Saint Augustine asked himself why Scripture had used such a daring image as intoxication. He concluded that it is because only the state of a man who has drunk so much as to lose his mind can give us an idea—even though it is a negative one—of what happens to the human mind when it receives the ineffable joy of the Holy Spirit. The mind recedes and becomes divine, becoming intoxicated with the abundance in the house of God, i.e., tasting something of the goodness that is to come in the heavenly Jerusalem.[5] When spiritually intoxicated, a person is out of his mind not because he is bereft of reason, as is the case with wine or drugs, but because he passes beyond reason into the light of God.

These quotations from Tradition are enough to give us an idea of the understanding of Christian life at that time. Notice that the remarks did not apply to the life of a privileged few, the mystics, but applied to all baptized believers. (The remarks were normally made to catechumens and neophytes!) We are clearly dealing with a charismatic Christianity in which people fervently believed, along with all of the New Testament, that *grace* is the beginning of *glory* and makes possible even now a kind of direct experience of God.

The pastors of the Church, far from being afraid of this enthusiasm and trying to rein it in, nourished it and became its promoters and its pastoral guides. Historians generally call this the golden age of Church history, but they do not seem to wonder where this extraordinary flowering of genius in the Church came from, that is, the magnificent doctrines in the writings of the Fathers, that incomparable ability to spiritually read the Scripture so as to draw out nourishing food for the life of the whole people of God.

All of that happened because the Holy Spirit flowed freely in the Church—like honey in a honeycomb, to use an image that was well known at the time. Required procedures (the channels of grace!) had not yet been rigidly institutionalized by human treatises, laws and canons. The confidence of the Church was not in the efficiency of its organization—in being a perfect society—but in the presence of the Holy Spirit in her midst. The Church was a spiritual society, a body animated by the Holy Spirit while visibly structured around the bishops.

The complete and definitive acknowledgement of the divinity of the Holy Spirit that occurred at this time gave the Church—almost as a reward—the experience of a "new Pentecost." This was a time when a bishop (and not just a simple theologian!) like Gregory of Nazianzen could exclaim to his people:

> How long are we going to keep our light hidden under a bushel? Now is the time to set the light [the Holy Spirit!] in the lampstand so that it can give light to the whole church, to souls, and to the whole world.[6]

Less than two years later, in the Ecumenical Council at Constantinople in 381, the profession of faith in the full divinity of the Holy Spirit finally entered into the Apostles' Creed; the great light was placed on the highest lampstand of the Church.

Troubles, however, were many at that time, and some were serious: heresies, conflicts between churches and minor schisms. These did not stop the work of God or cause the Church to retreat. In Saint Paul's words, the Church was more than a conqueror, thanks to the One— the Holy Spirit—who comforted her, who gave her strength and consolation. It was as though there was a fiery volcano at the center of the Church, which purified and cleansed everything with its molten lava and did not allow the weeds created by the sins of human beings to grow on its slopes.

When Paul VI proposed the ideal of a sober intoxication, the highest leader of the Church was asking us—as well as all Christians—to revive an experience of spiritual enthusiasm in today's Christianity similar to that which made the fourth century the golden age of Christian history.

Spiritual Sobriety in the New Testament

The Fathers of the Church spoke about intoxication, but they did not elaborate very much on what they meant by "sober." Rather they referred to Scripture itself, which often speaks of the virtue of sobriety or temperance. It was clear to them what "a sober intoxication" meant because they were using the same language as the Bible; their words had the same meaning as they had for Paul.

This is not the case for us. We have lost the sense of that combination of attitudes that the Bible calls sobriety. The meaning of this word has been reduced to a vague kind of moderation in speaking or in drinking. We must therefore rediscover its meaning, examining the New Testament with the help of the Holy Spirit.

"Sober"(*sōphrōn*) simply means "healthy," "whole" or "prudent." In the Bible, however, the word signifies something more than simple common sense, balance or self-control. In Romans Paul says, "Do not be haughty [*phronyntes*], but associate with the lowly; never be conceited [*phronimoi*]" (see Romans 12:16). In this text being sober is the equivalent of being humble, of not exalting oneself, of keeping a realistic sense of one's limitations, of not forgetting that everything is a gift and that every good thing has been received (see 1 Corinthians 4:7). So, "let the one who boasts, boast in the Lord" (1 Corinthians 1:31).

Elsewhere Paul speaks about moderation when dealing with the "pneumatics," that is, the charismatics who, in their enthusiasm for the Holy Spirit and for His powerful manifestations, have a tendency to let themselves drift into a certain kind of quietism or into superficiality, thus neglecting active participation in the community:

> For if we are beside ourselves [thus, intoxication or spiritual ecstasy], it is for God; if we are in our right mind [sober], it is for you. For the love of Christ urges us on, because we are convinced that one has died for all; therefore all have died. And he died for all, so that those who live might live no longer for themselves, but for him who died and was raised for them. (2 Corinthians 5:13–16)

What does the apostle mean here? He means that the spiritual intoxication from God, through prayer, should be translated into active, charitable commitment to the brothers and sisters. If it is not, it is suspect.

Paul himself understood the spiritual ecstasy of praying in tongues (he said he spoke in tongues more than all of them) and of prophecy. He knew rapture up to the third heaven, but he knew he could not boast about these things (since they are gifts from God who initiates and receives the glory for them). Rather, he could only boast about the cross (see Galatians 6:14), that is, about the fact that he no longer lived for himself but for others, like Jesus. For that reason he intoned the hymn that should never be forgotten: "If I speak in the tongues of mortals and of angels, but do not have love..." (see 1 Corinthians 13:1–13).

Another meaning of sobriety that can be found in the pastoral epistles is purity, the health of one's emotional and sexual life. A chaste, transparent life, in accordance with one's state in life, should be a natural reflection of life in the Spirit. It should show, according to these epistles, the beauty of a Christian vocation.

For older people this means a moderation that is dignified and temperate, for example, in drinking (see Titus 2:2). For newly married people it means a chastity that expresses itself in love and fidelity to a spouse and children (see Titus 2:4–6). For unmarried people sobriety involves the ability to control their passions and to live in a manner worthy of the faith (see Titus 2:6). In fact, in the pastoral epistles we find this rich statement: "God did not give us a spirit of timidity, but a spirit of power and of love and of self-control [sobriety]" (see 2 Timothy 1:7). It is a spirit, then, of courage and enthusiasm, which expresses itself in brotherly love and in temperance. It is the "spirit of sonship" (see Romans 8:15)!

We can ask at this point, what exactly is this sober intoxication of the Spirit? It is a state in which a person feels possessed by and led by God, a state that, rather than driving us away from participation in the community, leads us precisely to commitment, requires it of us and often even makes it easier and more joyful. To describe sobriety in more traditional terms, it is an enthusiasm (from *entheos*, meaning "filled with God") but an enthusiasm based on the cross. (Here *cross* includes all the things listed above: humility, charity, chastity.) It is a kind of enthusiasm that does not entail the reservations that the word raises among believers who are zealous defenders of reason, efficiency and the middle road.

In summary, the Fathers of the Church instilled in Christians of their age, and the pope urges upon Christians of today, an enthusiasm based on the cross and nourished by the cross.

How to Become Spiritual

Are we sure this is what Scripture really says? Are we sure we are not going backward or quenching the Spirit when we tie Him to things that also depend on men, like humility, service to one another and chastity?

Yes, there is no doubt. We are faced with a specific request from God that is among the clearest in the New Testament. It is an obligatory path: If we do not begin to walk on it, we will not move toward God but rather toward ourselves and our own whims. In fact, we will move toward spiritual defeat. The gift of God, which is the Holy Spirit, requires free acceptance—precisely because He is a gift—just as the marital gift of the bridegroom requires a free "yes" from the bride. But our "yes" is not genuine or profound unless it has been declared by way of the cross.

The stakes, as we can see, are serious. It remains to be seen whether this movement, which is spreading among the people of God for a profound renewal, will end as a will-o'-the-wisp (as was the case for "enlightened and charismatic" movements in the past) or will take root and renew Christians, as in that golden age referred to earlier.

There is no need to renounce our songs, the lifting of hands, speaking in tongues (when the Lord gives it—and it is up to Him to give it), joy or enthusiasm. We merely need to avoid focusing all our attention on these things. We must not think of them as breezes that have come to caress us gently. Rather, they are sturdy winds that swell the sails so that the Church advances with strength and courage, pulling behind it a confused and hopeless world.

I said we should search the Scriptures a second time. We need to investigate one point in particular: Why must our enthusiasm necessarily go through the cross of humility, brotherly love and purity?

The answer throughout the New Testament is that Jesus Christ attained the glory of the resurrection and a life "according to the Spirit" by His cross. He was "put to death in the flesh, but made alive in the spirit" (1 Peter 3:18). He himself asked the two disciples on the road to Emmaus, "Was it not necessary that the Messiah should suffer these things and then enter into his glory?" (Luke 24:26).

We proclaim that "Jesus is Lord." That proclamation made "in the Spirit and in power" at the Kansas City Conference in 1977 is proving to be the heart of the charismatic renewal and its biggest strength. But we must keep clearly in mind that the Jesus we proclaim as "Lord" with Paul (see Philippians 2:11) is not any kind of Jesus. He is not a Jesus of sentimental paintings or a perfumed Jesus. He is Jesus Crucified! It is this Jesus, and not any other, whom the Father presents to us as Lord.

In Jesus' life the cross was not merely the wood upon which he was hung at the end. Thomas à Kempis emphasized in the *Imitation of Christ* that Jesus' whole life was the cross and suffering. His life of humility and obedience to the Father, His role as a "servant" of men (see Mark 10:45; John 13:13–16) and His proclamation of the Good News—all these comprised the cross. To accomplish these things Jesus received the Holy Spirit (see Luke 3:21–22; 4:18–19), and by His faithful fulfillment of all these things He Himself became, through the Resurrection, "a life-giving spirit" (1 Corinthians 15:45), the giver of the Spirit to the Church.

No one comes to Pentecost other than by way of Easter. It is moving to see how, immediately after Pentecost, the Christian community is led to turn back to Jesus, to rediscover Him, to gather together His sayings and His remembrances. Every kind of Pentecostalism that is healthy and Catholic or even simply Christian is also evangelical: It includes the need to know and imitate Christ, the concrete Christ of the Gospels. God gives the Holy Spirit only to those who look like Jesus and only in order that they might become more like Jesus.

And how are we to become more like Jesus? This is another answer that is found in the whole New Testament: by denying the flesh to live according to the Spirit. The flesh belongs to the old man, which is egotistical, inclined to evil and disordered desires, rebellious toward God and surrendered to the world. "Those who belong to Christ Jesus have crucified the flesh with its passions and desires. If we live by the Spirit, let us also be guided by the Spirit" (Galatians 5:24–25). If "by the Spirit you put to death the deeds of the body, you will live" (see Romans 8:13). As in the days of Elijah (see 1 Kings 18:38), the fire that comes down from heaven only falls on the wood that is prepared for burning!

What is this death we are talking about? It is nothing depressing or sad; it is "being born again" to new life, a "new birth," as Jesus said to Nicodemus. More concretely, in Paul's words, it signifies no longer living only for ourselves but living in conformity with the resurrected

Christ. It means opening ourselves to others with humility, obedience, charity and brotherly service—all the things, actually, that were listed above concerning the meaning of sobriety in the New Testament.

Tradition offers us concrete examples of people who have lived the ideal of sober intoxication that has now been proposed to us. I am thinking of Saint Ignatius of Antioch, who implored the community in Rome not to stand in the way of his pending martyrdom:

> It is beautiful to pass from this world in order to be raised up in God.... I am God's grain of wheat; I must be crushed by the teeth of wild beasts to become the pure bread of Christ.... Now I am beginning to become a true disciple.... Let me imitate the passion of my God; let me join the pure light.... My earthly desires [the works of the flesh] have been crucified; there is no desire left in me for the things of this world. The living water [that is, the Spirit] which speaks inside me says, "Come to the Father! [the same words that the Spirit says to the Bride in Revelation]."[7]

What Ignatius speaks of is certainly spiritual intoxication; this is the voice of a real charismatic. This is an intoxication that leads to martyrdom. It is foolishness, but it is the folly of the cross (see 1 Corinthians 1:18), the only folly that can be attributed to the Holy Spirit and that confers citizenship in the Church.

I am also thinking of Saint Francis, traveling to Assisi in winter, with bare feet half frozen, explaining to Brother Leo what perfect joy is: It is not in doing miracles or raising the dead; it is not in prophecy or in speaking all languages. Rather, it consists in being prepared to endure insults even from brothers in the monastery while maintaining charity. Francis explained that "above all the graces and gifts of the Holy Spirit which Christ gives to His friends is that of conquering oneself and willingly enduring sufferings, insults, humiliations and hardships for the love of Christ."[8] We could insert "renewal in the Spirit" in place of "perfect joy" here to learn what is, and what is not, perfect renewal.

The secret of renewal, which is also the secret for holiness, is thus balance between enthusiasm (or abandonment to the action of the Spirit) and active, personal commitment. This balance does not remove anything legitimate from enthusiasm or commitment but makes each aspect complement the other, with God Himself always taking the initiative. The wine of the cross is the only wine that produces the intoxication of the Spirit!

A Vision for the Renewal

From Pope Paul VI's words and our reflections on the Bible, a vision emerges for the future of the renewal. The renewal must move past its initial phase of understandable intoxication to that of sobriety or, even better, to that of sober intoxication. Alongside spontaneous and creative prayer, songs, tongues and the joy of being with the brothers and sisters and of being nourished by the pure milk of the Word of God, there should develop an increasingly firm commitment to building the kingdom of God within us and in the Church—in other words, to growing. *Growing* should become the watchword for charismatics today—"growing up in every way into Him who is the head, into Christ," as the apostle says (see Ephesians 4:15).

One day this dialogue occurred between Jesus and some of His disciples:

> *Disciples*: "Grant us to sit, one at your right hand and one at your left, in your glory."
> *Jesus*: "Are you able to drink the cup that I drink or to be baptized with the baptism with which I am baptized?"
> *Disciples*: "We are able."
> *Jesus*: "The cup that I drink you will drink; and the baptism with which I am baptized you will be baptized." (See Mark 10:37–39)

This dialogue, like all the others in which Jesus was involved, is not in the past but is always occurring. To every disciple who asks Him—as we ourselves do—to be at His right hand in glory and to have the joy of His Spirit, Jesus lovingly shows the way: to drink His cup, to receive the baptism *He* received!

We need to discover, then, how the Spirit is calling Jesus' disciples today and then move courageously in that direction. We need to listen to "what the Spirit says to the Churches" (Revelation 2:7) because He reminds us of the things Jesus required "if any one wants to be my disciple."

The first requirement is *a life of personal holiness*, especially in the area of sex. This area is underestimated today in terms of its importance in spiritual growth (or nongrowth). We need to demonstrate that Jesus is Lord of our lives even in this intimate and generally hidden

grave need
for Chastity

area. Here, as one author has said, the battle occurs every day and the victory is difficult. We must live purity as a gift, as a charism, but we must live it!

There may be someone in a prayer group or fellowship group who, over a period of time, continues to fall into grave disorders in this area without much spiritual discomfort. Perhaps the person violates the requirements of his or her state in life, whether that is engagement, marriage or celibacy. I would go so far as to say that such people should refrain from going to prayer meetings. Paul wrote about one member in the community at Corinth, "Let him who has done this be removed from among you. Do you not know that a little leaven leavens the whole lump?" (see 1 Corinthians 5:2, 6).

As Cardinal Leo Josef Suenens once said in an interview about the renewal, when a light is turned on at night, there is always the risk of attracting flying insects. There are still many insects flying around the renewal. They can do great harm to the work of the Spirit, especially if they are not acting in good faith.

The second requirement is *humility*. I am speaking specifically of the humility that resists the temptation to take over God's work and to always want to be in the place where the action of the Spirit is most evident. It is a humility that understands *service* to mean *at the service of* the community. It prevents any imperceptible increase of power and dominion over the other members. It is a humility that makes others avoid becoming attached to us, remembering that there is only one Master and that we are all brothers and sisters. It stands against the factions that plagued the Corinthian church and can plague Christian bodies today: "I belong to Paul" or "I belong to

Apollo" or "I belong to Cephas" (see 1 Corinthians 1:12).

The third requirement is *brotherly love* within the group but not restricted to the group. It should be evident not only at home or at work but everywhere. It is not just any kind of love but the kind Paul speaks of in the context of the charisms. He describes this love as patient, kind, not jealous, not boastful. It bears all things, believes all things, hopes all things, endures all things (see 1 Corinthians 13:4–7).

In line with this kind of love, there is also a commitment to the poor, especially to those who are closest to Jesus' heart and whom no one else cares for today: those who are oppressed in various kinds of slavery to sin and to the devil, the outcasts, the afflicted in spirit, those deprived of hope rather than of material goods.

Service to the Church is also part of this type of love: serving whenever it is requested or possible in parishes, in the works of the Church. This service extends not just to parish activities, trips and concerts, but to the truly spiritual works that concern the real life of the community: evangelization, catechesis, prayer, liturgical life and service to the poor. In a word, this service involves active participation in the mission of the Church.

We should be able to move naturally from the intoxication that is "for God," as Paul said, to a sobriety with respect to the brothers and sisters. This is a vigilant state in which our eyes and ears are open to discern a brother's or a sister's need.

We should think about starting *new Christian communities* wherever the signs of the Spirit seem to indicate it. These are to be communities in which the renewal can be lived out in all its richness and strength, in full communion with the bishops and with their consent. The community has always been the instrument that the Spirit uses to bring about the great renewals throughout the history of the Church: monastic communities in the fourth century; Franciscan and Dominican mendicant friars in the Middle Ages; militant Jesuit communities after the Reformation.

Perhaps even before creating new communities, the Spirit might wish to renew some old existing ones, to give new life to the "dry bones" that are scattered throughout the Church. We need to pray that pastors, parish priests and religious superiors might be renewed. Today it is community that should be the lampstand on which the great light, the Holy Spirit, is placed, so that "it gives light to all in the house" (Matthew 5:15). He has already been placed in the lampstand of the Creed, but that is no longer enough!

On a national level, on a regional level and, in some places, on a local level, we are already a community, even if it is only a spiritual and not a formalized community. In fact, we share so many things that we feel ourselves united by profound bonds of charity. Above all we aspire to have the presence of the Holy Spirit in our midst because He Himself—in the Church as in the Trinity—is the bond of peace and the joy of communion.

Our sense of belonging to the Church, however, does not depend on this kind of community or on the communities we hope are coming forth. Our fundamental community already exists, and it is the Catholic Church. We are a living part of it, even if we are unworthy. We don't want to be "our own little church" but to be in *the* Church!

I know of some brothers who are suffering because of the mistrust or rejection they encounter in certain church circles. I want to tell them to remain peaceful; we are not orphans. Yes, we were orphans at one time, but now we have become the sons of God and thus sons of the Church. We were not a people, but now we are a people—a priestly, prophetic people whom God has called forth from great darkness into the light so that we might proclaim His marvelous deeds (see 1 Peter 2:9–10). We have a roof, a house and a home—the bosom of Holy Mother Church—and a mother cannot reject a child who clings to the hem of her dress. We should nestle into the bosom of the Church; that is the place for anyone who is seeking the Holy Spirit. We must say of the Church what (according to the ancient Latin version of the Bible) Job said about his God: "Though he slay me, yet I will trust him" (see Job 13:15).

We know that the Church will not kill us. Rather it will make us live, if only we demonstrate an enthusiastic acceptance of the cross. The Church is like a body of water, a sea. Like water, it has the marvelous capacity of weighing the objects that are thrown into it: The heavy materialistic things go straight to the bottom, but the light things, those that are devoid of themselves, that are humble, don't sink. If a certain thing is from the Holy Spirit, it will keep afloat in the Church.

All that we need to do is to love the Church and to be ready to suffer and die for her. No one, then, should quench the Spirit or suppress authentic charisms in order to please someone else or even the hierarchy of the Church. That is not, in any case, what the hierarchy wants; it wants to know us as we are and to know our goals and plans. In good time it will pronounce judgment, and then we must obey. This is always the way that authentic spiritual movements emerge in the history of the Church.

This is the path that Paul VI has mapped out. He has urged us to say "yes" to sobriety but with intoxication; "yes" to the cross but with enthusiasm. *Laeti bibamus sobriam profusionem Spiritus,* he said to us. "Let us drink the sober intoxication of the Spirit with joy."

— This is true Christian living/ living the life of the Spirit, which is the Christian life. Full of love + seeking the things that are above, but doing them here. w/ God's grace, and truly w/ Him in us in the Person of the Holy Spirit.

CHAPTER TWO

Humility

I would like to recall the section from Luke that deals with the parable about choosing the place of honor at the table and ends this way: "for all who exalt themselves will be humbled, and those who humble themselves will be exalted" (Luke 14:11).

Humility had, and has, a role to play in Pentecost. Pentecost is an important event for the whole Church. What can we ourselves do to make Pentecost happen? Absolutely nothing! Only God makes a Pentecost. The power descends from on high, and nothing on earth can stop it. All that is positive and all that is a gift in Pentecost comes from God. It is the Father who decides the manner, the time and the measure of the Spirit for everyone.

What can we do, then, to experience our own Pentecost if we can't do anything positive? We can make ourselves empty to allow the Holy Spirit to come! Making our-selves empty means having an attitude of profound, sincere humility before God.

This is how Mary prepared the apostles to receive the first Pentecost. She helped them make themselves lowly, humble and docile. We can read that between the lines. Before the Passion of the Lord, when the apostles were together for the last time in that same upper room, they were discussing who was the greatest among them (see Luke 22:24). Mary, "the humble handmaid," taught them about humility during that memorable "novena" between the Ascension and Pentecost. Now we find those same men again in the upper room, but they are no longer discussing who is the greatest. Instead they are "constantly devoting themselves to prayer together" (see Acts 1:14).

Humility, then, seems to be the best preparation for receiving the Holy Spirit. To fully understand the expression "sober intoxication of the Spirit," we need to understand the precise meaning of *sober*. An intoxication of the Spirit, in the way it happened on the Day of Pentecost, depends on God; being sober, however, is our part. So let's see what being humble means.

The Humility of Jesus

Jesus finished His parable about the dinner guests by saying that he who exalts himself will be humbled and he who humbles himself will be exalted. But how do we humble ourselves?

I am sure that if I asked different people what humility means, I would get many different answers, each containing part of the truth but each incomplete. If I asked a man who is temperamentally prone to violence and to forcefully insisting on his own point of view, he might answer, "Humility means not raising my voice, not being overbearing to the family, being more gentle and flexible." If I asked a young girl, she might answer, "Humility is not being vain, not wanting to get people's attention, not living only for myself or for how I look." A priest might answer, "Being humble means knowing myself to be a sinner, having a low opinion of myself." But it is easy to see that these answers do not yet touch the core of humility.

To discover the real root of humility, we need, as always, to turn to the only Teacher, Jesus. He said, "Learn from me; for I am gentle and humble in heart" (Matthew 11:29). I must confess that for a while I was quite astounded by that saying of Jesus, for where exactly does Jesus show Himself to be humble? Nowhere in the Gospels does Jesus make the least admission of wrongdoing. That is actually one of the most convincing proofs of the uniqueness and divinity of Christ. Jesus is the only man who has lived on earth who, in His dealings with friends and with enemies, never had to say, "I was wrong." He never had to ask anyone for forgiveness, not even the Father. His conscience was clear as crystal; no sense of guilt marred it. We do not read that about any other man or any other founder of a religion.

Therefore, if being humble means having a low opinion of oneself and admitting wrongdoing, Jesus was not humble. "Which of you," He could ask with confidence, "convicts me of sin?" (John 8:46). And yet this same Jesus could say with equal confidence, "Learn from me; for I am gentle and humble in heart." Humility is not what we often think it is. We need to discover what it is in the Gospels.

Humility = abasement
lowering

What did Jesus do to be and to call Himself humble?
A very simple thing: He abased Himself. He "came
down," but not in His thoughts and speech—no, in
His actions! Jesus actually descended, thus humbling
Himself. Finding Himself in the form of God in glory,
He descended from that state in which nothing can be
desired and nothing better can be had. He took the form
of a slave and humbled Himself, being obedient unto
death (see Philippians 2:6–8).

Once Jesus initiated that dizzying descent from God
to slave, He did not stop; He continued to abase Himself
all His life. He knelt down to wash the feet of His
apostles; He said, "I am among you as one who serves"
(Luke 22:27). He did not stop until he reached the point
beyond which no creature can go—that is, death. But
precisely then, at the ultimate point of His abasement,
the power of the Father, the Holy Spirit, joined Him,
snatched His body from the tomb, made Him alive again,
exalted Him to the highest heaven, gave Him the Name
that is above all names and commanded that every knee
should bow before Him. This is a concrete example and
the greatest demonstration of Jesus' saying that "He who
humbles himself will be exalted" (see Luke 14:11).

Seen in this light, humility does not seem to be a question of feelings—of feeling bad about ourselves—but
rather a question of concrete action. It is not a matter of
words but of actual deeds. Humility is the readiness to
abase oneself, to lower oneself and serve the brothers and
sisters; it is having a will to serve. This is all done out of
love, not out of any other motives.

Unbelievers can also have an attitude of service. We
have to admit that there are people around us who do

not claim to be Christians and yet, in certain cases, are an example to us in relating to the poor and the marginalized. The difference is that with Christians such a readiness for service should be inspired by and should express love.

In a certain sense we can say that humility is gratuitous; it is self-abasement without self-interest or calculation. The parable about the dinner guests continues: "But when you give a banquet, invite the poor, the crippled, the lame, and the blind. And you will be blessed, because they cannot repay you" (Luke 14:13–14). This is a service with no strings attached because nothing is expected in return. Here humility reveals itself to be the twin sister of charity, to an aspect of that *agape* that Saint Paul eulogizes in 1 Corinthians 13. When the apostle says that charity is not "boastful or arrogant or rude," he means that charity is humble, and humility is charitable.

According to Jesus' illustration, then, to be humble means to pour ourselves out freely and not to live only for ourselves (see 2 Corinthians 5:15). When we look for applause and recognition, we lack humility because we cancel out the gratuitous aspect. We are seeking our own reward. I can go speak someplace and come home rewarded either by money or by being pleased with myself. In both cases Jesus says to me, "You have received your reward."

Humility and Soberness

Humility, abasing ourselves to serve in love, is rarely transparent and pure in us. It always involves something negative, for example, self-denial, a renunciation of anything that is wrong in our intentions and our actions, an abasement of ourselves before we move in the direction of others. When Jesus "descends," He does so from a real and objective height because He is the Holy One of God (see John 6:69). When it is we who descend, we lower ourselves only from a false or pseudo-height, a height to which we were unlawfully elevated by pride, vanity, anger, and so forth. Thus humility is always a "negative" virtue because it condemns the base instinct in us to elevate ourselves above our neighbors.

In this sense it is correct to say that humility is truth. Humility reestablishes the truth about ourselves; it acknowledges that our place is not over others but under them. Saint Teresa of Ávila wrote:

> I was wondering once why Our Lord so dearly loved this virtue of humility; and all of a sudden—without, I believe, my having previously thought of it—the following reason came into my mind: that it is because God is Sovereign Truth and to be humble is to walk in truth.[1]

Saint Paul also speaks of humility in these terms: "For if those who are nothing think they are something, they deceive themselves" (Galatians 6:3). According to the apostle, we could say that humility is, above all, spiritual sobriety, that is, a sober, healthy, non-inflated, non-exalted view of ourselves. "I say to every one among you not to think of yourself more highly than you ought to think, but to think with sober judgment" (Romans 12:3). In the original Greek the last phrase means "to evaluate yourselves soberly." A little further Paul insists, "Do not be haughty" (Romans 12:16).

This humility-soberness consists, then, in a healthy

realism that allows us to be truthful before God. We are not pursuing an abstract truth; we do not want to be like the psychoanalyst who tries to help people realize a truth about themselves so that they can be freed of their complexes. We are aiming at another truth, one that allows honesty before God, even before being honest with ourselves and with others (since this is the consequence of honesty with God). It is written that God shows Himself good and generous to the pure-hearted but shows Himself "perverse" to the unrighteous, the one who has a deceitful heart (see Psalm 18:27). One thing that God requires above all from those who draw near to Him is "truth in the inward being" (Psalm 51:6).

The Humility of God

I noted previously that humility includes some negative aspects for us—self-denial, sacrifice and the cross—precisely because we are sinners who need to remove the evil that is present in our every action. But if that is the case, where will we find humility in its pure state and with no connection to sin?

The answer that spontaneously springs to our lips is "in Jesus of Nazareth!" But if we really reflect on it, we have to say that humility in its pure state, without any connection to sin, is not even found in Him. It is, indeed, true that Jesus is the man without sin, innocent and holy; it is true that He had no sin Himself. However, He took upon Himself the sins of all men, and He became "sin" in God's eyes. Even in Jesus, then, His humbling of Himself, His making Himself obedient unto death, presents an aspect of atonement and thus of connection to sin. Only in His second coming, at the end of time, will He come without any kind of dealings with sin (see Hebrews 9:28).

So, we must ask again, where do we find humility, that gratuitous self-abasement to serve others in love, in its pure state? We must get to its source, because the virtue of humility draws all of its strength and power from it. We find it in God, in the Trinity!

There is a prayer by Saint Francis of Assisi, which is preserved in the Basilica of Saint Francis and in his own handwriting, entitled "Praises of God." The *Poverello* sings a magnificent praise to the One and Triune God:

> You are love,
> You are wisdom,
> You are humility,
> You are endurance,
> You are rest,
> You are peace.
> You are joy and gladness.
> You are justice and moderation.[2]

When I first read the phrase "You are humility," I said to myself, Saint Francis, my Father, I do not understand what you are saying here! Maybe you let yourself get carried away. You were making a list of the virtues found in God, and you put humility in there, without thinking that humility is a virtue that cannot be found in the Trinity because the Trinity is glorious, holy and full of light.

But I was mistaken and Saint Francis was right! He has given us, with these words, one of the most sensitive and sublime definitions of God: God is humility!

If humility means abasing oneself out of love, then God is humility because He can do nothing but lower Himself. There is nothing above Him, and thus He cannot climb up or lift Himself up higher. When He does something "outside of Himself" *(ad extra)*, God can only "lower Himself," humble Himself. That is what He has done since the creation of the world. The story of salvation is none other than the story of successive humble acts by God. This is, in fact, how Saint Francis sees it:

> Every day he humbles himself just as he did when he came from his heavenly throne (Wis 18:15) into the Virgin's womb; every day…he descends from the bosom of the Father into the hands of the priest at the altar.[3]

Francis exclaims of the Eucharist, "Look at God's condescension, my brothers!"[4]

I have come to realize that this was already a familiar idea among the Fathers of the Church. They spoke of the *synkatabasis* of God, a word that means "condescension." God made Himself small so that He could approach man and descend to his level. Saint John Chrysostom—who particularly liked the word *synkatabasis*—said that creation itself is already an act of condescension by God and that biblical revelation—the fact that God Himself learned to stammer in the human language—is another. This is especially true of the Incarnation.

Even Pentecost is an act of humility by God. Why do we speak of the *descent* of the Holy Spirit? It is because every intervention by God to bless man is a condescension, a humbling of Himself. At Pentecost the Holy Spirit humbled Himself, taking on lowly signs like fire, wind and tongues. He humbles Himself to dwell in needy creatures of flesh, making them His temples.

I understood later why Saint Francis, in his "Canticle of Brother Sun," wrote, "All praise be yours, my Lord, through Sister Water, so useful, lowly [humble], precious and pure."[5] Water, like God, does not flow upward but always descends, until it reaches the lowest place, which it always tends to occupy.

God is humility; what have we discovered from that? Only another theological idea? No, we have discovered the real reason that we should be humble. We must be humble to be sons and daughters of our Father, to resemble our legitimate Father.

If we are not humble, we do not resemble our Father in heaven but we imitate a much different father. Who in the universe always wants to ascend, to climb up? Who says, "I will ascend to heaven; / I will raise my throne above the stars of God; /..../ I will make myself like the Most High" (Isaiah 14:13–14)? Let's not even give him the honor of naming him, because we all know very well who it is.

We need to be humble, then, in order to resemble our Father. Otherwise, Jesus needs to say to us what he said to the Pharisees who believed they were the sons of Abraham: "You are doing the works of a father, but he is not Abraham" (see John 8:38–47).

The Exercise of Humility

Now we can ask the initial question—"What is humility?"—from another point of view, a more profound one: Is humility an attitude toward ourselves, toward others or toward God?

A number of years ago I wrote a meditation maintaining that humility is not an attitude toward ourselves or toward others but only toward God. Now I need to correct what I said. Humility encompasses all these at once: It is a way of relating to ourselves, to others and to God, yet it remains profoundly unified.

I said earlier that humility is the twin sister of charity. Just as charity expresses itself in two intimately linked attitudes—"Love the Lord your God with all your heart and your neighbor as yourself"—so too does humility. True humility consists in being humble simultaneously before God and our neighbor. We cannot be humble before God in prayer if we are not humble before our brothers and sisters.

Being humble before God means being like children, the biblical *anawim*, that is, the poor who have no one but God to rely on. It means not trusting in chariots or horses, or in our intelligence or our own righteousness. If you cannot be humble with the brother you see, how can you be humble before God whom you cannot see? If you do not wash the feet of the brother you see, what does your willingness to wash the feet of God, whom you do not see, mean? God's feet are your brothers and sisters! We can say the same things about humility that John said about charity (see 1 John 4:20).

There are people (and I am certainly among them) who are able to talk about all the things that could possibly be wrong with them and who confess their faults in prayer with admirable frankness and courage. Thus, they are humble before God and themselves. But if a brother begins to take their confessions seriously or dares to agree about even a small part of what they confessed on their own, they bristle. Theirs is not true humility. The truly humble man is the one who evaluates himself in God's light, discovering in Him who he really is and then transferring that truth into his relationships with brothers and sisters.

That kind of humility is a good that comes down from heaven; it is that "perfect gift which is from above, coming down from the Father of lights" (see James 1:17). It is not a plant that springs forth naturally from the earth; the world does not recognize it. It is the wisdom of the gospel, which confounds the wisdom of the world. On earth these two wisdoms meet head-on, and so Saint Paul could say, "If you think that you are wise in this age, you should become fools so that you may become wise. For the wisdom of this world is foolishness with God" (1 Corinthians 3:18–20).

We see clearly that the world around us, instead of cultivating humility, exalts pride. If we want to compliment someone, we say he *prides* himself on this or that. The world is structured on the values of ambition and career and encourages us to keep climbing the social ladder. From elementary school on, what is instilled in young people is the importance of having careers, of asserting themselves, even at the expense of others, and of being first.

Jesus' way of thinking is 180 degrees different. Yet we must be discerning here. What does evangelical humility aim for? To create a community of passive, inactive people who lack initiative and do not use their gifts? Absolutely not! The philosopher who said that—Nietzsche—understood nothing about the gospel. Evangelical humility does not mean you do not use your gifts; it means just the opposite. It means we do not use our gifts for ourselves or to dominate others. Instead, we use our gifts for the service of others—not to be served but to serve.

Humility in Marriage

There are some specific areas in which humility is particularly necessary. First of all, the family: It is necessary to be humble in marriage.

I believe that God invented humility for the salvation of marriages. Marriage, the bond of love between a man and a woman, is born out of humility. To fall in love with another person—when it is a genuine love—is the most radical act of humility that one can imagine. It means going toward another and saying, "I am not enough; I am not sufficient for myself; I need you." It is like stretching out one's hand for alms and begging another creature for part of himself or herself. That is indeed the most radical act of humility.

God made human beings poor and needy; He even inscribed humility in human flesh when he created male and female, that is, incomplete creatures. He made them, from the very beginning, two beings, moving in search of one another, each one "unsatisfied" with only himself or herself. God has positioned human beings on a plane that inclines upward, not downward, so that the union between man and woman should move them beyond the other sex upward to the supreme Other, God Himself.

Therefore, since marriage is born out of humility and finds its source in the lowliness of the human condition, it cannot survive except by humility. Saint Paul says to Christian couples, "Clothe yourselves with compassion, kindness, humility, meekness, and patience. Bear with one another and, if anyone has a complaint against another, forgive each other" (Colossians 3:12–13). Humility and forgiveness are like a lubricant that, day by day, dissolves every friction and the walls of misunderstanding and resentment before they become high walls that cannot be torn down.

Spouses should be on guard lest the "other father," the spurious one, set up a pattern of retaliation and revenge between them. We do not need to listen to that voice inside that shouts, "Why do I always have to be the one who gives in and who is humble?" To give in is not to lose but to win—to win over the true enemy of love, which is our egoism, our "I."

The Church needs renewed families, and families become renewed through humility. It is love, of course, that renews the family, but it is humility that makes love possible.

Humility in the Renewal

The renewal has been described very correctly as "giving the power back to God," so it is obvious why humility is urgently necessary in the renewal of the Spirit. Humility prevents the renewal from becoming a purely human work. We periodically need to put the power back in God's hands, and that is done through humility. We need to learn to say, with the Book of Revelation and the liturgy of the Church, "For the kingdom, the power, and the glory are Yours, now and forever!"

Every time we forget this and put our focus on people, it is a disaster, as it was in Corinth. In our prayer meetings there is sometimes not enough purification of what is merely human.

Humility in the renewal is as important as insulation in electricity. The higher the level of current that goes through a wire, the thicker and more efficient the insulation needs to be; otherwise, there is a short circuit!

I dimly remember some of the ideas my physics professor in high school taught us about this. He told us that insulation is made of inert, worthless material, but it is as absolutely indispensable as the copper wires that carry the current. The wires carry the current, but the insulation protects it. Progress in the technology of electrical conduction must always be accompanied by a proportional progress in the technology of insulation. Otherwise, there is a short circuit!

In particular, humility must shine in renewal leaders and in anyone who ministers in some way. We need to let ourselves be challenged without immediately taking offense. We need to let ourselves be admonished and corrected by brothers and sisters. We need to let others replace us and even to anticipate that directive from our leaders, rather than having to be told several times before we understand.

One possible temptation in the renewal is to want to be in the exact spot where, in our opinion, the Holy Spirit is flowing. We can want to be in the eye of the cyclone, the place where the most famous person or the most gifted group is. If the Lord shows this weakness to us, it is because He wants to free us from it.

It is good to want to be where the Spirit of God is working, but the Spirit of God prefers hiddenness. The place where He is working is not necessarily where the most famous person is. If we really want to be in the eye of the cyclone of the Spirit, let's hurry to find the lowest place. That is where the Spirit found Mary when He filled her with His power.

The renewal needs vocations to the hidden life. If any of us feel that this is our vocation, we should immediately say a "yes" together with Mary. It should not be difficult for us to move out of the highest place. Others should experience resistance in moving us out of the lowest place and not out of the highest place.

The renewal also needs humility in its relationships with others who serve the Lord, in other church groups and situations. We should never have a mentality of being "the chosen" because that spoils everything. We should not think of ourselves as "charismatics" in the sense of being people gifted with certain powers, but rather in the sense of being servants of the Spirit.

The Fruit of Humility

We have found the root of humility in God; we have studied its trunk and its branches. Now let's look for its fruit. Of the many wonderful fruits of humility, I want to dwell on two in particular.

One excellent fruit of humility is the approval of God. God watches over the humble person with a father's eye, with tenderness and affection. The prophet Isaiah tells us that God's glance goes throughout the universe, looking for a place to rest and not finding one, because everything is His and has been made by His hands. However, when He finds a "humble and contrite heart" (see Isaiah 66:2), there He can rest.

Psalm 138:6 tells us, "For though the LORD is high, he regards the lowly; / but the haughty he perceives from far away." Just as the Lord, from His position, cannot go up higher, so too, it can be said, He cannot look higher than Himself. Just as He can only descend, so too He can only look down. As Augustine said, "If you lift yourself up, He will withdraw from you; if, instead, you humble yourself, He will incline toward you."[6] This is the reason Mary says, "He has looked with favor on the lowliness of his servant" (Luke 1:48).

Another fruit of humility is reconciliation with our brothers and sisters. Humility wins other people over. It is a strange thing: The world does not try to develop humility, and people are generally not humble; nevertheless, they can instantly recognize someone who is humble, and they cannot resist such a person. There is no stronger argument for the renewal or for the Church than a genuine act of humility.

I conclude with Psalm 131:1–2, which sings about the fruits of humility:

> O Lord, my heart is not lifted up,
>   my eyes are not raised too high;
> I do not occupy myself with things
>   too great and too marvelous for me [sobriety!].
> But I have calmed and quieted my soul,
>   like a weaned child with its mother;
>   my soul is like the weaned child that is with me

— humility is con-descension. To go down to be w/ another in the lower regions & meet God working in the hiddenness

? What is the hiddenness of the diocesan priest?

37

The Outpouring or Baptism in the Spirit

Before speaking about the baptism, or outpouring, in the Spirit, I think it is important to understand what the renewal in the Spirit is, where this experience happens and what constitutes its strongest effect. Then we will better understand that the outpouring is not an event in and of itself but rather the beginning of a journey whose aim is the profound renewal of life in the Church.

Renewal in the Spirit

The expression *renewal in the Spirit* has two biblical equivalents in the New Testament. To understand the soul of the charismatic movement, its profound inspiration, we must primarily search the Scripture. We need to discover the exact meaning of this phrase that is used to describe the experience of the renewal.

The first text is in Ephesians 4:23–24: "Be renewed in the spirit of your minds and…clothe yourselves with the new self." Here the word *spirit* is written with a small s, and rightly so, because it indicates *our* spirit, the most intimate part of us (the spirit of our minds), which Scripture generally calls the heart. The word *spirit* here indicates that part of ourselves that needs to be renewed in order for us to resemble Christ, the New Man *par excellence.* "Renewing ourselves" means striving to have the same attitude that Christ Jesus had (see Philippians 2:5), striving for a new heart.

This text clarifies the meaning and the aim of our experience: The renewal should be, above all, an interior one, one of the heart. After the Second Vatican Council, many things were renewed in the Church: liturgy, pastoral care, the *Code of Canon Law* and religious constitutions and attire. Despite their importance, these things are only the antecedents of true renewal. It would be tragic to stop at these things and to think that the whole task had been completed.

What matters to God is people, not structures. It is souls that make the Church beautiful, and therefore she must adorn herself with souls. God is concerned about the hearts of His people, the love of His people, and everything else is meant to function as a support to that priority.

Our first text is not enough, however, to explain the phrase *renewal in the Spirit.* It highlights our obligation to renew ourselves ("be renewed!") as well as what must be renewed (the heart), but it doesn't tell us the "how" of renewal. What good is it to tell us we must renew ourselves if we are not also told *how* to renew ourselves? We need to know the true author and protagonist of the renewal.

Our second biblical text, from Titus, addresses that precise issue. It says that God "saved us, not because of any works of righteousness that we had done, but according to his mercy, through the water of rebirth and renewal by the Holy Spirit" (Titus 3:5).

Here *Spirit* has a capital S because it points to the Spirit of God, the Holy Spirit. The preposition "by" points to the instrument, the agent. The name we give to our experience signifies, then, something very exact: renewal by the work of the Holy Spirit, a renewal in which God, not man, is the principal author, the protagonist. "I [not you]" says God, "am making all things new" (Revelation 21:5); "My Spirit [and only He] can renew the face of the earth" (see Psalm 104:30).

This may seem like a small thing, a simple distinction, but it actually involves a real Copernican revolution—a complete reversal that people, institutions, communities and the whole Church in its human dimension must undergo in order to experience a genuine spiritual renewal.

We often think according to the Ptolemaic system: its foundation consists in efforts, organization, efficiency, reforms and good will. The earth is at the center of this scheme, and God comes with His grace to empower and crown our efforts. The sun revolves around the earth and is its vassal; God is the satellite of man.

However, the Word of God declares, "We need to give the power back to God" (see Psalm 68:35) because the "power belongs to God" (Psalm 62:11). That is a trumpet call! For too long we have usurped God's power, managing it as though it were ours, acting as though it were up to us to govern the power of God. Instead, we need to revolve around the sun. That's the Copernican revolution I'm talking about.

Through that kind of revolution, we recognize, simply, that without the Holy Spirit we can do nothing. We cannot even say, "Jesus is Lord!" (see 1 Corinthians 12:3). We recognize that even our most concerted effort is simply the effect of salvation, rather than its cause. Now we can begin to really "lift up our eyes" and to "look up," as the prophet exhorts (see Isaiah 60:4), and to say, "I lift up my eyes to the hills— / from where will my help come? / My help comes from the LORD, / who made heaven and earth" (Psalm 121:1–2).

The Bible often repeats the command of God, "You shall be holy, for I the LORD your God am holy!" (Leviticus 19:2; see Leviticus 11:44; 1 Peter 1:15–16). But in one place in that very same book of Leviticus, we find a statement that explains all the others: "I am the LORD; I sanctify you!" (Leviticus 20:8). I am the Lord who wants to renew you with My Spirit! Let yourselves be renewed by My Spirit!

Baptism: An "Unreleased" Sacrament

Now let's move on to the theme of the baptism of the Spirit. This outpouring is not a sacrament, but its name implies a connection to a sacrament and even more than one: the sacraments of Christian initiation. The outpouring actualizes or, in other words, renews Christian initiation. The fundamental connection, however, is with the sacrament of baptism.

The term "baptism in the Spirit" indicates that there is something here that is basic to baptism. We say that the outpouring of the Spirit actualizes and revives our baptism. To understand how a sacrament received so many years ago and usually administered in infancy can suddenly come alive and be revived and release such energy as we see on the occasions of outpouring, we must recall some aspects of sacramental theology.

Catholic theology can help us understand how a sacrament can be valid and legal but "unreleased." A sacrament is called "unreleased" if its fruit remains bound, or unused, because of the absence of certain conditions that further its efficacy. One extreme example would be the sacrament of marriage or of holy orders received while a person is in the state of mortal sin. In those cases, such sacraments cannot confer any grace on a person. If, however, the obstacle of sin is removed by repentance, the sacrament is said to revive *(reviviscit)* due to the faithfulness and irrevocability of the gift of God. God remains faithful even when we are unfaithful, because He cannot deny Himself (see 2 Timothy 2:13).

There are other cases in which a sacrament, while not being completely ineffective, is nevertheless not entirely released: It is not free to works its effects. In the case of baptism, what is it that causes the fruit of this sacrament to be held back?

Here we need to recall the classical doctrine about sacraments. Sacraments are not magic rites that act mechanically, without people's knowledge or collaboration. Their efficacy is the result of a synergy, or collaboration, between divine omnipotence (that is, the grace of Christ and of the Holy Spirit) and free will. As Saint Augustine said, "He who created you without your consent will not save you without your consent."[1]

To put it more precisely, the fruit of the sacrament depends wholly on divine grace; however, this divine grace does not act without the "yes"—the consent and affirmation—of the person. This consent is more of a *conditio sine qua non* than a cause in its own right. God acts like the bridegroom, who does not impose his love by force but awaits the free consent of his bride.

God's Role and Our Role in Baptism

Everything that depends on divine grace and the will of Christ in a sacrament is called *opus operatum*, which can be translated as "the work *already* accomplished, the objective and certain fruit of a sacrament when it is administered validly." On the other hand, everything that depends on the liberty and disposition of the person is called *opus operantis*; this is the work yet to be accomplished by the individual, his or her affirmation.

The *opus operatum* of baptism, the part done by God and grace, is diverse and very rich: remission of sins; the gift of the theological virtues of faith, hope and charity (given in seed form); and divine sonship. All of this is mediated through the efficacious action of the Holy Spirit. In the words of Clement of Alexandria:

> Once baptized, we are enlightened; enlightened, we are adopted as sons; adopted, we are made perfect; made perfect, we receive immortality.... The operation of baptism has several names: grace, enlightenment, perfection, bath. It can be called a "bath" because through it we are purified of our sins; "grace" because the punishments

deserved for our sins are removed; "enlightenment" because through it we can contemplate the beautiful and holy light of salvation, and see into divine reality; "perfection" because nothing is lacking.[2]

Baptism is truly a rich collection of gifts that we received at the moment of our birth in God. But it is a collection that is still sealed up. We are rich because we possess these gifts (and therefore we can accomplish all the actions necessary for Christian life), but we do not know what we possess. Paraphrasing a verse from John, we can say that we have been sons of God until now, but what we shall become has yet to be revealed (see 1 John 3:2). This is why we can say that, for the majority of Christians, baptism is a sacrament that is still unreleased. So much for the *opus operatum*. What does the *opus operantis* consist of in baptism?

It consists of faith! "The one who believes and is baptized shall be saved" (Mark 16:16). With regard to baptism, then, there is the element of a person's faith. "But to all who received him, who believed in his name, he gave power to become children of God" (John 1:12).

We can also recall the beautiful text from the Acts of the Apostles that tells about the baptism of Queen Candace's court official. When their journey brought Philip and the official near some water, the official said, "'Look, here is water! What is to prevent me from being baptized?' Philip said, 'It is permitted if you believe with all your heart'" (Acts 8:36–37). (Verse 37 here, an addition from the early Christian community and not usually included in modern translations, testifies to the common conviction of the Church at that time.)

Baptism is like a divine seal stamped on the faith of man: "When you had heard the word of truth, the gospel of your salvation, and had believed in him, [you] were marked with the seal [this refers to baptism] of the promised Holy Spirit" (Ephesians 1:13).

Saint Basil wrote, "Truly, faith and baptism, these two modes of salvation, are bound indivisibly to one another, because if faith receives its perfection from baptism, baptism is founded on faith."[3] This same saint called baptism "the seal of faith."[4]

The individual's part, faith, does not have the same importance and independence as God's action because God plays a part even in someone's act of faith: Even faith works by the grace that stirred it up. Nevertheless, the act of faith includes, as an essential element, the response— the individual's "I believe!"—and in that sense we call it *opus operantis,* the work of the person being baptized.

Now we can understand why baptism was such a powerful and grace-filled event in the early days of the Church and why there was not normally any need for a new outpouring of the Spirit like the one we are experiencing today. Baptism was administered to adults who were converting from paganism and who, after suitable instruction, were in a position to make an act of faith, an existential, free and mature choice about their lives. (We can read about baptism in the *Mystagogical Catecheses,* attributed to Cyril of Jerusalem, to understand the depth of faith of those who were prepared for baptism.)

They came to baptism by way of a true and genuine conversion. For them baptism was really a font of personal renewal in addition to a rebirth in the Holy Spirit (see Titus 3:5). Saint Basil, responding to someone who had asked him to write a treatise on baptism, said that it could not be explained without first explaining what it means to be a disciple of Jesus, because the Lord commands,

> Go therefore and make disciples of all nations, baptizing them in the name of the Father and of the Son and of the Holy Spirit, and teaching them to obey everything that I have commanded you. (Matthew 28:19–20)

In order for baptism to operate in all its power, anyone who desires it must also be a disciple or have a serious intention of becoming one. According to Saint Basil:

> A disciple is, as the Lord Himself taught us, anyone who draws near to the Lord to follow Him, that is, to hear His Words, to believe and obey Him as one would a master or a king or a doctor or a teacher of truth.... Now, whoever believes in the Lord and presents himself ready to be discipled must first set aside every sin and everything that distracts from the obedience which is owed to the Lord for many reasons.[5]

The favorable circumstance that allowed baptism to operate in such power at the beginning of the Church was this: The action of God and the action of man came together simultaneously, with perfect synchronism. It happened when the two poles, one positive and one negative, touched, making light burst forth.

Today this synchronism is not operative. As the Church adopted infant baptism, little by little the sacrament began to lack the act of faith that was free and personal. The faith was supplied, or uttered, by an intermediate party (parents and godparents) on behalf of the child. In the past, when the environment around the baby was Christian and full of faith, the child's faith could develop, even if it was slowly. But today our situation has become even worse than that of the Middle Ages.

The environments in which many children now grow up do not help faith to blossom. The same must often be said of the family, and more so of the child's school and even more so of our society and culture. This does not mean that in our situation today normal Christian life cannot exist or that there is no holiness or no charisms that accompany holiness. Rather, it means that instead of being the norm, it has become more and more of an exception.

In today's situation, rarely, or never, do baptized people reach the point of proclaiming "in the Holy Spirit" that "Jesus is Lord!" And because they have not reached that point, everything in their Christian lives remains unfocused and immature. Miracles no longer happen. What happened with the people of Nazareth is being repeated: Jesus was not able to do many miracles there because of their unbelief (see Matthew 13:58).

The Meaning of the Outpouring of the Spirit

The outpouring of the Spirit, then, is a response by God to the dysfunction in which Christian life now finds itself. In these last few years we know that the Church, the bishops, have also begun to be concerned that Christian sacraments, especially baptism, are being administered to people who will make no use of them in their lives. Thus, they have considered the possibility of not administering baptism when the minimum guarantees that this gift of grace would be valued and cultivated are absent.

We cannot, in fact, "throw our pearls before swine," as Jesus said, and baptism is a pearl because it is a fruit of the blood of Christ. But we can say that God is concerned, even more than the Church is, about this dysfunction. He has raised up movements here and there in the Church that are proceeding in the direction of renewing Christian initiation among adults.

The renewal in the Spirit is one of those movements, and its principal grace, without doubt, is tied to the outpouring of the Spirit and what precedes it. Its efficacy at revivifying baptism consists in this: Finally a person is doing his or her part, making a decision of faith that is prepared through repentance. This allows the work of God to "be released" in all its power.

It is as though God's outstretched hand has finally grasped the hand of the individual, and through that hand clasp, He transmits all His creative power, which is the Holy Spirit. To use an image from physics, the plug has been inserted into the outlet, and the light has been turned on. The gift of God is finally unbound, and the Spirit permeates Christian life like a perfume.

For the adult who has been a Christian for many years, this faith decision necessarily has the characteristic of a *conversion*. We could describe this outpouring of the Spirit, insofar as the person is concerned, either as a renewal of baptism or as a second conversion.

We can understand something else about this outpouring if we also see its connection with confirmation, at least in the current practice of separating it from

Actualizing Sacraments

the sacrament of baptism and administering it later. In addition to being a renewal of the grace of baptism, the outpouring is also a *confirmation* of baptism itself, a conscious "yes" to it, its fruit and its commitments. As such it parallels (at least in its subjective aspect) the effects of confirmation on the objective, sacramental level.

Confirmation is understood as a sacrament that develops, confirms and fulfills the work of baptism. The outpouring is a subjective and spontaneous—not sacramental—confirmation in which the Spirit acts not from the power of the sacramental institution but through the power of His free initiative and the openness of the person.

The meaning of confirmation sheds light on the special sense of greater involvement in the apostolic and missionary dimension of the Church that usually characterizes someone who has received the outpouring of the Spirit. That person feels impelled to help build up the Church, to serve the Church in various ministries, clerical or lay, and to give testimony to Christ. All of these things recall Pentecost and actualize the sacrament of confirmation.

Jesus, "the One Who Baptizes in the Holy Spirit"

The outpouring of the Holy Spirit is not the only occasion in the Church for this renewal of the sacraments of initiation and, in particular, of the coming of the Holy Spirit at baptism. Other occasions include the renewal of baptismal vows during Easter vigils; spiritual exercises; the profession of vows, called "a second baptism"; and, on the sacramental level, confirmation.

It is not difficult, then, to find the presence of a spontaneous outpouring in the lives of the saints, especially on the occasion of their conversion. For example, we can read about Saint Francis at his conversion:

> After the feast they left the house and started off singing through the streets. Francis' companions were leading the way; and he, holding his wand of office, followed them at a little distance. Instead of singing, he was listening very attentively. All of a sudden the Lord touched his heart, filling it with such surpassing sweetness that he could neither speak nor move. He could only feel and hear this overwhelming sweetness which detached him so completely from all other physical sensations that, as he said later, had he been cut to pieces on the spot he could not have moved.
>
> When his companions looked around, they saw him in the distance and turned back. To their amazement they saw that he was transformed into another man, and they asked him, "What were you thinking of? Why didn't you follow us? Were you thinking of getting married?"
>
> Francis answered in a clear voice: "You are right: I was thinking of wooing the noblest, richest, and most beautiful bride ever seen." His friends laughed at him saying he was a fool and did not know what he was saying; in reality he had spoken by a divine inspiration.[6]

Although I said the outpouring of the Spirit is not the only time of renewal of baptismal grace, it holds a very special place because it is open to all of God's people, big and small, and not just to certain privileged people who do the Ignatian spiritual exercises or take religious vows.

Where does that extraordinary power that we have experienced in an outpouring come from? We are not, in fact, speaking about a theory but about something that we ourselves have experienced. We can also say, with Saint John, "What we have heard, and what we have seen with our...eyes and touched with our own hands...we declare to you...so that you may also have fellowship with us" (1 John 1:1–3). The explanation for this power lies in God's will: It has pleased Him to renew the Church of our day by this means, and that is all there is to it!

There are certainly some biblical precedents for this outpouring, like the one narrated in Acts 8:14–17. Peter and John, knowing that the Samaritans had heard the Word of God, came to them, prayed for them and laid hands on them to receive the Holy Spirit. But the text that we need to begin with to understand something about this baptism in the Spirit is primarily John 1:32–33:

> And John [the Baptist] testified, "I saw the Spirit descending from heaven like a dove, and it remained on him. I myself did not know him, but the one who sent me to baptize with water said to me, 'He on whom you see the Spirit descend and remain is the one who baptizes with the Holy Spirit.'"

What does it mean that Jesus is "the one who baptizes in the Holy Spirit"? The phrase serves not only to distinguish the baptism of Jesus from that of John, who baptized only with water, but to distinguish the whole person and work of Christ from His precursor's. In other

51

words, in all His works, Jesus is the one who baptizes in the Holy Spirit.

"To baptize" has a metaphoric significance here: It means "to flood, to bathe completely and to submerge," just as water does with bodies. Jesus "baptizes in the Holy Spirit" in the sense that he "gives the Spirit without measure" (see John 3:34), that He has "poured out" His Spirit (see Acts 2:33) on all of redeemed humanity. The phrase refers to the event of Pentecost more than to the sacrament of baptism, as one can deduce from the passage in Acts: "John baptized with water, but you will be baptized with the Holy Spirit not many days from now" (Acts 1:5).

The expression "to baptize in the Holy Spirit" defines, then, the essential work of Christ, which already in the messianic prophecies of the Old Testament appeared oriented to regenerating humanity by means of a great out -pouring of the Holy Spirit (see Joel 2:28–29). Applying all this to the life and history of the Church, we must conclude that the resurrected Jesus baptized in the Holy Spirit not only in the sacrament of baptism but in different ways and at different times as well: in the Eucharist, in the hearing of the Word of God, in all other "means of grace."

The baptism in the Spirit is one of the ways that the resurrected Jesus continues His essential work of "baptizing in the Spirit." For this reason, even though we can explain this grace in reference to baptism and Christian initiation, we need to avoid becoming rigid about this point of view. It is not only baptism that revives the grace of initiation, but also confirmation, first Communion, the ordination of priests and bishops, religious vows, marriage—all the graces and charisms. This is truly the grace of a new Pentecost. It is, like the rest of Christian life, a new and sovereign initiative, in a certain sense, of the grace of God, which is founded on but not exhausted in baptism. It is linked not just to initiation but also to the perfection of Christian life.

Only in this way can we explain the presence of the baptism in the Spirit among Pentecostal brothers and sisters. The concept of initiation is foreign to them, and they do not invest the same importance in water baptism as do Catholics and other Christians. In its very origin the baptism in the Spirit has an ecumenical value, which is necessary to preserve at all costs. It is a promise and an instrument of unity among Christians, helping us to avoid an excessive "catholicizing" of this shared experience.

Brotherly Love, Prayer and Laying on of Hands

In the outpouring there is a hidden, mysterious dimension that is different for each person because only God knows us intimately. He acts in a way that respects the uniqueness of our personalities. At the same time, there is also a visible dimension, in the community, that is the same for all and that constitutes a kind of sign, analogous to the signs in the sacraments. The visible, or community, dimension consists primarily in three things: brotherly love, prayer and the laying on of hands. These are not sacramental signs, but they are indeed biblical and ecclesial.

The laying on of hands can signify two things: invocation or consecration. We see, for example, both types of laying on of hands at Mass. There is the laying on of hands as invocation (at least in the Roman rite) at the moment of epiclesis, when the priest prays, "May the Holy Spirit sanctify these gifts so that they may become for us the body and blood of Our Lord Jesus Christ." Then there is the laying on of hands when the concelebrants pray over the offerings at the moment of consecration.

In the rite of confirmation, as it now occurs, there are also two occasions for the laying on of hands. The first has the character of invocation. The other, which accompanies the anointing with the oil of chrism on the forehead, by which the sacrament becomes actualized, has the character of consecration.

In the outpouring of the Spirit, the laying on of hands has only the character of invocation (similar to what we find in Genesis 48:14; Leviticus 9:22; Mark 10:13–16; Matthew 19:13–15). It also has a highly symbolic significance: It recalls the image of the Holy Spirit's overshadowing (see Luke 1:35); it also recalls the Holy Spirit as He "swept over" the face of the waters (see Genesis 1:2). In the original the word that is translated "swept over" means "to cover with one's wings," or "to brood, like a hen with her chicks."

Tertullian clarifies the symbolism of the laying on of hands in baptism: "The flesh is covered over by the laying on of hands so that the soul can be enlightened by the Spirit."[7] This action is a paradox, like many things in God: The laying on of hands enlightens by covering, like the cloud that followed the chosen people in Exodus and like the one that surrounded the disciples on Mount Tabor (see Exodus 14:19–20; Matthew 17:5).

The other two elements are brotherly love and prayer, or "brotherly love that expresses itself in prayer." Brotherly love is the sign and vehicle of the Holy Spirit. He, who is Love, finds a natural environment in brotherly love, His sign *par excellence*. (We can also say this love is like a sacramental sign, even if it is in a different sense: "a signifying cause.") We cannot insist enough on the importance of an atmosphere of brotherly love surrounding those who are going to receive the baptism of the Holy Spirit.

Prayer is also closely connected with the outpouring of the Spirit in the New Testament. Concerning Jesus' baptism, Luke writes, "While he was in prayer, the heavens opened and the Holy Spirit descended upon him" (see Luke 3:21). It was Jesus' prayer, we could say, that made the heavens open and the Holy Spirit descend upon Him.

The outpouring at Pentecost happened this way too: While they were all continuing in prayer, there came the sound of a violent wind, and tongues of fire appeared (see Acts 1:14–21). Jesus Himself said, "I will ask the Father, and he will give you another Advocate" (John 14:16). On every occasion the outpouring of the Spirit is connected to prayer.

These signs—the laying on of hands, brotherly love and prayer—all point to simplicity; they are simple instruments. Precisely because of this, they bear the mark of God's action. Tertullian writes of baptism: "There is nothing which leaves the minds of men so amazed as the simplicity of the divine actions which they see performed and the magnificence of the effects that follow.... Simplicity and power are the prerogatives of God."[8]

This is the opposite of what the world does. In the world, the bigger the objectives are, the more complicated are the means. When people wanted to get to the moon, the necessary apparatus was gigantic.

If simplicity is the mark of divine action, we need to preserve it in our prayer for the outpouring of the Spirit. Simplicity should shine forth in prayers, in gestures, in everything. There should be nothing theatrical, no excited movements or excessive words.

The Bible records the glaring contrast between the actions of the priests of Baal and the prayer of Elijah during the sacrifice on Mount Carmel. The former cried out, limped around the altar and cut themselves until they bled. Elijah simply prayed, "O LORD, God of Abraham, Isaac, and Israel,…answer me, so that this people may know that you, O LORD, are God, and that you have turned their hearts back!" (1 Kings 18:36–37). The fire of the Lord fell on the sacrifice prepared by Elijah but not on the one prepared by the priests of Baal (see 1 Kings 18:25–38). Elijah later experienced that God was not in the great wind, or in the earthquake, or in the fire but in the still, small voice (see 1 Kings 19:11–12).

From where does the grace of the outpouring come? From the people present? No! From the person who receives? Again, no! It comes from God. It makes no sense to ask if the Holy Spirit comes from inside or from outside of the person: God is inside and outside. We can only say that such grace has a connection to baptism because God always acts with consistency and faithfulness; He does not contradict Himself. He honors the commitment and the institutions of Christ. One thing is certain: It is not the brothers and sisters who confer the Holy Spirit. Rather, they invite the Holy Spirit to come upon a person. No one can give the Spirit, not even the pope or a bishop, because no one possesses the Holy Spirit. Only Jesus can actually give the Holy Spirit. People do not possess the Holy Spirit, but, rather, are possessed by Him.

When we talk about the mode of this grace, we can speak of it as a new coming of the Holy Spirit, as a new sending of the Spirit by the Father through Jesus Christ or as a new anointing corresponding to a new level of grace. In this sense the outpouring, although not a sacrament, is nevertheless an event, a *spiritual event.* This definition corresponds most closely to the reality of the thing. It is an *event,* something that happens and that leaves a sign, creating something new in a life. It is a *spiritual* event, rather than an outwardly visible, historical one, because it happens in a person's spirit, in the interior part of a person, where others may not recognize what is happening. Finally, it is spiritual because it is the work of the Holy Spirit.

There is a wonderful text from the apostle Paul that speaks specifically of the renewing of the gift of God. Let's hear it as an invitation addressed to each of us: "I remind you to rekindle the gift of God that is within you through the laying on of my hands; for God did not give us a spirit of cowardice, but rather a spirit of power and of love and of self-discipline" (2 Timothy 1:6–7).

Outpouring of HS as God aiding us to live out the Christian life? God present in / through Church & aiding this!

or

Call to "more"? Tongues, loud praise ... type of Christianity.

CHAPTER FOUR

Charisms

But each of us was given grace according to the
measure of Christ's gift. Therefore it is said, "When he
ascended on high he made captivity itself a captive; he
gave gifts to his people." (Ephesians 4:7–8)

These verses from the apostle point to the fundamental
event on which every discussion about charisms should
begin: Christ, resurrected and ascended into heaven, has
sent the Holy Spirit and has distributed gifts to men.
Therefore it is Christ the Lord who should be the center
of our attention, He who, not only then but forever and
even now, gives His Spirit to His Church. He is the fountain to whom we should look, the "spiritual rock" from
which sprang that "river whose streams [the charisms!]
make glad the city of God" (see Psalm 46:4).

The best way to speak of charisms is to comment on
some of the major texts in the New Testament on this
issue. The first of these is in Ephesians: "There is one
body and one Spirit,…one God and Father of all.… The
gifts he gave were that some would be apostles, some
prophets, some evangelists"(Ephesians 4:4, 6, 11).

58

Unity

Diversity

Charisms here

This text indicates that the essence of the Church has two aspects—unity, or communion (*koinonia*), and diversity, or service (*diakonia*)—and that the charisms belong to the second aspect. In other words, on one hand the Church is made up of certain realities shared by all and identical for all, such as one God and Father, one Lord Jesus Christ, one Spirit, one faith, one hope and one baptism. On the other hand, the Church encompasses other realities that are different for each person, that is, ministries and charisms. These are expressions of the richness, the dynamism, the variety in the Church. They make the Church not only a well-structured and connected body but also a body structured according to the strength of each member.

Charisms and Sacraments

Among the things that are shared, Saint Paul listed baptism and then all the sacraments. In fact, the difference between unity and diversity is reflected in the difference between sacraments and charisms.

In 1 Corinthians we read:

> Now there are varieties of gifts, but the same Spirit; and there are varieties of services, but the same Lord; and there are varieties of activities, but it is the same God who activates all of them in everyone. (1 Corinthians 12: 4–6)

The same distinction appears in this text between what is diverse in the Church (charisms, ministries and activities) and what is "one and the same." Among the things that are the same for all, the apostle listed the sacraments and wrote further on, "For in the one Spirit we were all baptized into one body,…and we were all made to drink of one Spirit" (1 Corinthians 12:13). The expression "made to drink of one Spirit" could be a veiled allusion to the Eucharist, which in early Christian initiation was received at the same time as baptism. It is certain, in any case, that Eucharist is in the category of things that are shared. Immediately before this passage, in fact, the apostle says, "Because there is one bread, we who are many are one body" (1 Corinthians 10:17).

What is the connection, then, between charisms and sacraments? The sacraments are shared in common; there is no objective distinction among believers who receive them in the same manner. The only distinction depends on an individual's personal faith and holiness and not on his or her position in the Church. The Eucharist that the pope receives is the same Eucharist that the bishops, priests and lay people receive. Baptism is the same, whether it is administered by the pope, a priest or, in an emergency, a layperson. The sacraments, then, are those shared realities that enable the Church to be above all a communion and a unity.

A charism, on the other hand, is a particular manifestation of the Spirit given to each person (see 1 Corinthians 12:7). Charisms are, for that reason, not all equal. In fact, none is really equal to another.

In His infinite wisdom God has established two distinct channels to sanctify the Church or, one could say, two different directions from which the Spirit blows. There is the Spirit who comes from above, so to speak, and who is transmitted through the pope, the bishops and the priests. He acts through the magisterium of the Church, through the hierarchy, through authority and especially through the sacraments. It is through these channels, instituted by Christ and entrusted to the institutional Church, that the Spirit, or grace, comes to us. No one, not even the hierarchy of the Church, can make changes to these channels.

We can compare the sacraments to the switches for electrical current, placed in specific places throughout a house. Up in the mountains an electrical generator produces electricity. It travels over mountains and valleys through thick wires and reaches the city. There, branching out, it reaches the outlets that are in each house. Every time a switch is turned on, heat, energy or light come forth from the outlet.

This is the way it is with grace: There is a main center for grace, which is the redemptive sacrifice of Christ consummated on the cross. From that center grace flows uninterruptedly to us through the channels established by Christ, and we draw upon that grace in the sacraments.

Up to this point I have spoken of the direction "from above." However, the Spirit also blows from the opposite direction, "from below," that is, from the foundation or the cells of the body, which is the Church. This is truly the wind that Jesus said "blows where it chooses" (John 3:8).

Paul seems to take up this concept from Jesus when, speaking of charisms, he says, "All these are activated by one and the same Spirit, who allots to each one individually just as the Spirit chooses" (1 Corinthians 12:11). "As the Spirit chooses": Here the freedom of God reigns supreme, not bound by choices made once and for all at the beginning of the Church but always new and unforeseen. Charisms are the concrete manifestations of this Spirit who blows "where He chooses" and whom no one can foresee or determine ahead of time. If the sacraments are the established outlets of grace, the charisms are the surprise outlets of grace and of the Holy Spirit.

The complete Church—the living organism that is watered and given life by the Holy Spirit—is the combination of these two channels or the result of these two directions of grace. Sacraments are the gifts given to all for each one's use, while the charisms are gifts to each one for the use of all. The sacraments are gifts given to the Church as a whole to sanctify individuals; charisms are gifts given to individuals to sanctify the whole Church.

It is easy to see, then, what a loss it would be for the Church if, at a certain point, it decided to do without one or the other of the two channels—to forego either the sacraments or the charisms, that is, either the Spirit who descends from on high or the Spirit who is diffused throughout the Church. Unfortunately, this has happened in the Church, at least on the practical level if not in principle.

After the Second Vatican Council everyone acknowledged that in the past there had been a certain diminishment of the sanctifying organism of the Church, especially with regard to the charisms. Everything was flowing only through the so-called vertical channels constituted by the hierarchy and entrusted to it. It was through these channels that the Christian people received the Word of God, the sacraments and prophecy (generally understood as the charism of infallible teaching and inerrancy in the magisterium of the Church!). This was the "pyramid" Church, in which everything was supposed to follow a very precise and one-directional course: from God to the pope, from the pope to the bishops, from the bishops to the priests and from the priests to the faithful. It was inevitable that this would cause some kind of inertia among the laity.

At the root of this doctrinal impoverishment was a certain conception of the Church that was formed in the modern age and is called, by analogy, the "deist" conception of the Church.[1] Descartes held a deist conception of the world: God had created the world, and after He had put it in motion, so to speak, He withdrew, leaving it to function on its own according to laws written into it once and for all. This is also called a mechanical view of the world. It negates, on a practical level, Providence and the actual, ongoing governance of God over the world.

By analogy, a deist conception of the Church is one that considers it a perfect organism created by Jesus, gifted at the very beginning with all the power and the means (sacraments, hierarchy, magisterium) to journey to the *parousia* by itself. This concept inadvertently obscures the actual, ongoing lordship of Christ over His Church, which expresses itself in His freedom to intervene in the Church by His Spirit moment by moment, and to prepare ever-new surprises for His Bride.

In practice this deist conception severely diminished the space in which the charisms are found. In fact, no one talked about the charisms anymore—or when they did, they talked about them only in the narrow context of identifying the graces and extraordinary phenomena in the lives of certain saints.

With the Second Vatican Council this somewhat static and mechanical image of the Church was changed. The

Church came to recognize that it could not do without the immense richness of the grace that is spread through the capillaries of the body of the Church—in all of its members—and that manifests itself in the gifts, the charisms, of each person. Thus the Council wrote the now-famous text on this issue:

> It is not only through the sacraments and the ministrations of the Church that the Holy Spirit makes holy the People, leads them and enriches them with His virtues. Allotting His gifts according as he wills (1 Corinthians 12:11), he also distributes special graces among the faithful of every rank. By these gifts he makes them fit and ready to undertake various tasks and offices for the renewal and building up of the Church, as it is written, "the manifestation of the Spirit is given to everyone for profit" (1 Corinthians 12:7). Whether these charisms be very remarkable or more simple and widely diffused, they are to be received with thanksgiving and consolation, for they are fitting and useful for the needs of the Church.[2]

The dual movement of the Spirit is reestablished in this text. It says that the Holy Spirit acts not only through the sacraments, or from on high, but also from below, through the network of grace established by the charisms of all the baptized. In both cases the Spirit's action intends to sanctify the people of God, to do something essential and constitutive of the Church, and not simply to add a casual embellishment or enrichment.

Charisms and Service

According to this section of the Council's text, the purpose of charisms is clear: They are to make the faithful fit and ready to assume the responsibilities of renewing and building up the Church. The Council was only restating the very clear teaching of the New Testament on charisms. Saint Paul writes that it is God who has determined that "some would be apostles, some prophets, some evangelists, some pastors and teachers, to equip the saints for the work of ministry [service], for building up the body of Christ" (Ephesians 4:11–12). Saint Peter, on his part, recommends, "Serve one another [*diakonia*] with whatever gift [*charisma*] each of you has received" (1 Peter 4:10).

The purpose of the charisms, then, is *diakonia*, or service or ministry. This last word, *ministry*, is the one most used in our translations of the Bible. Unfortunately, the word is used ambiguously today so that it is sometimes misleading. For example, there are political and governmental ministries that are not always departments of service, or at least not experienced by people as such.

The word *ministry* in the New Testament simply means "service" (from *ministrare*, which means "to serve"). The purpose of the charisms, then, is not to give glory, prestige or a reputation of holiness to those who receive them or to give people a position or power over others. Absolutely not! If they are used in this way, the goal of the charisms is distorted.

When Jesus, ascending up to heaven, poured out, like a rain, His gifts on men, He had in mind His body, the Church. He loved and wanted to edify the Church. Commenting on Ephesians 4:8, Augustine notes that the apostle says, "He gave gifts to his people," while at the same time a verse from the Psalms says that He "receives gifts from people" (see Psalm 68:19). Augustine explained that both things are true in Christ: He has given gifts to men insofar as He is the Head, and He has received gifts insofar as He is the Body—since the totality of Christ is the Head and the Body together, Christ and the Church together. Whatever someone receives as a gift from the Holy Spirit is also a gift to the Church.[3]

The charisms, then, are for the Church, for the enrichment of the Church, for the vitality and variety of the Church. This helps us understand how Saint Paul could call love "the more excellent way," the charism of all charisms. Here too Saint Augustine can guide us. After recalling the various charisms listed by the apostle in 1 Corinthians 12:8–10, he wrote:

> Perhaps you don't have any of these gifts that are listed; but if you have love, that is not a small gift. If, in fact, you love unity, everything that is possessed by someone else is possessed by you as well! Banish envy and all that is mine will be yours, and if I banish envy, all you possess is mine! Envy separates, while love unites. Only the eye, in the body, has the function of seeing, but does the eye really only see for itself? No, the eye sees for the hand, the foot and all the other members; if, in fact, the foot is about to strike a certain obstacle, the eye certainly does not look elsewhere, in order to avoid preventing the accident. Only the hand acts in the body, but does it really act only for itself? No, it also acts for the eye; in fact, if a blow were aimed only at the face and not at the hand, would the hand say, "I am not moving because the blow is not directed at me"? In the same way, the foot serves all the members by walking; while the other members are silent, the tongue speaks for all. We have, then, the Holy

Spirit if we love the Church, and we love it if we continue to remain within its unity and its charity. In fact, the same Apostle, after having affirmed that men were given different gifts—just as different members of the body are assigned different tasks—continues, saying, "... *I will show you a still more excellent way*" (1 Cor 12:31), and he begins to speak of charity. He places it ahead of tongues of men and angels; he prefers it to miracles done in faith, to knowledge, and to prophecy. He even puts it before the great works of mercy which consist in giving all that one has to the poor; he prefers it, lastly, even to martyrdom. He puts charity ahead of all these other great gifts. If you have charity, then, you have all, because whatever other thing you might have, it will profit you nothing without charity.[4]

Here is the secret as to why charity is "the more excellent way": It makes me love unity (that is, the Church and, concretely, the community in which I live). In the context of unity, all the charisms, and not just certain ones, become mine.

And there is another reason: If you really love unity, the charism that I possess is more yours than mine. Suppose I have the charism of an evangelist or of announcing the Word of God. I can delight in it myself and boast about it, but then I become "a clanging cymbal," and the charism, says the apostle, "profits me nothing." On the other hand, for those of you who hear the proclaimed Word, that Word continues to be profitable, in spite of my sin. Through charity you possess without danger what I possess with danger to myself. What an extraordinary invention from the wisdom of God! Charity multiplies the charism; it makes one person's charism a charism for everyone.

But because this miracle happens, we need to banish envy, said Augustine. We need to die to our own individual, egotistical "I," which seeks its own glory, and assume instead the great, expansive "I" of Christ and the Church. This presupposes a state of profound conversion. The charisms, in fact, presuppose that a person is in a continuous state of conversion and remain healthy and righteous only in a person who is in that state.

When Saint Paul affirmed that without charity, even if I have the most sublime charism, "I gain nothing," this does not mean that without charity the charisms profit no one and become worthless. It only means that they do not profit me. Charisms profit the Church even if they do not profit those who possess them and exercise them.

The Exercise of Charisms

To discuss the final point, the concrete exercise of charisms, I want to return to Saint Paul's words: "To each is given the manifestation of the Spirit for the common good" (1 Corinthians 12:7). I want to emphasize the words, "the manifestation of the Spirit." A charism is a manifestation, or epiphany, of the Spirit—a partial but genuine mode of manifestation. (The Greek word here is the same word used to indicate the manifestation of Christ in the New Testament, *phanerōsis*.)

This is a serious point. Unless the charisms are spontaneous manifestations and natural reflections of the Spirit dwelling in a person's heart and life, then they either are not truly present or will be quickly spoiled. The charisms can be detached from, or artificial in, the life of the one who exercises them. In fact, Jesus tells us that it is possible for a person with charisms to end up in hell:

> Not everyone who says to me, "Lord, Lord," will enter the kingdom of heaven, but only the one who does the will of my Father in heaven. On that day many will say to me, "Lord, Lord, did we not prophesy in your name [a charism], and cast out demons in your name [a second charism!], and do many deeds of power in your name [athird charism!]?" Then I will declare to them, "I never knew you; go away from me, you evildoers." (Matthew 7: 21–23)

How is it that people who prophesy, cast out demons and do many miracles could hear, "Go away from Me!" on Judgment Day? It is because these charisms were not the authentic manifestations of a life guided by the Spirit of Jesus. They were, if anything, *demonstrations* of the Spirit but not *manifestations* of the Spirit. This is what happens when the gifts of God are abused for one's own glory or used without the acceptance of the stringent requirements that the Spirit Himself has set in place and that the gospel sums up in the word *cross*.

We must, therefore, enter into a perspective of real conversion, no longer thinking of charisms as wonderful gifts that, thanks to the outpouring of the Spirit, have landed on the tree of our lives at a certain point. Such a tree would be a Christmas tree, not a living tree. The Christmas tree is an artificial or cut tree under which gifts are placed. It is put away or thrown out after the gifts have been opened and the holiday is over. Christians who have charisms without lives characterized by the cross resemble these trees—good for nothing and discarded as soon as the gifts have been collected.

Christians who are like trees that grow along streams of water are very different. They always bear new fruit in season, and their leaves do not wither (see Psalm 1:3). They will indeed go through the winter—that is, through periods in which they don't seem to have any fruit and are stripped of everything—but in spring they will begin to bud, and in time they will produce abundantly.

Saint Paul expressed this very well when he affirmed that the charisms should be an expression of a life "in the Spirit." The charisms, in fact, can only be counted on in those who, "by the Spirit,...put to death the deeds of the body" (see Romans 8:13). This explains why, after a brilliant beginning in the renewal, some people stopped along the road or even turned back.

What has happened to some people is similar to what happens when a fire is lit in a fireplace in a house. At first, the fire moves through material like paper, straw and dry twigs. But after this initial flame, either the fire succeeds in enkindling large pieces of wood and lasts until the following morning to warm the whole house, or it does not continue to burn and accomplishes nothing. This latter fire is a "flash in the pan." In the context of spiritual renewal, either the initial flame engulfs the heart and transforms it from a heart of stone to a heart of flesh, or it does not reach the heart but remains on the periphery and soon burns out, leaving no trace of itself.

If there is a scarcity of "burning coals" in our groups—of lives really penetrated by the fire of the Spirit, burning for the Church—this is the reason: The fire did not reach the heart. These people did not go through what Saint Paul calls "the circumcision of the heart" (see Romans 2:29).

We need to be more serious about certain fundamental rules concerning holiness, which can be specifically observed in the lives of saints who are recognized as such by the Church. I am astounded, I suffer, and sometimes I feel righteous indignation when I hear people in the renewal say that the joy of the Resurrection should be proclaimed but the cross and self-denial should be downplayed. They say we need to avoid returning to a certain kind of outdated spirituality that is too oriented toward suffering. It is true that we should emphasize faith and the joy of the Resurrection to the extreme, but the balance does not lie in scaling back to moderate doses of self-denial and of the cross. That is an entirely human way of thinking. The balance comes only in carrying both to extremes: fully accepting the cross in the depths of our souls so that we can fully experience the Resurrection in the depths of our souls.

The Church does not contradict itself, and Jesus does not contradict Himself. For twenty centuries this is how saints have become holy. At the beginning of a spiritual journey, grace is experienced in gifts and great consolations, so that a person may become detached from the world and make a decision for God. But afterward, once a person is detached from the world, the Spirit urges that individual to go the "narrow way" of the gospel, the way of mortification, obedience and humility. There is no reason that the Lord today would radically change His method and make saints in a different way, a way paved with sweetness and lofty experiences from beginning to end. It is impossible to see why or how He would have them go from glory to glory without having them go from cross to cross.

Jesus saved us by going from cross to cross and has made His saints go from cross to cross, but with the joy that is a foretaste of the Resurrection. The charisms should display the fruits of the Spirit, and if that is not happening, we need to stop and reflect. Jesus said, "You will know them by their fruits" (Matthew 7:16), and the fruits He was talking about were those of the Spirit: love, joy, peace, kindness, patience, humility, obedience, and so forth.

Now that I have mentioned obedience, I would like to dwell on that virtue for a moment. The charisms should be exercised in obedience. Saint Paul told us that the charisms belong to those who, by means of the Spirit, put to death the works of the flesh. These are those who, through obedience, put to death self-love, pride and their own point of view. In any group where there is not an atmosphere of obedience and submission (to whomever presides—to the priest or simply to one another), everything is in danger; everything is ambiguous. Factions arise and then disappointments. Obedience is the mark by which we recognize whether brothers and sisters are operating in genuine charisms or not. All we need to see is their readiness—whenever a voice of authority calls them—to move aside and submit their charisms to the community.

Saint Teresa of Ávila had visions that truly were of Jesus. But from the moment a certain confessor told her that the devil was deceiving her and that she should sprinkle holy water on any vision, she obeyed. She sprinkled holy water on Jesus, and Jesus was glad that she obeyed her confessor.

How can we allow someone among us to say, "People are holding me back and forbidding me, but I sense that the Lord is asking me to do this or that"? You "sense," dear sister, you "sense," dear brother, but you do not realize that your "feeling" has gotten you off track. The important thing is not what you sense; the important thing is what the Church senses. If you really want to have "senses," then take on the same mentality that Jesus had, as Paul said: obedience and humility (see Philippians 2:5–8).

One final point about the exercise of charisms: they do not go together with sin. Therefore, there is a need for a definite break with sin. It is truly important to offer the Lord a contrite and humble heart, a heart that has no attachment to sin. Blessed are you if, in a moment of meditation, you succeed in saying to Jesus, "Lord, I know that the very root of my sin is the bondage that still prevents me from running to you freely. Therefore, trembling at my unrighteousness, but full of faith in your grace, I say, 'There is nothing in common between me and that sin. It's over! I break forever with my sin!'"

On the topic of sin, let me express a heartfelt grief that I have carried for some time. There is deception in some groups, in some people, and there are situations that seem to trifle with God. Saint Paul said, "God is not mocked" (Galatians 6:7). Even now there are people who do not seem to have understood how seriously God regards sin.

I am not talking about the sins that we all commit, which overtake us by surprise and which we repent of and confess. I'm talking about the "state" of sin: situations clearly identified long ago as representing a serious break with God and with the Church, but in which people nevertheless live contentedly while continuing to attend weekly prayer meetings. It is a terrible thing: The Letter to the Hebrews says that whoever lives in this kind of sin is "crucifying again the Son of God again and [is] holding him up to contempt" (see Hebrews 6:6). A person who lives this way and, without repenting, goes to a church service or a prayer meeting and claps his or her hands and praises Christ the Lord crucifies Him anew. If there are such cases among us, repentance, repentance, confession, confession! "O that today you would listen to his voice! Do not harden your hearts" (Psalm 95:7–8).

Lord, help us to have contrite and humble hearts, which have burned all the bridges to willful sin, so that You can pour out on us Your Spirit and enrich us with His gifts for the glory of the Father and for the building up of Your Church. Amen!

CHAPTER FIVE

Anointed

In the first centuries of Christianity, the week that followed Easter was the time when the bishop presented "mystagogical catechesis," which is so named because it introduced people to an understanding of the mysteries of the faith.

The neophytes, baptized at the Easter Vigil and dressed in white, returned for seven days for teaching from the bishop. He revealed to them the profound significance of the rites and mysteries that they had just received. It was like being introduced to the treasure-house of the Church. The "rule of secrecy" *(disciplina arcani)* kept these most sacred rites of the faith hidden from the catechumens until the moment of this solemn instruction by the bishop. It was a long-awaited and unforgettable moment.

Tertullian referred to it when he wrote that the converts from paganism seemed to be "overwhelmed at the light of so much truth."[1] It was probably in the same kind of circumstance that Peter imparted mystagogical teaching to the neophytes in one of his letters: "Like newborn infants, long for the pure, spiritual milk, so that by it you may grow into salvation" (1 Peter 2:2).

One of the mysteries that was explained during that week was that of anointing, today called confirmation. At that time confirmation was conferred immediately after baptism in the context of the rites of Christian initiation. In the liturgy of the hours for the sixth day within the octave of Easter, there is an excerpt from the *Mystagogical Catecheses*, attributed to Saint Cyril, bishop of Jerusalem, which explains the rite and the sacrament of anointing and of consecration:

> Baptized in Christ and clothed in Christ, you have assumed a nature similar to that of the Son of God. Having become partakers in Christ, you are properly called "christs" that is, consecrated, because God has said of you, "...Do not touch my anointed ones..." (Psalm 105:15). You were consecrated when you received the sign of the Holy Spirit. Baptized in the Jordan River, after imparting the fragrance of His divinity to the waters, Christ emerged from the waters and the con-substantial Holy Spirit descended upon him. The same thing happened to you, after you were immersed in the sacred waters and received the chrism, which is a figure of that which anointed Christ, i.e., the Holy Spirit.... Thus, while the body is anointed with visible ointment, the soul becomes sanctified by the holy and life-giving Spirit.[2]

As we meditate on the mystery of the anoint-ing and consecration of a Christian, let's turn to the Church. Let's climb up, so to speak, onto the knees of our mother so that we may "nurse and be satis-fied / from her consoling breast" (see Isaiah 66:11).

Most of us have never had our mystagogical instruction, that is, a deep initiation into the mysteries of our faith the way it used to happen at adult baptism. The renewal in the Spirit is really the place where the introduction to the most profound and life-giving truths of faith occurs for many today. We ourselves, at this point, are the newborn infants who long for the pure milk of the Spirit.

"You Are a People Holy to the Lord!"

All the great Christian truths are prefigured in the Old Testament; they are announced ahead of time and prepared for through symbols and prophecies. Easter is prefigured in the slaying of the paschal lamb, baptism in circumcision, the Eucharist in the manna and so on.

The same is true of consecration. It is the act by which a thing, a person or a whole people is chosen, separated from everything else and appointed to the worship and service of God in a special way. Consecrated people enter into a relationship with God that is special when compared to His relationship with other nations or categories of people within the same nation. Consecration is the act by which they are "made holy" and leads to the status of being consecrated.

Israel, as a people, was consecrated to the Lord and, as such, was different from all other peoples. Moses instructed them:

> For you are a people holy to the Lord your God; the Lord your God has chosen you out of all the peoples on earth to be his people, his treasured possession.

> It was not because you were more numerous than
> any other people that the Lord set his heart on you and
> chose you—for you were the fewest of all peoples. It was
> because the Lord loved you. (Deuteronomy 7:6–7)

Israel was, therefore, among the peoples of the earth, the priest within the family of nations. God told Moses to tell the people: "Now therefore, if you obey my voice and keep my covenant, you shall be my treasured possession out of all the peoples. Indeed, the whole earth is mine, but you shall be for me a priestly kingdom and a holy nation" (Exodus 19:5–6).

Within this consecrated people there were some who were consecrated in a special way. The rite of this consecration was an anointing with perfumed oil. To understand this action, we need to remember that oil, for the ancients, was a rare and precious element. One psalm refers to "oil to make the face shine," alongside the wine that gladdens the heart and the bread that strengthens people (see Psalm 104:15). People would anoint themselves with this oil to make their faces more beautiful, and wrestlers would anoint themselves to be more agile and more prepared for their matches. It is not surprising, then, that in the religious sphere this element would come to signify the dignity and the beauty conferred by contact with God and to symbolize the Holy Spirit.

Those appointed for the anointing essentially belonged to three categories: kings, priests and prophets. We know, for example, that Samuel anointed King Saul and later David by pouring a vial of perfumed oil over their heads (see 1 Samuel 10:1; 16:13). Exodus describes the unction to anoint Aaron as high priest, specifying all the spices that were to be combined to make the anointing oil (see Exodus 30:22–25). Elijah anointed Elisha as the prophet to succeed him (see 1 Kings 19:16); Isaiah said the Spirit of the Lord anointed him to bring the good news to the poor (see Isaiah 61:1–3); and Jeremiah said that he was consecrated as a prophet in his mother's womb (see Jeremiah 1:5). In the case of the prophets, however, the anointing was usually only spiritual and metaphorical.

Moving from the Old to the New Testament, we suddenly find the great and solemn affirmation that now the Church is the new holy nation and the new kingdom of priests: "But you are a chosen race, a royal priesthood, a holy nation, God's own people, in order that you may proclaim [His] mighty acts" (1 Peter 2:9). Every single baptized person has received the anointing and is consecrated: "God establishes us with you in Christ" wrote Saint Paul, " and has anointed us, by putting his seal on us and giving us his Spirit in our hearts as a first installment" (2 Corinthians 1:21–22). In turn, John wrote, "You have been anointed by the Holy One" (1 John 2:20). All Christians, then, have been consecrated or sanctified, that is, declared and made holy to serve God: "You were washed, you were sanctified" (1 Corinthians 6:11).

Christ, the Anointed One

But what does it mean that Christians have been consecrated? What kind of anointing have they received?

We need to start with Jesus, who is the first Consecrated One, the One to whom all the consecrations in the old covenant pointed. The very name "Messiah," in Greek *christos* and for us "Christ," means the "Anointed One," the "Consecrated One." The transition from the letter to the Spirit, from the type to the reality, from the external and temporal to the interior and eternal, all occurred in Him. Jesus used Isaiah's words to declare, "The Spirit of the Lord is upon me, / because he has anointed me" (Luke 4:18).

The event Jesus referred to in these words is the baptism in the Jordan, when "God anointed Jesus of Nazareth with the Holy Spirit and with power" (Acts 10:38). It is precisely from this anointing that the name of Christ is derived. "He is called Christ because He was anointed by the Father with the Holy Spirit," explained Tertullian.[3] According to Saint Irenaeus it is an action that involves the whole Trinity:

> In the name of "Christ" is implied the one who anointed, the one who was anointed and the unction itself with which He was anointed. It is the Father who anointed, the Son who was anointed, and the Holy Spirit Himself who was the anointing.[4]

The Father consecrates, Jesus is consecrated, and the Holy Spirit is the consecration. The role of the Holy Spirit in consecration becomes very clear here. He Himself is the oil of gladness (see Psalm 45:7) with which "the most handsome of men" (see Psalm 45:2) is anointed.

What does this mean, and why was Jesus only consecrated at the Jordan at the age of thirty? Jesus was certainly full of the Holy Spirit from the time of His conception in Mary! That is true, but that was His personal, incommunicable grace due to the hypostatic union between the Word and the humanity of the Savior. In baptism Jesus was anointed and consecrated as the head

of the mystical body in view of the mission He needed
to fulfill. He received the anointing that He would trans-
mit to His body, the Church. He was anointed Messiah,
receiving a kind of official investiture.

This profound truth can be found in the most ancient
teachers of the faith, the Church Fathers. Let's no longer
be content with dull devotional practices but rather
nourish ourselves with solid food. "The Lord," wrote
Saint Ignatius of Antioch, "received ointment on His
head that He might breathe the odor of incorrupt-
ibility into the church."[5] Saint Irenaeus clarified, "The
Spirit of God descended on Jesus and anointed Him
so that we, drawing from the fullness of His anointing,
would be saved."[6] Another great doctor, Saint Athanasius,
expressed the same conviction:

> It was for our sake that the Holy Spirit descended upon
> Jesus in the Jordan. It was for our sanctification so that
> we might share in His anointing and so that it might be
> said of us, "Do you not know that you are the temple of
> God and that the Holy Spirit dwells in you?"[7]

If the anointing of Christ was for us, why doesn't it come
to the Church immediately? Why is there a long interval
between the time when Jesus received the Spirit at Jordan
and the time when, at Easter and at Pentecost, He gave it
to His disciples?

The Spirit, as Saint Irenaeus said, needed to become
accustomed to dwelling among men. He needed first to
find a place in which He could dwell. The Spirit was completely present in the purest humanity of Christ, like a
perfume in an alabaster vase, but He could not be poured

out until Christ had been "glorified" (see John 7:39). In His passion the alabaster vase was broken—that is, Jesus' humanity was broken—and the perfume filled the whole house, the Church. He "gave up his spirit" (John 19:30), and His last breath became the first breath of the Church. The very evening of Easter Jesus breathed on His disciples and said, "Receive the Holy Spirit" (John 20:22).

There are three walls of separation between the Holy Spirit and us: nature, sin and death. Jesus tore down the first wall when He united within Himself the divine nature and human nature, the Spirit and flesh, in the Incarnation. He tore down the second wall when He died on the cross in expiation for the sins of the world. He tore down the third wall when He was raised from the dead. There is now no impediment to the oil of anointing.

The precious oil on Aaron's head—on Christ, the new High Priest—is poured out over the whole body to the hem of His robe (see Psalm 133:2). The Church, as such, is the place *par excellence* where the psalmist's wonderful image is made real, the place in which brothers and sisters "live together in unity!"

Christians, the Anointed Ones

At baptism each of us began to share in this consecrating ointment. In the early days of Christianity, when baptism was generally administered to adults, there was a special rite of anointing that expressed this particular meaning of the sacrament. It remains, even today, a complementary rite to baptism. But with the prevalence of infant baptism, it became detached from baptism and became a sacrament on its own called confirmation or chrismation, which means "anointing with chrism."

The words of Saint Cyril of Jerusalem that we read earlier refer to this rite when it was still closely tied to baptism. According to Cyril, just as Jesus became fully Christ—that is, consecrated—by His anointing in the baptism at Jordan, so too those who believe in Him become and are called "christs," or Christians, through their anointing. By this anointing they participate in the anointing of Christ.

For the early Church Fathers the name "Christians" did not primarily mean "followers of the doctrines of Christ," as it did for the pagans, who first gave them that name at Antioch (see Acts 11:26). Rather, the name *Christian* meant "anointed, consecrated," in imitation of Christ, the Consecrated One *par excellence.* According to Theophilus, "We are called Christians [*christianoi*] because we have been anointed [*chriometha*] with the oil of God."[8]

The result of all this is that we have in ourselves the same Spirit who was in Jesus of Nazareth. The Holy Spirit whom we have received is indeed the Third Person of the Trinity, but He has become, through the Incarnation, the Spirit of the Son. "God has sent the Spirit of his Son into our hearts" (Galatians 4:6). We have received the Spirit of the Son and not any other spirit. We are, so to speak, permeated by the Spirit's anointing and have therefore become "the aroma of Christ" (see 2 Corinthians 2:14–16).

What a joy to think that the same Spirit who was in Jesus during His days on earth is in me, and that He whom Saint Basil called His inseparable companion is now also my inseparable companion, the sweet guest of my soul! When we sense an inspiration, it is the voice of

Jesus who speaks to us (who exhorts us and counsels us) through His Spirit.

Because of the consecration that we have received, we carry a mark in the deepest part of our being, a mysterious seal (see Ephesians 1:13) engraved by the fire of the Holy Spirit, a royal seal. Because of that seal we are again made in the image of God and of Christ. The splendor of that image is so great that when Saint Catherine of Siena once saw a soul full of God's grace in a vision, she would have fallen to her knees in worship if she had not been warned that the soul was a creature and not God.

Kings, Prophets and Priests

But consecration is not an end in itself. Someone is always consecrated for something, for a purpose. Why have Christians been consecrated?

We can discover that in Jesus, who is the source and model of our own consecration. Jesus combined and fulfilled within Himself a triple consecration as king, as prophet and as priest.

In His baptism Jesus was first of all anointed as *king* to fight against Satan and to establish the kingdom of God: "But if it is by the Spirit of God," He said, "that I cast out demons, then the kingdom of God has come to you" (Matthew 12:28). The Old Testament kings were anointed to fight in physical battles against visible enemies: the Canaanites, the Philistines, the Amorites, and so on. In the New Testament Jesus is anointed with a kingly anointing to fight spiritual battles against invisible enemies: sin, death and the one who had dominion over death, Satan.

Second, Jesus was anointed as *prophet* to bring the good news to the poor. He applied to Himself the words with which Isaiah described his own prophetic consecration: "The Spirit of the Lord is upon me, / because he has anointed me to bring good news to the poor" (Luke 4:18; see Isaiah 61:1).

Finally, Jesus is anointed as *priest*, both through His incarnation and His baptism, to offer Himself in sacrifice. According to the Letter to the Hebrews, Jesus, "through the eternal Spirit, offered himself…to God [to] purify our conscience from dead works" (see Hebrews 9:14).

We too have been consecrated kings, prophets and priests. At the time of anointing with the sacred chrism in the rites that follow baptism, the Church declares, "Almighty God, Father of our Lord Jesus Christ, you have delivered us from sin and have given us new life through the water of the Holy Spirit." And to the baptized the priest says, "He Himself consecrates you with chrism and salvation as priest, king and prophet in Christ, and as a member of his body forever."

As *kings*, Christians are anointed to fight against sin—"do not let sin exercise dominion in your mortal bodies" (see Romans 6:12)—and against all their spiritual enemies, especially Satan. They are anointed for spiritual battle (see Ephesians 6:10–20). They are consecrated as *prophets* insofar as they are called to "proclaim [God's] mighty acts" (see 1 Peter 2:9) and to evangelize. Finally, they are consecrated as *priests* to exercise their royal priesthood.

On this point, Pope Leo the Great said to the Christians of his time:

> All those who are reborn in Christ become kings through the sign of the Cross and are consecrated as priests

through the anointing of the Holy Spirit. Thus, apart from the specific service of our ministry, all Christians are clothed with a spiritual and supernatural charism which makes them participants in a royal race and a priestly office. What is as royal as a soul who, submitted to God, governs his own body? What is as priestly as consecrating a pure conscience to the Lord and offering Him pure sacrifices on the altar of one's heart? Through the grace of God, these functions now belong to all of you. [9]

The Universal Priesthood of Christians

I will dwell only on the third anointing, that of priesthood. There is, in fact, a universal and shared priesthood that unites us all, both priests and laypeople. Today we can rejoice that we can affirm this, knowing that it expresses the authentic thinking of the Church. In the constitution *Lumen gentium* from Vatican II we read:

> The baptized, by regeneration and the anointing of the Holy Spirit, are consecrated to be a spiritual house and a holy priesthood, that through all the works of Christian men they may offer spiritual sacrifices.... Therefore all the disciples of Christ, persevering in prayer and praising God,... should present themselves as a sacrifice, living, holy and pleasing to God.[10]

From the point of view of personal sanctification, the priesthood that is shared by all is more important than the ministerial priesthood that is exercised at the altar. What Paul says about charity and the charisms (see 1 Corinthians 13) is relevant to that priesthood. Saint Gregory Nazianzen asked, "What does it profit me to offer the body of Christ at the altar if I don't offer myself with Christ?"[11]

In fact, this universal priesthood consists principally in offering oneself with Christ. This is the "spiritual sacrifice" of the priestly people. "I appeal to you," Paul wrote, "by the mercies of God, to present your bodies as a living sacrifice, holy and acceptable to God, which is your spiritual worship" (Romans 12:1). The word "body" here means all of one's life, since human life is lived in the body. "Body" here has the same meaning it did when Jesus instituted the Eucharist.

All of life, and not just certain parts of it, constitutes the substance of this sacrifice: the joys as well as the sorrows. Saint Augustine wrote:

> Every work...tending to effect our beatitude by an holy conjunction with God is a true sacrifice....[A] man, consecrated wholly to God's name, to live in Him and die to the world, is a sacrifice.[12]

A living sacrifice is the life of a mother who does a thousand things for her children and her family. A living sacrifice is a day's work for the Christian worker. A living sacrifice is the life of a sister, a priest or a religious whom the Church recognizes as consecrated in a very particular way. A living sacrifice is the life of a young man or woman who must face many battles and resist the seductions of the world. A living sacrifice for an elderly person is the long days often spent alone.

Finally, a living sacrifice is the life of a person who is ill. He or she can pray that the cup of suffering be removed, as Jesus prayed, and those around the sick person can and should pray for healing. But if, through the powerful grace of God, a person succeeds in accepting the illness, blessed is that man or woman. That life, although it is imposed upon the person and is limiting, can expand into marvelous fruitfulness. Thus, every life can be rescued from banality and from emptiness if only it is consecrated.

The meaning and the purpose of human existence become clear when we present ourselves to God as a pure and holy sacrifice. For what reason, in fact, did God give us the gift of life and of existence if not so that we would have something precious to offer Him, which we could return to Him as a gift? The same dynamic occurs in the Eucharist: We offer back to God the sacrifice of bread that we have received through His bounty. In the Offertory we say, "Through your goodness we have this bread to offer." We are each consecrated as a priest to return our life to God as a gift, "burning it" before Him as sweet-smelling incense.

Making small sacrifices in life is the path to a life of sacrifice. In *The Imitation of Christ* we find this beautiful prayer, which we can use to daily renew the offering of our lives to God:

> Lord, all things in heaven and in earth are Yours. I desire to offer myself to You in free and perpetual oblation, so that I may forever be with You. Lord, in simplicity of heart, I offer myself this day to You, to be Your servant in service and sacrifice of perpetual praise. Accept me with the oblation of Your precious Body, which this day I offer You.[13]

"Do Not Be Conformed to This World"

There is no sacrifice without a death. In the Mass the Offertory precedes the consecration; every oblation becomes perfected when the victim has been sacrificed. We cannot deceive ourselves about offering the whole world as a sacrifice if we ourselves do not die to the world. Saint Paul, after his exhortation to offer our bodies as a living and holy sacrifice, continued, "Do not be conformed to this world" (Romans 12:2), and elsewhere he declared, "The world has been crucified to me, and I to the world" (Galatians 6:14).

Here we discover the original and fundamental meaning of "consecrated" and "holy," which in Hebrew is the word *qadosh*. Because of their consecration, Christians are qadosh, that is, different, separate, set apart. We need to reacquire a sense of being *qadosh*.

Speaking prophetically of those who would be living in eschatological times—meaning us—Isaiah said someone will declare, "I belong to the Lord!" and another will write on his hand, "The Lord's" (see Isaiah 44:5). Revelation shows the counterpart to this: The mark of the beast inscribed on one's forehead or hand (see Revelation 13:16) indicates belonging spiritually to the powers of this world that Satan directs.

The call here has never been more urgent. The world has become so invasive that it now follows us into our homes. It assails us with messages that are diametrically opposed to the Word of God. This warning in Revelation is relevant: "Come out of her, my people, / so that you do not take part in her sins" (Revelation 18:4). Babylon, as Saint Augustine explained, is the opposite of the City of God. It is the city of Satan, the city built on love of self, with extreme contempt for God. We need to come out of that Babylon, which we also carry inside of ourselves, without leaving human society and solidarity with brothers and sisters. Since the principle of the world is egotism, not being conformed to this world means not being egotistical but loving and being a neighbor to all men and women.

We need to make this separation from the world real and concrete through specific actions. We cannot pretend to die to the world and then continue on just as before, swallowing everything the world says, thinks and does, surrendering to all its demands and its lusts. "No man can serve two masters," Jesus said (see Matthew 6:24). For example, how much time do we spend reading about the world's activities reported in newspapers, and how much time do we spend reading about God's activities reported in the Bible?

The world has need of "separated" ones, so that it does not collapse from its own spiritual emptiness and barrenness. It needs "the salt of the earth" in order to be spared the consequences of its own corruption.

Consecration and Purity

There is one aspect to this separation from the world that is especially urgent: purity. Saint Paul wrote to the Christians at Corinth:

> Do you not know that your body is a temple of the Holy Spirit within you, which you have from God, and that you are not your own?... [T]herefore glorify God in your body. (1 Corinthians 6:19, 20)

The reason for Christian purity lies precisely in consecration. We are not our own; we belong to the Lord. We cannot use our bodies for our own pleasure, for some personal satisfaction as an end in itself. That is a defilement of the temple of God; it is desecration, the exact opposite of consecration. And how much defilement and desecration we see in the world today!

Christian purity is not a refusal of or disdain for love. On the contrary, it is the cultivation of love—of true love, that is. What the world calls love is usually nothing more than empowered egotism most of the time. No one lives in love without sacrifice, without renunciation. The capacity that people have to give to another is equal to their readiness to deny themselves. Eroticism is the real tomb of love, because it is only an unbridled pursuit of oneself for oneself.

The appeal with which the apostle ends his exhortation on purity is addressed, in a special way, to young people: "Glorify God in your body." Therefore, I dare to entrust to young Christians a message on behalf of Jesus: Keep yourselves pure; fall in love with purity! Be the fragrance of Christ. The Word of God proposes this wonderful ideal to you: "Be blameless and innocent, children of God without blemish in the midst of a crooked and perverse generation, in which you shine like stars in the world,...holding fast to the word of life" (Philippians 2:15, 16).

This is not beyond your strength. John wrote, "the one who is in you is greater than the one who is in the world" (see 1 John 4:4). Do not let yourselves be subject to the world; believe that being pure is possible. I dare to make my own the words that the apostle John addressed to the young people in the early Christian community: "I write to you, young people, / because you are strong / and the word of God abides in you, / and you have overcome the evil one" (1 John 2:14). When he said that they *are* strong, not that they *should be* strong, it is an assertion and not simply a desire or a wish.

One important aspect of this call to purity is modesty. Modesty, by itself, proclaims the mystery that the body is united to a soul. It says that we do not belong to ourselves and that there is something in us that goes beyond our bodies. Modesty reflects respect for oneself and for others.

Wherever a sense of modesty is lacking, human sexuality becomes fatally trivialized. It is stripped of spiritual consideration and reduced to consumer merchandise. The world laughs at modesty and induces young people to be ashamed of the very thing they should take the most pride in and protect. The world is perpetrating real violence on the young.

We need to wake up. Saint Peter urged the Christian women of his time:

> Let your adornment be the inner self with the lasting beauty of a gentle and quiet spirit, which is very precious in God's sight. It was in this way long ago that the holy women who hoped in God used to adorn themselves. (1 Peter 3:4–5)

This is not a condemnation of adornment for the body or of efforts to take a concern for one's appearance. Rather, Peter urged that this adornment be accompanied by a pure heart and that it be done in order to give joy through the gift of self, rather than to seduce.

Modesty is a wonderful testimony to the world. One of the first Christian martyrs, young Perpetua, was placed on top of a wild cow in a Roman arena and was hurled into the air. After falling to the ground bleeding, she readjusted her dress because she was "mindful rather of modesty than of pain."[14] Testimonies like that helped to change the pagan world and introduced within it a respect for modesty.

Modesty is the most beautiful ornament of purity. Fyodor Dostoevsky wrote that the world would be saved through beauty, but that there existed only one beautiful person in the world, Christ. Purity allows the beauty of Christ to manifest itself in the face of a young Christian man or woman. Purity manifests the "beautiful" character of the Christian vocation. This beauty is not exclusively tied to age and does not fade as physical beauty does. How many times elderly cloistered sisters have elicited the exclamation from visitors, "What a face! What light!"

Let us ask God to renew in us, through His Holy Spirit, the consecration received in baptism and strengthened in us through the sacrament of confirmation. Let our prayer be the one the Church addresses to God in the consecration of the sacred chrism on Holy Thursday: "May this anointing sanctify us and free us from our corrupt human nature so that, consecrated as a temple for your glory, we may spread the fragrance of a holy life."

CHAPTER SIX

The Healing Power of the Spirit

He came down with them and stood on a level place, with a great crowd of His disciples and a great multitude of people from all Judea, Jerusalem, and the coast of Tyre and Sidon. They had come to hear him and to be healed of their diseases; and those who were troubled with unclean spirits were cured. And all in the crowd were trying to touch him, for power came out from him and healed all of them. (Luke 6:17–19)

A Power That Heals Everyone

What was this power, this *dynamis*, that came out of Jesus? A magnetic fluid, a hypnotic current, a power of suggestion or something like that? Certainly not; it was the Holy Spirit! Luke said it, once and for all, at the beginning of Christ's ministry: "Then Jesus, filled with the power [*dynamis*] of the Spirit, returned to Galilee" (Luke 4:14), and "the power of the Lord was with him to heal" (Luke 5:17).

This power, which is the Holy Spirit, still *now* comes out of Jesus. Now that He is resurrected and is "declared to be the Son of God with power according to the spirit of holiness" (see Romans 1:4), that power comes forth from Him even more truly and more powerfully, if we can say that, than when He walked the earth.

This power heals *everybody*. This is the decisive point we need to understand and to believe right now. We should say, as Jesus did in the synagogue at Nazareth, "Today this scripture has been fulfilled!" (Luke 4:21).

The Holy Spirit does not have problems with numbers. A human doctor in front of a crowd of people with many and varied ailments would throw up his arms and say he was unable to heal everybody. But not the Holy Spirit. Just as the sun can bring light to one person or to a billion people, so too the Holy Spirit can do the same in the spiritual realm.

The early Christians were enthused and amazed when they discovered this characteristic of the Holy Spirit. Saint Cyril of Jerusalem said during a liturgical gathering:

> The Holy Spirit is great, omnipotent in His charisms, and wonderful. Calculate how many of us are seated here. Well, He does what is best for each one. Being in our midst, He sees the conduct of each person, and He also sees our thoughts, our hearts, what we say, and what we think. He is truly as great as I have said so far, but that is still too little. Picture in your minds, enlightened by Him, how many Christians there are in this diocese, and how many are scattered throughout Palestine. Travel in your minds beyond this province to the whole Roman Empire and from there to the whole world. Observe the races of Persians, the peoples of India, the Goths, the

Sarmatians, the Garbs, the Spaniards, the Moors, the Libyans, the Ethiopians and all the other peoples whose names we don't even know.[1]

The Holy Spirit, he concluded, comes to all of them. We should expect and ask for general healing. I do not mean that some people want to hear the Word of God and that others want to be healed of their infirmities. We cannot accept that kind of truncation. The text from Luke says about the great crowd that followed Jesus, "They had come to hear Him *and* to be healed"—not to hear *or* to be healed.

We need to have both: to hear the Word of God and to be healed of our infirmities or, even better, to be healed precisely by listening to the Word. In fact, it is the Word that heals. Scripture clearly says, "For neither herb nor poultice [a fancy word meaning "plaster"] cured them, / but it was your word, O Lord, that heals all people" (Wisdom 16:12). We, along with the Roman centurion, articulate this at every Mass: "Only say the word and I shall be healed" (see Matthew 8:8). The word, I repeat, is the privileged instrument of healing.

This means that we should all receive healing. When the Lord heals physically, it confirms what He does for everybody on the spiritual, interior, invisible level. Physical healings are a benefit for all, a gift to all, and not an exception or a privilege for the fortunate few. A healing liturgy is not a lottery in which there are two or three lucky winners and many losers.

We read that there was a wonderful pool in Jerusalem called Bethsaida. Whoever first lowered himself into the pool when the waters were stirred up by an angel would come out healed. "Even greater things" happen today, as Jesus Himself predicted, since He is risen and lives in the Spirit. The pool of Bethsaida is any place where Christians gather. And the wonderful thing is that not only the first but all who "lower themselves into the water" come out restored.

Let no one say, as the paralytic did, "Sir, I have no one to put me into the pool when the water is stirred up" (John 5:7). Everyone who exercises a ministry today—preaching, healing, leading songs or prayer—is an "angel" commissioned through his or her service to "stir up" the water and to "lower into it" all those who will let themselves be immersed. Which water? The water of faith, of course.

Not only does Jesus want to heal *all* men and women through the power of His Spirit, He also wants to heal the *whole* person in all his or her constitutive aspects and dimensions. You have certainly heard of holistic medicine, which aims not only to heal the sick part but the whole person (*holos* in Greek means "whole"). This medical approach is not satisfied, we would imagine, to heal an infection in a leg without curing everything else.

Medicine to heal an infection can be so strong that it damages the heart or causes an ulcer. This certainly does not do the sick person any good. An incompetent doctor might say, "You came to have your infection cured; well, I've cured your infection. What else do you want from me?"

The Holy Spirit does not do things this way. He does not want to heal the infection on a finger and bypass curing the heart. What good would it do someone to have a knee joint healed but still have a heart, mind and soul diseased or even dead?

Spiritual Therapy

Since the Holy Spirit wants to heal the whole man, we should know how man is constituted, that is, what the components are that need healing. A stanza in the hymn *Veni Creator* says,

> Light a light in our minds,
> Pour out love into our hearts,
> Healing what is sick in our bodies
> By your eternal power.

Within these apparently simple words is an outline of a specific vision of the human being (in scholarly terms, an anthropology). It sees every individual in three existential dimensions. First is the sphere of *rationality*, expressed in the word *sensus*, which does not mean "senses" in ecclesiastical Latin but "the mind" or "intelligence." Then comes the sphere of *affectivity* or *will*—the part of ourselves that is usually called the *heart*. Finally, there is what Saint Francis of Assisi called *brother body*. The body is not the whole person (as modern materialism presumes), but neither is it a provisional appendage that can be ignored (as ancient Platonic spirituality held). We do not each "have" a body; each of us "is" a body.

What will we ask of the Holy Spirit concerning each of these three components? For our minds we ask for *light*—certitude, truth—from the One who is the "Spirit of truth." For our hearts we ask for *love*. Finally, for brother body we ask for *healing*, for a strengthening of what is sick or weak. Perhaps the author of *Veni Creator* alludes to these words of Christ, "The spirit indeed is willing, but the flesh is weak" (Matthew 26:41).

What we all need now is special therapy. As heliotherapy makes use of the sun to heal, I will call this special therapy *pneumatherapy*, a therapy based on Pneuma, the Holy Spirit. Heliotherapy consists in exposure to the beneficial rays from the sun over a period of time. Pneumatherapy consists in exposing our whole being, bit by bit, to the spiritual "Sun," that is, the Holy Spirit.

"Mental" Illnesses

We should give names to our sicknesses, so let's begin with naming the illnesses of the mind. We will discover, to our surprise, that we are all mentally ill.

Our worst mental illness is not insanity. That is certainly a horrible sickness that we would wish on no one, but in comparison to other mental illnesses, it is at least "innocent."

Our first mental illness is called *unbelief.* Saint Paul described some people with this illness: "The god of this world has blinded the minds of the unbelievers, to keep them from seeing the light of the gospel of the glory of Christ" (2 Corinthians 4:4). The unbelieving mind is the closed mind, the mind that sees this world and nothing else and believes that it knows everything. Unbelief is a kind of mental atrophy, an inability to see anything beyond and above our own minds.

A great philosopher from the nineteenth century who was also a believer, Søren Kierkegaard, said that the supreme act of human reason is to acknowledge that there is something more supreme. It is precisely this leap that many refuse to make. They believe in defending the rights of reason and do not realize that they humiliate and offend reason by negating its capacity to transcend and to project beyond itself.

Another mental illness that is just as terrible is *idolatry*. It consists in exchanging the creature for the Creator, in putting something else in God's place, something that keeps "truth as the prisoner of injustice." The truth is that only God is God and we are creatures of God. He is the Creator and we are the creatures. Idolatry reverses the two roles: Man does not accept God and instead makes himself a god. He becomes the potter, and God becomes the vessel that he shapes according to his pleasure. He is the one who determines God's place rather than the reverse. This is a mental disease: "Their senseless minds were darkened. Claiming to be wise, they became fools" (Romans 1:21–22). Foolishness, not madness, is the real mental illness here.

Do we think that idolaters existed only in Paul's time but not today? And even today, do we believe idolaters exist only outside of our churches and prayer groups? No. Idols have become more subtle, but they are still here. For one person his idol is his "I": Me, myself, and I!

For others the idol is money. Oh, money, money! How much evil this dreadful god has done in the world, this "idol of molten metal" for which people betray, corrupt others and let themselves be corrupted! It is a fearful, ruthless god, like Moloch in the Bible, to whom innocent victims were sacrificed, or the god of the Aztecs, who demanded the daily sacrifice of a certain number of human hearts.

For others the idol can be sports: soccer, football, and so on. If the Sunday game at the stadium is the most important thing of your week, if you live in anticipation of each game, if your only thrill in life is when you shout and scream in that stadium, then you are an idolater and need healing.

There is another sickness that coils around us on all sides. It is called *superstition*—resorting to wizards, sorcerers, fortune-tellers, occult arts and spiritualists. This too is a mental sickness. In Deuteronomy we read, "No one shall be found among you...who practices divination, or is a soothsayer, or an augur or a sorcerer, or one who casts spells, or who consults ghosts or spirits or who seeks oracles from the dead. For whoever does these things is abhorrent to the Lord" (Deuteronomy 18:10–12).

Isaiah wrote this terrifying prophecy: The Lord is about to bring judgment on this land because it is overflowing with soothsayers and diviners from the east (see Isaiah 2:6, 12).

"Diviners from the east": How modern our ancient Isaiah is! Yes, unfortunately, our world is overflowing with sorcerers and diviners. Most of the time it is a case of charlatanism and nothing else. Thieves trade on the naïveté and credulity of people, and often on their desperation as well when they are faced with overwhelming health or financial problems. The godless intention of practicing this art and of resorting to occult arts is enough to make people fall into the snares of the evil one.

We have only two ways to be healed or to improve: through nature or through grace. *Nature* includes science, medicine, technology and all the resources that man has received from God to govern the earth and his own life in obedience to Him. *Grace* includes faith and prayer, through which healing and miracles are sometimes obtained—always, however, from God, because "that power belongs to God" (Psalm 62:11).

When a third way appears—whether it is recourse to occult powers through occult means, secretly concealed from God without any need for His approval, or the direct abuse of His name or of some of His signs (like the pictures of certain saints)—then the master and pioneer of this third way enters immediately on the scene. He is the one who said one day that all power on earth was his and that he could give it to whomever he pleased if he were adored (see Luke 4:6). Devastation in such cases is inevitable. The fly is caught in the web of the "great spider" and will not easily come out alive.

"Heart" Diseases

Let's move on now to the second sphere of our being, the heart. What will we ask of the Holy Spirit concerning our affections, our will, our capacity to love and be loved? We ask for love: as the line from the *Veni Creator* says, "Pour out love into our hearts."

And now I need to tell you another unpleasant thing: Not only are we all mentally ill, but we all have heart diseases—some more, some less. We are all spiritual cardiopaths, aren't we? Let's do a bit of "anamnesis" in this case too. This is the point at which the doctor has the sick person describe his symptoms.

There is a heart disease called *abulia*. This is a Greek word: *Boule* means "will," and the initial "*a*" always means "lack." So *abulia* means "a lack of will" and the whole procession of things that derive from a lack of will: weariness, sluggishness, a belief that everything is too overwhelming or too difficult. It is a chronic state of spiritual laziness that is one of the biggest obstacles to holiness.

Then there is the opposite disease called "the will to power," which was theorized by Friedrich Nietzsche. According to him, when Christianity ends, a new gospel will come forth, the gospel of the superman. He will be guided not by a will to serve but by the will to power, by the will to conquer.

Hitler took up this message, and we know the things that his will to power produced, but let's not stop with the historical Hitler. There are many little Hitlers in our midst: authoritarian spirits who tyrannically impose their own wills on others in their families and at work. How many tears, how much sorrow, is produced by this sickness of the will!

Just as in the physical realm, so too in the spiritual realm there are illnesses that affect one sex more than the other. The will to power is a predominately male disease. Dear male colleagues, let's be careful. God did not intend to confer on our male sex the right to express our rage at every little thing, to raise our voices, to pound our fists on the table, to terrorize all those around us, as if this were the only way to demonstrate that we are real men. This is a symptom of weakness and not of virility. This is a real spiritual disease, the capital sin called anger.

Some men are said to be angels in public and devils at home, and I have to say I have known some of these men. We are now beginning to talk openly about domestic violence. This is a real problem that Christians at least should be able to resolve without calling the police. Many families live in a perpetual state of fear, holding their breath under the permanent threat of Dad's anger.

There is also a disease that is typically female: the spirit of slavery. Saint Paul wrote, "You did not receive a spirit of slavery to fall back into fear, but you have received a spirit of adoption" (Romans 8:15), and, "For freedom Christ has set us free. Stand firm, therefore" (Galatians 5:1).

I am speaking to women from many cultures where this spirit of slavery is still strong. After the brief dawn of their youth, when the world opens to them and everyone seems captivated by them, many women become wives and mothers and are reduced to slaves. They are slaves of their husbands, slaves of their children—without joy, without beauty. They often dress in black (because there is always some grief they are carrying).

You say to me, "But you are preaching against the gospel! Doesn't the gospel talk about self-renunciation, mortification and self-denial?"

Yes, but not this kind of mortification because this kind does not bring life; it prevents giving and receiving joy and also prevents freely suffering. The Holy Spirit is the Spirit who gives freedom. You have been set free by Christ, ladies, to remain free. If there is suffering or self-denial in caring for your children, your husband or your elderly parents, you will endure it but with joy and interior freedom.

The liberty I am talking about makes you free precisely to serve: "You were called to freedom...[so that you could] through love become slaves to one another" (Galatians 5:13). This is a "paschal" kind of freedom. The exodus from Egypt was, in fact, a transition "from slavery to service."

The world needs women not only until they are twenty but afterward as well. Let's be done with the spectacle of woman reduced to her body, to her breasts and not much else, making her a mere object.

My sisters, you are not only victims in this situation, you are also, in part, accomplices. In the Book of Genesis God says to Eve, "Your desire shall be for your husband, and he shall rule over you" (Genesis 3:16). That one statement, better than whole volumes, describes the reality of our world. You, woman, after the Fall, will be attracted to your husband and will be dominated by your instinct to please the man, and you will not notice how the man will use this situation to dominate you. This is exactly what has happened.

What is your part in complicity here, my sisters? You should not think of life only with a man in mind. You should not wager everything on trying to please and attract a man's gaze. If you do, the consequence is inevitable: You will remain slaves. Men will only see sex in you and will dominate you and use you for publicity, for pornography and for all sorts of evil purposes.

How can we cry out about scandal, then, when tragedies occur? Adolescents and others are seduced, especially the weaker ones, by this exhibition of the woman's body. But what right do the newspapers and television have to rend their garments the day after such tragedies? Given what they disseminate every day, aren't they themselves in large part responsible for all this?

The United Nations recently organized a World Conference on Women in Beijing. Today the whole world is talking about equal rights for men and women. It is certainly a sign of the times, a wonderful thing. However, if we limit ourselves to drafting documents on women's rights but a profound healing in the hearts of women does not occur, then the conference in Beijing will have been good for nothing, and all the talk about women's rights will be a dead letter. We should ask for healing of this from the Holy Spirit.

Let's look at the episode in Luke about the woman with curvature of the spine. She presented herself to Jesus on a Sabbath day, and Jesus said to her, " 'Woman, you are set free from your ailment.'...[I]mmediately she stood up straight and began praising God" (Luke 13:12–13).

Today I see women who are bent over, slaves, and Christ is calling out to each of them, "Woman, be free! Stand up, erect in all your dignity as a daughter of God! Be what the Creator meant you to be when He created Eve! The world needs you, and so does the kingdom of God. The Church needs you and your freedom!" The image of the bent-over woman in the Gospel of Luke speaks volumes on the situation of women in our society.

The Holy Spirit Heals Marriages

The Holy Spirit heals the hearts of men and the hearts of women, but He does more: He also heals the institution that makes a man and woman one flesh, *marriage*. In this case, to heal the individual (the man or the woman taken separately) without healing the family—the couple in which each takes part—would be like healing a part of the body and leaving the rest of the person sick. Even the healed part will continue to suffer and be sick.

I need to explain what the diseases of the couple are. There is a legal divorce, and there is a divorce of the heart. The *divorce of the heart* occurs when the wife and husband, although remaining together under the same roof, no longer love one another, no longer speak to each other and are estranged. It as though a glacial era has happened to them. Many families are a living hell, and we priests can talk about that because people confide the most fiery dramas and suffering to our ears and our hearts.

The Lord has many times performed the miracle of healing the entire family, of putting a dead, joyless marriage back on its feet. And He can do it today! Do you remember the great expanse of dry bones that Ezekiel saw? In this era of family crises, those dry bones are the couples who no longer have any vitality, love, understanding, openness or dialogue. But what did the Lord say to Ezekiel? "'Son of man,…prophesy to these bones'" (Ezekiel 37:3–4 [RSV]).

This "son of man," i.e., a nobody, refers to me right now because I dare to take the words of the prophet and make them mine. I cry out to today's dry bones: "O dry bones, hear the word of the Lord. Thus says the Lord God to these bones: I will cause breath to enter you, and you shall live.… [A]nd you shall know that I am the Lord" (Ezekiel 37:4–6).

Ezekiel said to the Spirit, "Come from the four winds, O breath" (Ezekiel 37:9), that is, from the four points of the compass. We no longer say this because we know where the Spirit comes from. We say instead, "Spirit, come from the side of Christ on the cross, and breathe on these dead ones!"—on dry couples throughout the whole world. Breathe on them, and make the love that has been extinguished come alive again. Only You can do it. You are "the gift of God"; renew in spouses the ability to make themselves gifts for one another.

I recently conducted a mission in the United States, and I would like to share one of my fondest memories of it. The evening before an important gathering, the couple who was hosting me took me out to eat. While we were waiting for the meal to be served, the husband shared:

Father, now you see me holding my wife's hand, but it wasn't always this way. We were on the point of separating and had been to see a lawyer three times, but every time we would hardly enter his office before we would start quarreling so much that the lawyer would be quite embarrassed. We couldn't take it anymore. We decided to divorce.

Then someone took me to a charismatic meeting one night, and I don't know what happened to me there, but I seemed to have a fire in my heart. My heart of stone was being shattered. I got home, woke my wife up late at night, embraced her and said, "You know, I love, I love you!" Perplexed, she looked at me and said, "What happened to you? Have you gone crazy?"

Later he convinced his wife to go to the charismatic prayer meeting, and today they are among the most committed people serving the Church. This man said:

I shudder today to think that I was about to lose my wife, my children and my grandchildren, who are my joy today, and to be deprived of them for the rest of my life. The Lord has given everything back to me, everything.

Who does these kinds of miracles today? The charismatic renewal? No. The difference in these charismatic meetings is not due to the men, women, or famous people there but to the Holy Spirit.

There is a Negro spiritual whose chorus consists of the repetition of only a few words:

There is a balm in Gilead
to make the wounded whole.
There is a balm in Gilead
to heal the sin-sick soul.

Gilead is often mentioned in the Old Testament as a place that was famous for its perfume (see Jeremiah 8:22). Listening to this song, one can think of a street vendor who goes down the street, shouting out the names and the prices of his merchandise. I can imagine myself to be like that street vendor now. But what is the balm that we claim to have? It is no longer the physical balm of Gilead; it is the Holy Spirit. Therefore I cry out: There is a balm in the Church that heals crushed souls and wounded hearts and that melts hearts of stone. Come, buy without cost. Take this oil, which comes to you through the Word, the sacraments and prayer. Take this balm, whether you are sick in heart or sick in mind. Let us all take this balm in massive doses, because the world needs massive doses of the Holy Spirit. With the words of the "Sequence of the Holy Spirit" let us say to the Spirit together:

Wounded lives to health restore!
Melt the frozen, warm the chill!
Guide the wayward home once more!

The Holy Spirit Heals "Brother Body"

What will we ask for *brother body* from the Holy Spirit of the *Veni Creator*? We will ask for healing of its infirmities!

There are diverse types of infirmities for the body as well. There are physical infirmities, pure and simple: paralyses, diseases of the bones, eyes, ears, and so on. These are things that carry no blame; they are not a punishment from God. We should all understand at least this by now. No one, I trust, who is suffering from some kind of sickness asks, "What did I do wrong for God to punish me like this?"

But there are sicknesses that imply a certain responsibility on our part. These hover between being sicknesses of the soul and those of the body. They are the consequences of abuses committed in the past against our bodies in excessive eating, drinking, promiscuous sex and drug abuse. We can ask the Lord to heal us of these sicknesses, but our cooperation is needed.

Before healing the paralytic at the pool of Bethsaida, Jesus asked him an apparently strange question: "Do you want to be made well?" (John 5:6). Wasn't it obvious that he certainly wanted to be healed? And yet Jesus wanted to hear him say that. Why? Because this is often the precise point: Do we want to be healed? Do we really want it? Are we ready to live without that certain something that we think of as part of ourselves?

Jesus often heals even physical sicknesses by means of His word. I remember this testimony by a man on a television show that I was part of:

> I was a last-stage alcoholic; I couldn't go for more than two hours without drinking. Whenever I would get on a

> train, the first thing I looked for was the club car. I made life impossible for my wife and my three children.
>
> One night we went to a meeting that was a Bible study. Someone read a passage, and when I heard one of the verses in that passage, I felt a kind of electrical charge go through me. It was as though a burst of flame went through my body. I felt myself healed. Afterward, every time I was strongly tempted to alcohol, I would run and open the Bible to that passage. Just seeing the words with my eyes gave me renewed strength until I was completely healed.

When the man tried to say what the particular verse was, his voice stuck in his throat. It was the verse from the Song of Songs, "Your love is better than wine" (1:2). That was it—the restorative power of the Word of God, heard in an atmosphere of faith and prayer!

The Holy Spirit does not cease to surprise us. I would like to give some teaching about healing at this point based on some recurring questions. What about the people who are not healed of physical ailments? What should we think about that? Did the person not have enough faith? Or did the people who prayed not have enough faith? Unfortunately, in some circles people think this way, but it is not true. Most of the time this only adds more suffering to the original difficulty.

I remember a consecrated lay woman I met in Africa who had a limp. People had prayed for her a lot but she was not healed. In the end, they sent her away, telling her that she probably did not have enough faith. She lived with her ailment and, in addition, with a strong sense of guilt for years. Finally one day she understood and changed her prayer: "Lord, it's okay; I accept living a life of limping. However, You must promise me one thing: When I enter Paradise, You must let me dance for several centuries because I was born to dance!"

If not being healed always indicates a lack of faith, then the saints are the people who had the least faith of anyone because some of them were sick all their lives. Doctors today calculate that when Saint Francis of Assisi died, he had about ten serious illnesses. Saint Paul himself prayed "three times," that is, an infinite number of times, for the Lord to remove a certain thorn from his flesh, but what did the Lord answer? "My grace is sufficient for you, for power is made perfect in weakness" (2 Corinthians 12:9).

There is another explanation for why some people do not get healed. God has two different ways of helping us and showing His power. Either He can remove the physical sickness, or He can give us the strength to carry it in a new, free and joyful way. He can unite us to Christ and complete "what is lacking in Christ's afflictions for the sake of his body, that is, the church" (Colossians 1:24). There are sick people who return from Lourdes not healed but happier than if they had been healed physically. When the Lord also heals physically, it is a visible sign to us that He can and wants to heal everyone spiritually.

Let's present our sick brothers and sisters to Jesus, as did the people who lowered the paralytic through the roof. Compassion, according to Saint Gregory of Nyssa, is the organ through which the charism of healing is exercised. Our attitude toward our own sufferings and those of our brothers and sisters should be different. For ourselves, we can accept sickness, but when it concerns our neighbor, we should dare much and be resolute with God. We read about a holy anchorite in antiquity who, concerning the sickness of a brother, dared to address God as only saints can: "O God, whether you want to or not, heal this brother!"[2]

We need to take the requests that people addressed to Jesus when He went through Palestine and make them ours:

"Lord, he whom you love is sick!"
"Lord, my daughter is cruelly tormented by the devil!"
"Lord, only say the word and my servant shall be healed!"

Lord Jesus, only say the word, and our diseases will be healed!

CHAPTER SEVEN

Pentecost: The Way to Conversion and Unity

What Kind of Unity?

When people want to start a pilgrimage, they need to first establish the destination, just as people who want to shoot an arrow need to know what their target is. We would like to make a kind of pilgrimage toward unity at this time, but we must first understand what kind of unity we are seeking.

In Acts of the Apostles we read:

> They devoted themselves to the apostles' teaching and fellowship, to the breaking of bread and the prayers.
>
> Awe came upon everyone, because many wonders and signs were being done by the apostles. All who believed were together and had all things in common; they would sell their possessions and goods and distribute the pro-

ceeds to all, as any had need. Day by day, as they spent much time together in the temple, they broke bread at home and ate their food with glad and generous hearts, praising God and having the goodwill of all the people. And day by day the Lord added to their number those who were being saved. (Acts 2:42–48)

This text describes the kind of unity for which we aim. There are various kinds of unity between Christians. There is a doctrinal unity, which official ecumenism is actively pursuing through dialogues and meetings on various levels today in the Church. However, this vertical kind of ecumenism is not enough; it needs to be accompanied by what Paul VI called an ecumenism from the ground up.

There is quite a difference between real water, which we drink and wash with, and the chemical formula for water, H_2O. The formula appears only in books, but the real water is for life. Something of the same kind can be said about unity: There is a unity that is a "formula" and a unity that is a lived reality.

The reality is what we hear described in the Acts of the Apostles at the end of the account of Pentecost: People lived together in simplicity and joy, sharing everything. These people came from different strata of society, and yet they were sharing meals and praying together.

Only a few days before they were profoundly different, and each person may have had many things about which to reproach one another. Among those who lived together now there were also some who had crucified the Lord but had recently converted. Executioners and victims, sinners and righteous, now find themselves reconciled. It is a miracle of the Spirit.

The text does not say up to this point that the apostles were preaching, and yet conversions were occurring: "And day by day the Lord added to their number those who were being saved" (Acts 2:48). Their unity itself was the great sermon. Their unity could be seen and touched by hands, so to speak. Tertullian reports that the pagans of his time, seeing the Christians come out of their meetings, exclaimed with amazement how much the Christians loved one another!

Now that we understand what the goal of our pilgrimage is, we need to begin moving toward it. Ours will be a pilgrimage through Pentecost. There will be four stages, which correspond to the number of pericopes that comprise the second chapter of Acts. At this point the most important thing is to listen carefully: The words are familiar to us, but now they must be heard in a new way. As we hear them, the Holy Spirit mystically renews His coming.

Something of the same kind happens in the Eucharist. At the moment of consecration during the Mass, the Church recounts what Jesus did at the Last Supper. The miracle is that while it is being recounted, what happened in the past happens all over again: The bread becomes the Body of Christ, and the wine becomes His Blood.

The recounting of the Pentecost event has an analogous power, even if it is not sacramental like the Eucharist. What we recount becomes real: The Holy Spirit mysteriously descends again and becomes present. It becomes not just a simple retelling but an event.

All Were Filled with the Holy Spirit

The first stage, recorded in the first four verses in the second chapter of Acts, is the infilling of the Holy Spirit:

> When the day of Pentecost had come, they were all together in one place. And suddenly from heaven there came a sound like the rush of a violent wind, and it filled the entire house where they were sitting. Divided tongues, as of fire, appeared among them, and a tongue rested on each of them. All of them were filled with the Holy Spirit and began to speak in other languages, as the Spirit gave them ability. (Acts 2:1–4)

It is God's style to prepare men to receive His interventions with signs and prophecies that draw His people's attention. He wants to ensure that these acts are noticed. All of the Old Testament was, in that sense, a preparation for the coming of Christ. Here too we have signs that are premonitions.

First there is a sign for *hearing*: They heard the rush of a violent wind. It was not just any kind of sound but the sound of a wind, and we know that in the Bible wind is a symbol for the Holy Spirit. Both Hebrew and Greek use only one word for wind and spirit: *ruah* in Hebrew and *pneuma* in Greek.

Then there is a sign for *sight*: They saw tongues, as of fire. Fire is another symbol often associated with the Spirit. John the Baptist had promised that a baptism of "the Holy Spirit and fire" (Matthew 3:11) was coming.

Finally comes the invisible reality that all the signs pointed to: "They were all filled with the Holy Spirit." The greatest event in the history of the world (along with the Incarnation and the Resurrection) is described in the simplest and most sober way. It is God's style to perform magnificent acts with the minimum of means and words.

But what profundity is hidden within these few words! To discover it, at least in part, we need to go beyond what was explicitly said. It is customary for the Bible to speak to us through references. Here Luke wanted to establish a parallel between Pentecost and the theophany at Sinai. He did it by creating a scenario very similar to the one at Sinai and by using the same symbols of storm and of fire.

Tradition has always been aware of this, so the liturgy on the Eve of Pentecost includes Exodus 19 among its various readings. That chapter narrates the decisive event for the chosen people: God gave a law, the Decalogue, and established a covenant with the people, who then became a "royal and priestly people" on the basis of that law.

Saint Augustine understood the meaning of this parallel very well. In one of his sermons on Pentecost he said to the faithful:

> Who is not struck by this coincidence and yet the difference? Fifty days transpire after the celebration of the Passover in Egypt...until the day when Moses received the law on stone tablets written by the finger of God. Similarly, fifty days after the sacrifice of the new Paschal lamb (Christ), the finger of God, i.e., the Holy Spirit, comes to the believers who are all gathered together.[1]

What does this mean? It is clear that the Holy Spirit is the new law of Christianity, the interior law, no longer written on stone tablets but on tablets of flesh. He is the very principal of the new covenant. What a magnificent revelation about the Holy Spirit and His role in Christian life! God gives the Holy Spirit not merely so that we might *carry* salvation to the ends of the earth, He *is* salvation. He is not only a help for that mission, He is life itself. Saint Paul said it clearly: "For the law of the Spirit of life in Christ Jesus has set you free from the law of sin and of death" (Romans 8:2).

The "law of the Spirit" means "the law which is the Spirit." This new law acts through love. It is nothing less than the new commandment of Christ, which is no longer a *commandment* now but a *gift*, a grace, a new capacity that is infused in us and permits us in turn to love God and our neighbor. The new *law* is the *grace* itself of the Holy Spirit.

Does this mean that the Holy Spirit dispenses us from all the other laws now, that is, from observing the Ten Commandments, the precepts of the gospel, the laws of the Church, canon law, and such? No! It means, rather, that from now on all the external and written laws—from that of Moses to our own simplest laws—should have their proper place as humble servants to the interior law of the Spirit.

If these laws pretended to substitute themselves for love and to give justification and life on their own, they would become the letter that kills. Saint Thomas has the boldness to affirm that without the interior grace of the Holy Spirit, even the precepts and the beatitudes of the gospel become the letter that kills.[2]

The Holy Spirit is the new law and, as such, is sufficient for the Christian. However, because we live in the flesh and are sinners, we also need all those other laws. They indicate to us what the will of God is in concrete and specific circumstances, helping us to discern the true from the false in the movements of the Spirit. In that sense, all the laws have become new, insofar as they participate in the newness of the Spirit.

In an ecumenical spirit, I would like to share an insight from Luther. In a sermon on Pentecost he affirmed that we are born with an old heart, a heart full of carnal desires and concupiscence. People desire prestige, power, money, their neighbor's goods, their neighbor's wife and so on, but God blocks their path with His command- ments: "You must…; you must not…!"

In this situation, said Luther, it is inevitable that they would begin to look at God with a sullen eye, as an enemy of their own happiness, as the one who is the obstacle to obtaining their desires. There is a silent bit- terness in sinful people against God, to the extent that, if it depended on them, they would rather that God did not even exist.

When the Holy Spirit comes, here is the miracle! He presents people with a different face for God: a God who is an ally, not an adversary; a good Father who did not spare even His own Son for them; a God, in short, who shows them favor. They understand that God has given the commandments for their good. A new feeling springs up in their hearts, that of sons or daughters, and from their lips at last comes the cry, "Abba, Father!"

This indicates regeneration and rebirth by the Spirit! Those who are reborn in the Spirit are those whose hearts of stone, hearts of slaves, have been removed and replaced with hearts of flesh, hearts of sons and daugh- ters. The Holy Spirit does a kind of surgical operation, a genuine heart bypass.

Generally, bypass surgeries are performed with total anesthesia, and people feel nothing. Only when the operation is over, after a period of time, do they realize they feel better. For the apostles it was not that way: Their heart bypass was not done with anesthesia! The things the apostles began to do very shortly afterward leave no doubt about that. A change like the one we see in their behavior—the spontaneous enthusiasm with which they faced the sneering of the crowd, even accepting being thought drunk at first—can only be explained by strong emotion. These are things that only love can make people do.

In fact, the disciples had a new experience at Pentecost as they were carried away by God's love. They felt themselves baptized—immersed—in the ocean of the Father's love. They discovered for the first time what the love of the Father was, this love that Jesus spoke to them about for so long and in vain. They discovered the tenderness that is in the name *Abba* which they had heard their Master share about many times.

How do we know all this? It is simple: The Holy Spirit is love. When He is poured out, love is poured out. The first thing He does when He enters people's hearts is to teach them to cry out, "Abba!" (see Galatians 4:6; Romans 8:15). To say that all "were filled with the Holy Spirit" is to say that all were filled to overflowing with love.

Paul makes this explicit: "God's love," he says, "has been poured into our hearts through the Holy Spirit that has been given to us" (see Romans 5:5). This is a historical affirmation, not a theoretical one, which refers to very specific events: Pentecost and baptism for each individual. It is at Pentecost that the love of God was poured out through the Holy Spirit!

It is striking how many times the following affirmation appears in the testimonies of those who have received the baptism of the Spirit: "At that moment I knew that I was loved by God, and I discovered for the first time the love of the Father." I remember an elderly lady around eighty who, having received prayer for the infilling, went around shouting out to everybody, "I feel like a little girl! I feel like a little girl! I have discovered that God loves me." This is also the most impressive thing in the accounts of those who participated in the retreat at Duquesne where the charismatic renewal in the Catholic Church began. One of those present wrote later, "For an instant, we were afraid we couldn't bear such excessive love."

With Pentecost the goal of the whole Bible is definitively accomplished. The goal that God was pursuing throughout all of revelation and the history of salvation was "to fill your creatures with every blessing."[3] Now it has been accomplished.

Telling God's Marvelous Deeds

The second stage of our pilgrimage through Pentecost is the proclamation of God's works:

> Now there were devout Jews from every nation under heaven living in Jerusalem. And at this sound the crowd gathered and was bewildered, because each one heard them speaking in the native language of each. Amazed and astonished, they asked, "Are not all these who are speaking Galileans? And how is that we hear, each of us, in our own native language? Parthians, Medes, Elamites, and residents of Mesopotamia, Judea and Cappadocia, Pontus and Asia, Phrygia and Pamphylia, Egypt and the

> parts of Libya belonging to Cyrene, and visitors from
> Rome, both Jews and proselytes, Cretans and Arabs—in
> our own languages we hear them speaking about God's
> deeds of power." All were amazed and perplexed, saying to
> one another, "What does this mean?" But others sneered
> and said, "They are filled with new wine." (Acts 2:5–13)

Here too the main teaching is hidden in a reference. In the column next to this passage in some Bibles, there is a reference to Genesis 11, the chapter about the tower of Babel. Something is happening here, Luke implied, that overturns the event of Babel, which was the origin of division, lack of communication and discord. This new event brings unity, harmony and communion.

Here too a city, an edifice, a tower, is being built—the Church. But there is a big difference. At Babel everyone spoke the same language, but at a given moment no one could understand anybody else. They had to abandon their project and go their separate ways. At Pentecost everyone spoke different languages, and yet they understood each other wonderfully, as if they were all speaking the same language.

We need to see what really happened at Babel in order to fully understand Pentecost. When the builders were ready to erect the tower, they said, "Come, let us build ourselves a city, and a tower with its top in the heavens and let us make a name for ourselves; otherwise we shall be scattered abroad upon the face of the whole earth" (see Genesis 11:4).

"Let us make a name for ourselves!"—this was the sin. The men of Babel were not atheists who wanted to scorn heaven. No, they were devout religious men like all the men of antiquity. What they wanted to do was build a temple to a divinity, one of those temples with graduated terraces called *ziggurats*, of which we can still find ruins in Mesopotamia. The builders at Babel wanted this temple to be the highest one, compared to those of their neighboring peoples, perhaps hoping they would obtain major favors from their god this way. They wanted to erect a temple *to* God but not *for* God; they wanted to make a name for themselves, not for God. They were using God.

At Pentecost, instead, everyone understood each other because they had forgotten about themselves. The apostles did not want to make a name for themselves but for God. They were no longer discussing among themselves who the greatest was. They were turned upside down by the Holy Spirit, dazzled by the glory of God. Everyone understood them because they did not speak about themselves but about "God's great deeds."

The apostles experienced the Copernican revolution: They became "decentralized" from themslves and were "recentralized" on God. We need to ask the Holy Spirit to perform this Copernican revolution in us too. Let's make Him our center and proclaim His great deeds. Only then can we say that the revolution has happened! In the fourth Eucharistic Prayer, at the moment of epiclesis, the celebrant says, "And that we might live no longer for ourselves but for him [Christ], / he sent the Holy Spirit from you, Father, / as his first gift to those who believe."[3] This is why the Holy Spirit was sent, and why there is a Pentecost, so that we might live no longer for ourselves but for the Lord.

Today we have an opportunity to demolish the various

towers of Babel in our midst. Woe to him who thinks he has nothing in common with the builders at Babel! (Remember, the men of Babel were also pious, religious men, "men of the church.")

If, for example, I am more concerned about giving a wonderful teaching than I am about God's glory, then I am a builder of Babel! If I form a new prayer group because I want one that is better than the others, if I plan out a renewal that will be the "true" renewal—different than the one the others have—I am a builder of Babel!

Babel is not only outside of us but also inside of us! Augustine, in his great treatise *The City of God,* wrote that there are only two spheres of activity in the world. The city of Satan—Babylon—is being built in one, and the city of God—Jerusalem, the Church—in the other. These two spheres are still out in the open and active, and all our actions, initiatives and programs are at the crossroads. Whether we will have a Babel or a Pentecost depends on us.

This is also an opportunity to call attention to the importance of the prayer of praise. The apostles proclaimed "God's mighty deeds." Their proclamation was more of a prayer of praise, of enthusiastic glorification of God, than actual preaching.

Praise is the antidote to sin. Saint Paul says that godlessness consists in knowing God but not giving Him the glory and the thanks that are His due (see Romans 1:21). If that is so, then the opposite of sin is not virtue but praise! The charismatic renewal has received the charism of praise; that is its secret weapon. Praise is what best helps us to decentralize and to recentralize on God.

Charisms

The third stage on our pilgrimage to unity is conversion:

> But Peter, standing with the eleven, raised his voice
> and addressed them, "Men of Judea and all who live in
> Jerusalem, let this be known to you, and listen to what
> I say. Indeed, these are not drunk, as you suppose, for it
> is only nine o'clock in the morning. No, this is what was
> spoken through the prophet Joel:
> 'In the last days it will be, God declares,
> that I will pour out my Spirit upon all flesh,
>   and your sons and your daughters shall prophesy,
> and your young men shall see visions,
>   and your old men shall dream dreams.
> Even upon my slaves, both men and women,
>   in those days I will pour out my Spirit;
>   and they shall prophesy.'" (Acts 2:14–18)

Here I need to explain a theological premise. All through
the Bible the Holy Spirit reveals Himself in two ways:
through His *sanctifying work*, which transforms a person
who receives Him and infuses him or her with a new
heart, and through His *charismatic action*. In the latter
case, He empowers certain people not so that He can
dwell in them and sanctify them from within, but so that
He can act through them in the community and for the
good of the community. He will give someone the spirit
of prophecy, someone else the ability to govern and
someone else the strength to overcome enemies.

These charisms are free gifts, given to people not
because they are holy and not even chiefly to make
them holy but for the service of the people of God.
That explains how someone can be charismatic without

necessarily being holy. The Scripture affirms that the charismatic Spirit is also an integral part of Pentecost by recalling the prophecy of Joel that foretold this outpouring of the Holy Spirit on all flesh: On young and old, on men and women (see Joel 2:28–29).

Saint Paul used two different approaches when speaking of charisms. When he addressed the church at Thessalonica, where it seems the charisms were not held in high regard, he exhorted them, "Do not quench the Spirit. Do not despise the words of prophets, but test everything; hold fast to what is good" (see 1 Thessalonians 5:19–21). When he addressed the Corinthians, who were enthusiastic about charisms, he gave another kind of teaching: He did not contradict them but rather disciplined them. He explained how the charisms should be used and put them in their proper place, establishing the right priorities. The charisms are necessary, but there is a better way. There is an action of the Spirit that is even more important: charity, that is, holiness.

I try to be a little like Paul in this regard. When I speak in circles where the charisms are held in high regard, I try to tone down some of the enthusiastic excesses, but when I speak in circles that are more like Thessalonica, I try to exhort people not to be afraid of charisms. I am convinced that it is important to reaffirm the importance of charisms today. They are fundamental to the charismatic renewal; if there were no charisms, there would be no charismatic renewal!

There is a tendency in theology today to broaden the arena of charisms. Everything is said to be a charism: My family life is a charism, my love for my wife is a charism, and even my sense of humor is a charism! Charisms and talents are put in the same category, but they are two different things, even if they are not opposite. Talent comes to me through my nature, while a charism comes from grace, as an unwarranted free gift from God. Both are works of the Spirit, but they are different modes.

Moreover, not all charisms are on the same level. If a charism is "a manifestation of the Spirit for the common good," then there are certainly some that fit that description better than others. Some are clear, unambiguous manifestations of the Spirit. The charismatic renewal has received a simple gift for demonstrating some of these manifestations of the Spirit which are so strong that they even make the world exclaim, "God is here!"

If the charisms disappear, the renewal in the Spirit will become like an inactive volcano whose streams of molten lava, which once burned so brightly, have become dull slate on which people can write whatever they wish.

What do we do to keep the charisms and the charismatic renewal alive? God freely gives the charisms to whom and when He wishes. It should not surprise us that there would be an era in which the Lord manifests the charisms more than in another. It would be limiting God's freedom to expect that charisms would manifest in all times and in all places in the same way and with the same intensity.

Having said that, however, I need to say that charismatic activity is based on sanctifying action, on a renewal of the heart, and that depends on us. The charisms do not continue if the people who received them do not live in the Spirit, that is, if they are not obedient, humble, chaste and pure! Saul, for example, received a powerful charism, but he did not obey the word of God, and he lost it.

Let us not deceive ourselves! The Lord is certainly faithful, and many times He maintains His grace and His charisms in us despite our sin. But that does not go on indefinitely. If there is dissonance between the two actions of the Spirit—the sanctifying and the charismatic—sooner or later there is a shipwreck, which drags others to ruin.

Grateful and joyful for the experience of charisms, we can repeat the prayer toward the end of the fourth chapter of Acts: "Stretch out your hand to heal, and signs and wonders are performed through the name of your holy servant Jesus" (see Acts 4:30). Nevertheless, remembering the times when we have misused the charisms, making them soles under our shoes to make us seem taller, let's say with David in a spirit of penitence, "Lord, do not take your holy spirit from me" (Psalm 51:11), even if we deserve it.

God Has Made Jesus Lord

Now for the fourth stage of the Pentecost event. After explaining the problem of charisms and dispersing the notion that these people were drunk, Peter dealt with the point that was most urgent to him. When we closely examine Peter's sermon at Pentecost, we get the strange impression that the apostle was in a hurry to resolve some minor problems, to clear away the chief point of potential misunderstandings so he could quickly reach the "therefore." Now it is time for the "therefore."

Beethoven's *Pastoral Symphony* comes to mind here. At a certain point there is a warning about the coming storm. Hissing and rumbling sounds come through the orchestra; we can tell the thunder is about to burst. In Peter's case the thunder is the name that he shouts out over the noise of the crowd, Jesus of Nazareth!:

> You that are Israelites, listen to what I have to say: Jesus of Nazareth, a man attested to you by God with deeds of power, wonders, and signs that God did through him among you, as you yourselves know—this man, handed over to you according to the definite plan and fore-knowledge of God, you crucified and killed by the hands of those outside the law....
>
> This Jesus God raised up, and of that all of us are witnesses....
>
> Therefore let the entire house of Israel know with cer-tainty that God has made him both Lord and Messiah, this Jesus whom you crucified. (Acts 2:22–23, 32, 36)

Luke's wording can make us wonder if it is only now that God has "made Jesus Lord." Wasn't He also Lord before the Resurrection?

Luke wanted to preserve the flavor of the first Christian sermon precisely for this reason. We are seeing *kerygma* here in its nascent state. "Let the whole house of Israel know...!" It is as though someone today would say, "Let the whole world know with certitude...!" What made Peter bold enough to speak like this when, only a few days before, he was afraid of the words of a serving girl? The Holy Spirit! The Holy Spirit gave him an experience of God's love and put the living Jesus in his heart. That is why what came out of his mouth was a surge of living Christology.

Our books and discussions are often full of a dead, theological and merely ideological Christ. We need to rediscover this living Christ, whom only the Spirit can stir up in us. We need to rediscover this personal experience of Jesus, who died and was raised for me. We need to have the same burning experience that Paul had on the road to Damascus when he asked, "Who are you, Lord?" (see Acts 9:5). From that moment on Paul considered everything as dung so that he might gain Christ.

The most vivid memory I have of that famous ecumenical charismatic conference in Kansas City in 1977 was the banner that filled the sky from one end of the stadium to the other: "Jesus is Lord." I knew this title belonged to Jesus, but to see His lordship lived and celebrated by all those people was a revelation for me. The Holy Spirit has raised up the charismatic renewal chieflyfor this: to rediscover and proclaim that Jesus is Lord. That is truly the defining act of our Pentecost.

A genuine unity that is lived out will begin only around this nucleus that proclaims that Jesus died, was resurrected and is Lord. If we really think about it, all the rest of the content of our faith is subject to some divergence among Christians. Even the doctrine of the Trinity is the subject of dispute between the East and the West (because of the dispute about *Filioque*). But there are no dissensions about Jesus among Christians. He is established as the indivisible nucleus of the faith around which a complete unity can be rebuilt.

Pope John Paul II, in his letter *Tertio Millenio Adveniente* about preparing for the third millennium, affirms that Christians of all denominations need to "come together."[4] What unites us is far more than what divides us. Let us come together, then, around the thing *par excellence* that unites us: the Lord Jesus.

Look at what happens to the lines within a circle. When they go from the circumference toward the center, they get closer to one another little by little until they form a single point at the center. For many centuries we have done the opposite. We went from the center of the circle, which is Jesus, toward our churches, our groups and our religious orders. We therefore became divided! We need to reverse direction and turn everything back in Jesus' direction. Pope John Paul II, in an ecumenical meeting with the heads of other churches, affirmed that the unity of Christians depends on a renewed, shared conversion to the Lord.

Kierkegaard, a philosopher who loved Jesus very much, affirmed that God has created two categories of people: heroes and poets. The hero is the one who accomplishes great deeds and even does battle with death. The poet does not do impressive deeds, but he sings about the hero and is enthusiastic about the hero; he is as happy as if he were the hero himself, because his own genius can be expressed in sheer admiration and devotion. When he has found his hero, the poet goes from city to city and tells people that they too should admire the hero.

For us, Jesus is our hero, and we should be his poets. I do not mean in the sense that we should write poems about Him but in the sense that we are in love with Jesus. The poets speak through their songs and succeed not only in convincing, but in taking others along with them.

Our evangelization should be Pentecostal: It should cause heartstrings to vibrate. In the place where the towers of Babel were first erected and people wanted to make a name for themselves, those towers are demolished and every one's name is forgotten. Let us, therefore, lift up the name that is above all names and proclaim Paul's words, "If you confess with your lips that Jesus is Lord and believe in your heart that God raised him from the dead, you will be saved" (see Romans 10:9).

Chapter Eight

"Repent, and You Will Receive the Gift of the Holy Spirit"

There are four stages in the events of Pentecost: They were all filled with the Holy Spirit; they proclaimed God's mighty works; God poured out His charisms on all flesh; and the Father made Jesus Lord. Let us see the disciples' response:

> Now when they heard this, they were cut to the heart and said to Peter and to the other apostles, "Brothers, what should we do?" Peter said to them, "Repent, and be baptized every one of you in the name of Jesus Christ so that your sins may be forgiven; and you will receive the gift of the Holy Spirit." (Acts 2:37–38)

The task before us is to put this text into practice. Like those three thousand people in Jerusalem at Pentecost, we should open our hearts to the Word of God and let it transform us. "You have crucified Jesus of Nazareth!" We can react to those words in two ways: either with repentance or with a hardening of our hearts.

But of what should we repent? The sin we should feel guilty about is the one Paul summed up in one word, ungodliness:

> For the wrath of God is revealed from heaven against all ungodliness.... So they [pagans] are without excuse; for though they knew God, they did not honor him as God or give thanks to him, but they became futile in their thinking, and their senseless minds were darkened...and they exchanged the glory of the immortal God for images resembling a mortal human being or birds or four-footed animals or reptiles. (Romans 1:18, 20–21, 23)

Ungodliness can be the sin of someone who knows God (not just atheists!) but who do not give Him the glory or the thanks that are His due. It is madness to put the creature in the Creator's place, in God's place, because at the core of every idolatry is "self-olatry."

After having said this about the pagans, the apostle suddenly addresses himself to a mysterious auditor: "Therefore, you have no excuse, whoever you are, when you judge others; for in passing judgment on another you condemn yourself, because you, the judge, are doing the very same things" (Romans 2:1).

The person is revealed as a judge, understood not so much as a member of a particular profession but as one type of human being. Unlike the pagan, this pious individual knows the law of God and thinks that merely knowing it ensures safety from God's wrath.

Christians are the ones today to whom the apostle addressed this word. We who know everything about Jesus Christ can judge today's pagans without realizing we are doing the same things they are—not the same things *materially* but in their *substance*. We also put the creature, *ourselves*, in the Creator's place.

We need to try to see what thing, what project, what person we have expended our lives for, which has become, without our realizing it, the thing that is the most important to us in the world—more than God Himself, at least in practice. That is the idol we need to destroy! It can be a son (especially if he is an only son), the prayer group or community that I started, the church that I built, the order that I founded (and today there are so many new ones founded!).

Until we have removed ungodliness from us, we can do whatever we want, but the Holy Spirit will never be able to bring about Pentecost inside of us. Let us begin by praying, "Have mercy on me, O God, / according to your steadfast love; / according to your abundant mercy blot out my transgressions. /.../ For I know my transgressions" (Psalm 51:1, 3).

Repent!

Now we come to the crucial word: *repent!* If we succeed, with the help of the Holy Spirit, in experiencing the kind of repentance that is being talked about in Psalm 51, rivers of living water will spring up in our lives. Despair will be transformed into hope, and remorse into an action of grace.

Let us invoke special assistance from the Holy Spirit, because Jesus said that repentance cannot happen without His action: When the counselor comes, He "will prove the world wrong about sin" (John 16:8). Only He can touch us in the neurological place that He alone knows and convince us of the seriousness of sin.

To repent means to change our way of thinking and judging. It is not a question, however, of abandoning our old way of thinking, the mentality of our age, to form a better one, perhaps more conformed to the gospel. That would be substituting our judgment for another judgment of ours. The miracle of repentance, then, would not occur.

The real *metanoia*, that is, change, occurs when we abandon *our* way of thinking and receive *God's* way of thinking, when we put aside *our* judgment and take on *God's* judgment. This is where the leap occurs. To repent means to take a running leap into the abyss of God's judgment! His judgments, says one of the psalms, "are like the great deep" (Psalm 36:6).

When this happens, a person begins to see his or her life and sins from within God's heart, and then things change. Seen in the light of the immense love of the Father, sin appears for what it truly is: a betrayal of His immense love, "crucifying again the Son of God and... holding him up to contempt" (see Hebrews 6:6).

Francis of Assisi entered into the heart of God and knew what repentance from sin was. One sign of his profound comprehension of repentance was the *tau* (the last letter in the Hebrew alphabet, shaped like the letter *t*). Francis had a special devotion to the *tau*: He would end whatever he was writing with it; he engraved it in the brothers' cells; and he would trace it on the people who came to him. The source of the *tau* was a vision of Ezekiel:

> Then he cried in my hearing with a loud voice, saying, "Draw near, you executioners of the city, each with his destroying weapon in his hand." And six men came from the direction of the upper gate, which faces north, each with his weapon for slaughter in his hand; among them was a man clothed in linen, with a writing case at his side. They went in and stood beside the bronze altar.
> Now the glory of the God of Israel had gone up from the cherub on which it rested to the threshold of the house. The LORD called to the man clothed in linen who had the writing case at his side; and he said to him, "Go through the city, through Jerusalem, and put a mark on the foreheads of those who sigh and groan over all the abominations that are committed in it." (Ezekiel 9:1–4)

Because of the *tau*'s shape, this Hebrew letter became a symbol of the cross for Christians. It is the same sign that the angel of the sixth seal places on the foreheads of the redeemed of the Lamb (see Revelation 7:2). Francis received the mission of being this "angel with the sixth seal" who signed the *tau* on the foreheads of those who were led to weep and to groan for the abominations that were occurring in the world and in the Church.

What kind of *tau* should we have on our foreheads? What is the *abomination* that we need to confess to the Lord? It is division, discord at all levels: between the different Christian churches, between groups, between ecclesial movements and within each movement, family and parish. All of this is an abomination for which we need to repent in a special way.

During the first great ecumenical charismatic conference in Kansas City in 1977, with about forty thousand people present, half of whom were Catholic and half from other churches, one night one of the primary leaders of the renewal said in prophecy, "You bishops, weep and groan, because the body of My Son is broken. You priests, you shepherds, you leaders, weep and mourn because the body of My Son is broken. All you people of God, mourn and weep, because the body of My Son is broken."

These words fell on the assembly like sparks of fire. One after another people fell to their knees, until the whole stadium was one soul and one heart that wept. It was a real Pentecost of repentance! That night we wept because the body of Christ was broken. The Lord is giving us the grace today to weep because the body of Christ is broken, through our own fault.

✳ ✳ ✳

"A broken and contrite heart, O God, you will not despise!" (see Psalm 51:17). God surely does not despise a broken and contrite heart, because for Him that is the precious pearl, the hidden treasure. Do you want to give God a gift? The best gift there is? One that would fill Him with joy? Let Him find a contrite heart within you!

After the exile, when the people of Israel began speaking about reconstructing the temple, Isaiah let us overhear a kind of soliloquy by God:

Heaven is my throne
   and the earth is my footstool;
what is the house that you would build for me,
   and what is my resting place?
All these things my hand has made,
   and so all these things are mine,
      says the Lord. But this is the one to whom I will
look, to the humble and contrite in spirit,
   who trembles at my word. (Isaiah 66:1–2)

He is saying, in other words, "If I build a temple for myself as high as the heavens, it would not be anything new for me; I made the heavens and it is my throne. If it were as vast as the earth, that is nothing new because the earth is my footstool." Then God says that what would please Him would be what people could give Him: contrite hearts! Here indeed would be something new and surprising for God! God's omnipotence is not enough to make a contrite heart. He can make the heavens and the earth, but He cannot, by Himself, make a contrite and humble heart. "The one who created you without your consent will not save you without your consent!" Augustine said.[1] He needs our free wills! Because He has no sin, He cannot assume the guilt. Only a person who has sin can make an admission of sin.

To offer this gift to God is not hard. Let us present ourselves to Him during a moment of profound meditation and say to Him, "Lord, I don't know myself; I don't know what my responsibilities are, what my real sins are or even to what point I failed concerning the unity of your body. No one knows what my part is in all this, neither friends nor enemies. There is only one in the whole universe who knows the truth about me, and it is you, Lord.

You are righteous in your words and in your judgments.
I accept your judgment about me!"

> Create in me a clean heart, O God,
> and put a new and right spirit within me.
> Do not cast me away from your presence,
> and do not take your holy spirit from me.
> Restore to me the joy of your salvation,
> and sustain in me a willing spirit.

> The sacrifice acceptable to God is a broken spirit;
> a broken and contrite heart, O God, you will not
> despise. (Psalm 51:10–12, 17)

*   *   *

Only the last step is lacking now to prepare ourselves for the conclusion of this repentance. So far we have tried to individualize our ungodliness; we have decided to be "finished with sin" (see 1 Peter 4:1), to cut down the wicked tree of guilt at its root. Now the time has come to throw it into the fire, so to speak. We need, to paraphrase one of Saint Paul's expressions, to destroy the body of sin (see Romans 6:6).

By way of example, I will share a personal experience. One day I was praying Psalm 139:

> O Lord, you have searched me and known me.
> You know when I sit down and when I rise up;
> you discern my thoughts from far away.
> You search out my path and my lying down,
> and are acquainted with all my ways.

Even before a word is on my tongue,
O LORD, you know it completely. (Psalm 139:1–4)

This is the psalm about God's omniscience: He sees all and searches every part of a person's being with His light—a kind of X-ray of someone's spirit. At a certain point something happened to me that I only understood later. I felt as though I were cut in two. One part of me was looking at myself, and the other part, my body, was lying on the ground. I was seeing myself from God's standpoint with God's eyes. At that point the image of a stalagmite came to me.

Stalagmites are columns of limestone that form in some very old caves when drops of limestone water fall from the ceiling. There are some in the Marches, my province, and in many parts of the world. The drops are chiefly composed of water, which drains off, but a small percent of limestone in each drop is deposited and begins to form a mass with the preceding one. Over the course of centuries, a limestone column is formed. The kind that rises from the bottom up is called a stalagmite; the kind that hangs from the ceiling is called a stalactite.

When I saw a stalagmite with the eyes of my mind, I immediately understood what the Lord wanted to tell me. My sins, from the first to the last, had fallen into the bottom of my heart like so many drops of limestone water. The majority had been drained off, thanks to confession, Eucharist and prayer. But because the repentance had not been perfect, there remained a particle of "limestone" each time—a bit of compromise, of resistance to God, of sin in short. This particle amassed with the preceding ones and, day after day, ended up creating a stalagmite. In an instant I understood then what the well-known heart of stone is that the Bible speaks about: It is the heart that we ourselves make, through small infractions of compromise and hardening of the heart.

How could I get free? I was immediately aware that I could not destroy the stalagmite by my will because it was precisely there—in my will. A new love was born in me for the blood of Christ then, because I understood that it is the only solvent that can remove this incrustation. I was filled with a new desire to enter into contact with that blood in the Eucharist! The expression "Lamb of God, who takes away the sin of the world" became precious to me in a new way.

That was also when I rediscovered the importance of confession. On the Day of Pentecost Peter said, "Repent, and be baptized for the remission of your sins." In that way he forever united *repentance* to the *sacrament*. The sacrament is the place in which pardon is proclaimed, celebrated and certified by the Church. Christ had said to the apostles, "If you forgive the sins of any, they are forgiven them" (John 20:23).

For the crowds at the first Pentecost, the sacrament was obviously baptism; for those of us who are already baptized, it is the sacrament of reconciliation. In it, the blood of Christ and the Spirit of Christ operate efficaciously. We Catholics have a great gift in this sacrament. It involves a special encounter with the Risen One who, with the gentle power of His Spirit, removes our sin.

If rocks are thrown into quicklime, they dissolve in very little time and are reduced to dust. We likewise should throw all our sins into this living furnace, which is the blood of the Redeemer, so that they can be dissolved.

Only in this way can we begin a new life—renewed, made clean again and granted amnesty! A universal amnesty! It is not, though, like the amnesties of this world that are always partial. *Amnesty* comes from a Greek word that means "to remember no longer, to cancel even the record about the thing." That is the kind of amnesty God gives. He sinks our sins into oblivion. Legal systems never do that; even if a sentence is remitted, the crime remains on the record. God, instead, forgets and invites us also to forget the things of the past.

$$* \quad * \quad *$$

There is a kind of absolution that comes from God Himself and that we can all receive: Catholics, Evangelicals and Protestants, even those whose tradition does not include the sacrament of confession. It is not a sacramental absolution, but it can prepare us for that. It concerns a vision that Zechariah had when he returned from exile.

The priests of Israel were clothed in filthy garments, which was a sign of mourning for the sin of the people. In the parable of the prodigal son, Jesus echoes many of the images in this prophetic text:

> Then he showed me the high priest Joshua standing before the angel of the Lord, and Satan standing at his right hand to accuse him. And the Lord said to Satan, "The Lord rebuke you, O Satan! The Lord who has chosen Jerusalem rebuke you! Is not this man a brand plucked from the fire?" Now Joshua was dressed with filthy clothes as he stood before the angel. The angel said to those who were standing before him, "Take off his filthy clothes." And to him he said, "See, I have taken

your guilt away from you, and I will clothe you with festal apparel." And I said, "Let them put a clean turban on his head." So they put a clean turban on his head and clothed him with the apparel; and the angel of the LORD was standing by.

Then the angel of the LORD assured Joshua, saying, "Thus says the LORD of hosts; If you will walk in my ways and keep my requirements, then you shall rule my house and have charge of my courts, and I will give you the right of access among those who are standing here." (Zechariah 3:1–7)

"I have taken your guilt away from you": That is an absolution. And so let us thank the Lord. Let's say with Micah: What God is as great as You who forgives sins? You have created the heavens and the earth; You have done great things, but nothing as great as this: You cast our sins into the depths of the sea (see Micah 7:18–19).

Yes, Lord, what God is like you? We thank you for Christ who, on the cross, has destroyed our sin! We thank you because you have drawn all men to Him. We thank you because you now pour out on Jerusalem, on your people, a mighty stream of grace and consolation. Amen.

CHAPTER NINE

We Were All Made to Drink of One Spirit

The Water from the Rock

The Book of Exodus has always constituted the principal nucleus of typological catechesis for the Church. Saint Paul, after reviewing all the major events of the Exodus—the passage through the Red Sea, the cloud, the manna, the water from the rock—concluded that all these things occurred "as examples [*typoi*] for us" and were written "to instruct us" (1 Corinthians 10:6, 11).

The Exodus, then, has always been read as a Christological and ecclesiological key—that is, in reference to Christ and to the Church. Saint John mostly emphasized the reading with reference to Christ. In the fourth Gospel Christ appears as the true Moses who gives the living water (see John 4), as the true manna from heaven (see John 6) and, on the cross, as the sacrifice prefigured by the paschal lamb sacrificed in Egypt (see John 19:36).

Saint Paul preferred to develop an ecclesiological reading, seeing figures of the sacraments of the Church and of the whole Christian life in the events of the Exodus. The Letter to the Hebrews combines both kinds of interpretation, speaking of Christ as "superior to Moses" and establishing a close comparison between the Hebrews freed from Egypt and the Christians freed from sin (see Hebrews 3–4). The Lenten liturgy, most especially, is full of these typological themes taken from Exodus.

However, apart from its typological value as a figure of Christian truths, Exodus also has a great existential significance and speaks to people in their most personal dimension. The very word *exodus* has a symbolic resonance with the great epics of literature: The exodus of the chosen people from Egypt is like a symbol and a parable for our condition as travelers, as pilgrims and strangers in this world, en route to a new homeland.

The Exodus, then, has great religious value. But to grasp it, we must identify ourselves with the people who went through it. We must realize that it is speaking about us—that we, on a spiritual and existential plane, are that oppressed people who groan and cry for help to God (see Exodus 3:7). One of the prayers in the liturgy says, "Long oppressed, long under the yoke of sin, we await our redemption."

The Hebrews of the New Testament would have recited this text from the Passover meal: "In every generation, each Jew should regard himself as though he too were brought out of Egypt."[1] This conviction continued in the Church after the Letter to the Hebrews spoke of a new "today" (*hodie*), which would last until the return of the Lord (see Hebrews 3:13).

With this in mind, let us reflect on one of the principal events and figures of the Exodus: the water that came forth from the rock (see Exodus 17:1–7). In the Book of Exodus there are two great events where water is the main feature. The first is the passage through the Red Sea, and the second is the water that came out of the rock. Water, however, plays quite a different role in these two events.

In the first case man entered the water; in the second, water entered man. The water of the Red Sea saved some and caused others to perish. It was the instrument of God's judgment. The water of the rock performed a different function: It quenched the people's thirst, restored their strength and enabled them to move ahead with their journey. This water was useful not only once but every day. In fact, according to rabbinic tradition, repeated by Saint Paul, the rock from which the water gushed "followed" or "accompanied" the people on their journey through the desert from that day on (see 1 Corinthians 10:4).

Christian typological catechesis very soon interpreted these two different functions of water as baptism and Eucharist, respectively: "And all were baptized into Moses in the cloud and in the sea,...and all drank the same spiritual drink" (1 Corinthians 10:2, 4). The two waters were interpreted, more precisely, in connection with the action of the Holy Spirit in baptism and in the Eucharist: "For in the one Spirit we were all baptized into one body,...and we were all made to drink of one Spirit" (1

Corinthians 12:13).

What does all this mean? It means there are two fundamental actions of the Spirit in Christian life. One action is unique, not to be repeated. It marks a new beginning and has a constitutive value corresponding to baptism. The other is a daily action, just like eating and drinking, which finds its highest—but not its only—expression in the Eucharist. The two things together represent the beginning and the growth of life: the new birth in the Spirit and living in the Spirit.

Intoxication and Sobriety

In Christian tradition the theme of the sober intoxication of the Spirit is connected to the Holy Spirit insofar as He is "spiritual drink." The text that moved the Church Fathers to take up the theme of "sober intoxication"—which had already been developed by Philo of Alexandria—and to give it a place in the Church was the one in which the apostle exhorted the Christians at Ephesus: "Do not get drunk with wine, for that is debauchery; but be filled with the Spirit, as you sing psalms and hymns and spiritual songs among yourselves, singing and making melody to the Lord in your hearts" (Ephesians 5: 18–19).

In the second part of this text, the way in which the apostle illustrated the behavior of those who are "filled with the Spirit" ("singing and making melody...") seems to allude to the very theme of sober intoxication.

Starting with Origen, there are countless texts from the Fathers that illustrate this theme, alternating between the comparison and the contrast of physical intoxication and spiritual intoxication. Both, they say, bring gladness, make us forget our sorrows and make us leave our senses.

But while physical intoxication makes a man staggering and unsteady, spiritual intoxication makes a man steady at doing good. While the first makes a man leave his senses to live below the level of reason, the other makes a man leave his senses to live above the level of reason and experience true spiritual "ecstasy." The first is "an intoxication of sin," and the second is "an intoxication of grace."

Developing the main point of the episode of the water gushing from the rock, Saint Ambrose wrote:

> The Lord Jesus made water gush forth from the rock and all drank from it. Those who drank it only according to its outward appearance were satisfied, but those who drank it in truth were immediately intoxicated. The intoxication that infuses joy is good. The intoxication which strengthens the steps of a sober mind is good.... Drink Christ who is life; drink Christ who is that rock from which the water gushed forth; drink Christ so that you can drink His words.... Holy Scripture can be imbibed, Holy Scripture can be devoured when the juice of the eternal word descends into the veins of the mind and into the energy of the soul.[2]

What does this suggestive theme of the sober intoxication of the Spirit tell us today? The first thing we can learn is that there are two different ways for a Christian to act: a human way and a divine way, a natural and a supernatural way. In the human mode the protagonist is a person using reason, even if it is enlightened by faith. In the divine mode the protagonist—or the "principal agent," as Paul VI called Him in *Evangelii Nuntiandi*—is the Holy Spirit. This second mode is what Saint Paul called being "led by the Spirit" (see Galatians 5:18) or acting "in the Spirit." The effects are also different, depending on whether a person acts wisely—relying on prudence, common sense, experience, organization and discretion—or acts in "a demonstration of the Spirit and of power" (1 Corinthians 2:4).

The Church has always demonstrated its greatest strength and vitality when it has acted on this charismatic and pnuematic level, that is, when it has performed actions that have the explicit mark of the Spirit.

The most important question for us now is how to take up again this ideal of sober intoxication and incarnate it in our current historical and ecclesiastical situation. Where is it written that such a "radical" way of living the gospel and of experiencing the Spirit was the exclusive prerogative of the Fathers and of the early days of the Church, but that it is not for us? On the contrary, "everything is yours," exclaims the apostle. All of it belongs to everyone in the Church because of the resurrection of Christ. The gift of Christ is not limited to a particular era but is offered in every era. There is enough for everybody in the richness of His redemption—not to mention that we need the sober intoxication of the Spirit even more than the Fathers did. The world has become so rebellious to the gospel, so sure of itself, so proud, that only the "strong wine" of the Spirit can win over its unbelief and lead it out of its human and rationalistic sobriety, which is sometimes called scientific objectivity.

In the past the usual order in which this dynamic occurred was from sobriety to intoxication. The word "sober" does not actually indicate only the quality of spiritual intoxication that distinguishes it from every other kind of intoxication (wine, drugs, success, for example) but pertains to all of life. "Sobriety" is the means through which spiritual intoxication is obtained; the part that man must accomplish is the ascetic change. The way to obtain spiritual intoxication, or fervor, is also sobriety, that is, abstinence from things of the flesh, moderation and fasting from the world.

In this sense the concept of sobriety was deepened in particular by Orthodox monastic spirituality, with its "Jesus Prayer." Here sobriety meant a spiritual method with vigilant attention to becoming free from lustful thoughts and from perverse speech, to removing all carnal satisfactions from the mind and leaving them behind, where the only activity was prayer and remorse for sin.[3]

Under different names—detachment, purification, mortification—this is the same ascetic doctrine found in the Latin doctors of the Church. Saint John of the Cross said that in order for a soul to have its will perfectly united with God's will, it must "detach and strip itself for God's sake of all that is not God."[4] We are at the second stage of spiritual life, called "purgative" or "illuminative." Here the soul frees itself painstakingly of its usual habits to prepare for union with God and for His transmissions of grace, which constitute the third stage, the unitive path.

We are heirs of a spirituality that conceived of the road to perfection in this sequence: First we remain in the purgative stage for a long time before entering into the unitive stage. We need to practice sobriety for an extensive period before being able to experience intoxication. Every fervor that manifests itself before that time is rendered suspect. Spiritual intoxication, with all that it signifies, thus comes at the end and is reserved for the "perfect." The others, the "progressives," should especially engage in mortification, without aspiring to a strong and direct experience of God in the Spirit while they are still struggling with their weaknesses.

There is great wisdom and experience behind all this. It must be said, however, that such an austere scheme also signifies the slow and progressive displacement of a focus on grace to a focus on man's effort. According to the New Testament, there is a circularity and simultaneity by which, if it is true that sobriety is necessary to achieve intoxication by the Spirit, it is also true that intoxication by the Spirit is needed to achieve the practice of sobriety. An ascetic path, undertaken without a strong initial leading from the Spirit, would be a deadly labor and would produce nothing except "boasting of the flesh." According to Saint Paul, we should "put to death the deeds of the body...by the Spirit" (see Romans 8:13). The Holy Spirit is given to us so that we can make progress in mortification by degrees rather than as the reward for having mortified ourselves.

One early Church Father, Macarius, said that a Christian life full of ascetic efforts and mortification but without the vivifying touch of the Spirit would be like a Mass where there were many readings, many rites and many offerings but no consecration of the species by the priest. Everything would remain as it had been. He concluded:

One must look on the life of the Christian in a similar way. He may have fasted, kept vigils, chanted the psalms, carried out every ascetic practice and acquired every virtue; but if the mystic working of the Spirit has not been consummated by grace with full consciousness and spiritual peace on the altar of his heart, all his ascetic practice is ineffectual and virtually fruitless, for the joy of the Spirit is not mystically active in his heart.[5]

This second path—from intoxication to sobriety—was the way that Jesus made His apostles follow. Even though they had Jesus as their teacher and spiritual director, they were not, before Pentecost, in a position to put into practice any of the gospel precepts. But when they were baptized with the Holy Spirit at Pentecost, then we see them transformed and able to undergo all kinds of hardships for Christ, including martyrdom. The Holy Spirit was the cause of their fervor rather than the effect of it.

There is another motive that impels us to rediscover this path from intoxication to sobriety. The Christian life is not only an issue of growing in personal holiness; it is also ministry, service, *diakonia* and proclamation. To accomplish these tasks we need "power from on high," the charisms or, in a word, a strong Pentecostal experience of the Holy Spirit. We need to be open to the Spirit to be capable of generosity and eagerness, that is, to "be ardent in spirit" (Romans 12:11), to reach that state in which service to God is done with eagerness, faithfulness and joy (as Saint Basil defined fervor).

The Penetrating Rain of the Spirit

Where are the places that the Spirit acts today in this Pentecostal way? Saint Ambrose exhorted us earlier with the words, "Drink, drink, drink." But where do we find this water?

Speaking of the Holy Spirit, whom those who believed in Him would receive, Jesus proclaimed one day, "Let anyone who is thirsty come to me, and let the one who believes in me drink" (John 7:37). But where is Jesus now? Where can we find Him now that He is risen and has left the earth?

We can find the answer in the very same Saint Ambrose who was the cantor *par excellence* of the sober intoxication of the Spirit. After discussing the two classic places, so to speak, in which one could receive the Spirit—"the intoxication of the cup of salvation and the intoxication that comes from the superabundant richness of Scripture"—he hints at a third possibility:

> There is also another intoxication which operates by means of the penetrating rain of the Holy Spirit. Such was the case in the Acts of the Apostles when those who spoke in different languages seemed to the hearers as though they were full of wine.[6]

After noting the "ordinary" way of being intoxicated by the spirit, Saint Ambrose adds an "extraordinary" way—extraordinary in the sense that it is not predetermined or instituted that consists in reviving the experience the apostles had on the Day of Pentecost. He obviously did not add this third possibility to tell his audience that it was not for them but had been reserved only for the apostles and the first generation of Christians. On the contrary, he intended to inspire the faithful to have the experience of the "penetrating rain of the Spirit" that occurred at Pentecost. The Second Vatican Council spoke from this same perspective when it declared:

> It is not only through the sacraments and the ministrations of the Church that the Holy Spirit makes holy the People.... He also distributes special graces among the faithful of every rank.[7]

The possibility of having the Spirit in this new, personal way, which depends solely on God's sovereign and free initiative, is therefore also open to us. And woe to us if we fall into the equivocation of the Pharisees and scribes of Jesus' time! "There are six days for us to work," they objected to Jesus, "so why heal and do miracles on the Sabbath?" (see Luke 13:14). We could be tempted to say to Him, "There are seven sacraments to sanctify and to give the Spirit, so why go beyond those for a new and unfamiliar way?"

In the Church there is a lot of discussion today about the Marian apparitions, some of which are genuine and some of which are at least dubious. People gather in great crowds at the places of these apparitions. I ask myself sometimes what would happen if the word spread one day that there was a place where what happened at Pentecost was happening again with the same phenomena...that the Upper Room was open again, and a "mighty wind" was moving again and shaking the house...that everyone returned from this place transformed, with a new fervor and love for the Church. Wouldn't there be a steady procession to that place?

For over twenty-five years that very news has been circulating through the Church. There are millions and millions of people who can testify to having known this place and having lived this Pentecost in their own humble way. And these are not just the voices of overexcited people, people who are easily enthused and naively credulous when it comes to miracles.

Pope Paul VI, in 1975, said that the renewal was a *chance* for the Church. Quoting a verse from a hymn by Saint Ambrose, he specifically recalled the ideal of "sober intoxication of the Spirit" and entrusted that ideal to the Catholic charismatic renewal as its plan. Our late supreme pontiff, John Paul II, on the tenth anniversary of that meeting between the renewal and Pope Paul VI, said that those past ten years had confirmed the accuracy of his predecessor's words.

The theologian Yves Congar, in his address to the International Congress of Pneumatology at the Vatican on the sixteenth centenary of the Ecumenical Council of Constantinople in 381, said,

> How can we avoid situating the so-called charismatic stream, better known as the Renewal in the Spirit, here with us? It has spread like a brushfire. It is far more than a fad.... In one primary aspect, it resembles revival movements from the past: the public and verifiable character of spiritual action which changes people's lives.... It brings youth, a freshness and new possibilities into the bosom of the old Church, our mother. In fact, except for very rare occasions, the Renewal has remained *within* the Church and, far from challenging long-standing institutions, it reanimates them.[8]

It is true that this renewal, like other new, analogous activities within the Church today, sometimes presents problematic and excessive sides, divisions and sins. But isn't that always what happens, even from the very outset, when the gifts of God are put into the hands of human beings? Is authority in the Church always exercised in a pure state, without the human taint of authoritarianism and the quest for power? And yet no one is trying to eliminate that charism from the life of the Church.

Even the first Christian communities, like the one at Corinth, were not exempt from disorders and weaknesses. The Spirit does not suddenly make everyone holy. He works in different stages and according to the openness He finds. Besides, we need to distinguish between the sanctifying grace of the Spirit *(gratia gratum faciens)* and His charismatic action *(gratia gratis data)*, which is for service and for the common good rather than for the individual.

The Baptism in the Spirit

The principal instrument by which the renewal in the Spirit "changes people's lives" is the baptism in the Spirit. This is a rite that occurs with gestures of great simplicity, in peace and joy, accompanied by an attitude of humility, repentance and openness to being children to enter the kingdom. It is a kind of *epiclesis*—that is, an invocation of the Spirit upon a member of the body of Christ. It recalls the invocation, in the Mass after the Consecration, for the Spirit to come on the assembly of the faithful and make them "a living sacrifice of praise."

It is a renewal and an actualization of the whole Christian initiation and not only of baptism. People prepare themselves for this by, in addition to making a good confession, availing themselves of teachings that put them in vital and joyful contact with the principal truths and realities of the faith: love of God, sin, salvation, new life, transformation in Christ, the charisms and the fruits of the Spirit.

But is it right to expect that everything will happen through this experience? Is this the only possible way to experience the grace of Pentecost? If by the baptism in the Spirit we mean a certain ceremony, done in a certain way in a certain context, we have to say no; it is not the only way to have a strong experience of the Spirit. There have been and are numerous Christians who have had an analogous experience without knowing anything about the baptism in the Spirit or who have received a "spontaneous outpouring of the Spirit," as we see in the lives of many saints.

Nevertheless, this baptism in the Spirit has come forth in a simple and powerful way to renew the lives of millions of believers in almost all of the Christian churches. We should think very carefully, then, before saying that this is not for us or before automatically dismissing it if the Lord offers us an opportunity to receive it.

I was on the verge of doing that myself, so I want to share my personal experience even if it costs me a great deal. It may be that my difficulties are like those of many other priests and theologians and therefore could help someone else not to succumb to the same danger. It would seem to me a lack of gratitude to God if I were silent about this whole experience, which has changed the course of my life. I have even thought that Providence might have placed me in my particular role precisely so that I could humbly testify to the heart of the Church about the rumblings of Pentecost, which in various forms are going through the body of Christ and which constitute a great sign of hope in the midst of all the trials that the Church must still go through in our day.

The first difficulty I had was this: I said to myself, "But I have Saint Francis as a father; I have inherited a wonderful spirituality, so many saints.... What else, what new thing do I need to look for? What can these brothers give me?"

I was thinking these things during a prayer meeting when, at the back of the room, a sister opened the Bible and began to read. John the Baptist was saying to the Pharisees, "Do not presume to say to yourselves, 'We have Abraham as our ancestor'" (Matthew 3:9). I understood that those words were directed to me. (This is a way the Spirit can speak, work and convict of sin.)

Another objection I had: "But I am a priest, ordained by a bishop; I have received the Holy Spirit. What else should I still receive, and from laypeople, no less?"

This time the answer came to me from my own theology. I imagined what Jesus would have answered: "And I, then? Wasn't I sanctified by the Father and sent into the world? Wasn't I full of the Spirit from the moment of my conception in Mary, my mother? And yet I went to the Jordan to be baptized by John the Baptist, who was just a layman!"

This is what led me to receive prayer for "a new outpouring of the Spirit." I received it as a conscious renewal of my baptism, as a definitive, first-person affirmation of the "Yes!" and "I believe!" that others had said in my stead at the moment of baptism. It was like surrendering the reins of my life to Christ.

When they invited me to reaffirm Jesus as the Lord of my life, I raised my eyes and saw the crucifix that was above the altar in the chapel. It was as though He were looking at me to make me understand a great truth: "This is the Jesus you choose as Lord, not a soft Jesus, a perfumed Jesus." This was enough to make me understand that this flow of grace that is called the charismatic renewal is totally different from superficial emotionalism. It goes right to the heart of the gospel and the *kerygma,* which is the cross of Christ.

I would like to conclude with the exhortation from Saint Ambrose that I cited at the beginning of this book as quoted by Paul VI. This hymn is from the liturgy of the hours and is, therefore, an invitation extended to the whole Church and not just to a few initiates: *Laeti bibamus sobriam profusionem Spiritus,* "Let us drink the sober intoxication of the Spirit with joy!"

Yes, Lord, we have great need of this spiritual intoxication. We need it to fulfill your commission, to convince our world of sin because they reject Jesus. We need it above all to become holy. And now, Lord, we say to you what Peter did: "Lord, not my feet only but also my hands and my head!" (John 13:9). Baptize us completely in Your Spirit!

(Note: Father Cantalamessa's phrasing in citations of Church Fathers has been followed by current translator unless otherwise noted.)

CHAPTER ONE: "LET US DRINK THE SOBER INTOXICATION OF THE SPIRIT WITH JOY!"

1. See "Pope Paul Addresses the Charismatic Renewal," *New Covenant,* July 1975, p. 25.

2. Saint Cyril of Jerusalem, *Catecheses,* "Lecture 17," 19.

3. Saint Ambrose, "On the Sacraments," V, 3, 17. See *The Fathers of the Church: Saint Ambrose: Theological and Dogmatic Works,* Roy J. Deferrari, trans. (Washington, D.C.: Catholic University of America Press, 1963), p. 314.

4. Augustine, *Sermons,* 225, *Patrologia Latina* 38, p.1098. See Saint Augustine, "Sermon 225," 4, in. *The Works of Saint Augustine: Sermons,* John E. Rotelle, ed., volume 6, Edmund Hill, trans. (New Rochelle, N.Y.: New City, 1993), p. 250.

5. Augustine, *Commentary on the Psalms,* 35, 14. See Saint Augustine, "On the Psalms," 35, 14, in *Ancient Christian Writers: St. Augustine on the Psalms,* Scholastica Hebgin and Felicitas Corrigan, trans. (Westminster, Md.: Newman, 1961), pp. 242–243.

6. Gregory of Nazianzen, *Orations,* 12, 6, in *Patrologia Graecae* 35, p. 856.

7. Saint Ignatius of Antioch, *Letter to the Romans,* 2–7.

8. *Little Flowers of Saint Francis,* ch. 8, in *St. Francis of Assisi: Omnibus of Sources,* 3rd edition, Marion

Habig, ed. (Chicago: Franciscan Herald Press, 1973), p.1320.

CHAPTER TWO: HUMILITY

1. Saint Teresa of Ávila, *The Interior Castle*, ch. 10, in *The Complete Works of Saint Teresa of Jesus*, E. Allison Peers, ed. (New York: Sheed & Ward, 1957), p. 323.
2. "Praises of God," in Habig, p. 125.
3. *Admonitions*, I, in Habig, p. 78.
4. "Letter to a General Chapter," in Habig, p. 106.
5. "Canticle of the Sun," in Habig, p. 130.
6. Saint Augustine, *Sermons*, 21, 2. See Saint Augustine, "Sermon 21," 2, in Rotelle, volume 3, p. 30.

CHAPTER THREE: THE OUTPOURING OR BAPTISM IN THE SPIRIT

1. Saint Augustine, "Sermon 169," 11, in *Patrologia Latina* 38, p. 923. See Saint Augustine, "Sermon 169," in Rotelle, volume 5, p. 231.
2. Clement of Alexandria, *Paedagogus* 1, 6, 26.
3. Saint Basil, "On the Holy Spirit," 12 in *Patrologia Graecae* 32, 117 B. See Saint Basil, "On the Holy Spirit," 12, in *Christian Classics Series: St. Basil the Great: On the Holy Spirit*, George Lewis, trans. (London: Religious Tract Society, 1888), p. 61.
4. Saint Basil, "Against Eunomius," 3, 5, in *Patrologia Graecae*, 29, p. 655.
5. Saint Basil, "On Baptism," 1, 1; in *Patrologia Graecae*, 31, pp. 1513ff. See Saint Basil, *On Baptism*, in *The Fathers of the Church: Saint Basil: Ascetical Works*, Sr. M. Monica Wagner, trans. (New York: Fathers of the Church, Inc., 1950), pp. 340–341.

6. *Legend of the Three Companions,* ch. 3, no. 7, in Habig, pp. 896–897.
7. Tertullian, "On the Resurrection of the Flesh," 8, 3.
8. Tertullian, "On Baptism," 2, 1ff.

Chapter Four: Charisms

1. See Heribert Mühlen, *Una mystica persona: Eine Person in vielen Personen* (Paderborn: Ferdinand Schöningh, 1964).
2. *Lumen gentium,* 12, in Austin P. Flannery, ed. *Documents of Vatican II* (Grand Rapids, Mich.: Eerdmans, 1978), p. 363.
3. Saint Augustine, "On the Trinity," XV, 19, 34.
4. Saint Augustine, *Tractates on John,* 32, p. 8.

Chapter Five: Anointed

1. Tertullian, "Apology," 39, 9.
2. Saint Cyril of Jerusalem, *Mystagogical Catecheses,* 3, 1–3.
3. Tertullian, *On Baptism,* 7, 1.
4. Saint Irenaeus, *Against Heresies,* III, 18, 3.
5. Saint Ignatius of Antioch, "Letter to the Ephesians," 17.
6. Saint Irenaeus, *Against Heresies,* III, 9, 3.
7. Saint Athanasius, *Discourses Against the Arians,* 1, 47.
8. Theophilus of Antioch, "To Autolycus," 1, 12.
9. Pope Leo the Great, *Discorsi* 4, 1–2, in *Patrologia Latina,* 54, pp. 148ff.
10. *Lumen gentium,* 10, in Flannery, pp. 360-361.
11. Saint Gregory Nazianzen, "Oration 2," 95.
12. Saint Augustine, *The City of God,* 10, 6, John Healey, trans., volume 1 (New York: E. P. Dutton & Co., 1945), p. 279.

13. Thomas à Kempis, *The Imitation of Christ*, 4, 9 (New York: Doubleday, 1976), p. 197.
14. *The Passion of Ss. Perpetua and Felicity*, W.H. Shewring, trans. (London: Sheed and Ward, 2002), p. 40.

CHAPTER SIX: THE HEALING POWER OF THE SPIRIT

1. Saint Cyril, *Catecheses*, 16, 22.
2. *Apophthegmata Patrum* 19, 14, in *Patrologia Latina*, 73.

CHAPTER SEVEN: PENTECOST: THE WAY TO CONVERSION AND UNITY

1. Saint Augustine, *The Spirit and the Letter*, 16, 28.
2. See Saint Thomas Aquinas, *Summa Theologiae*, volume 30, I–IIae, question 106, article 2 (New York: McGraw-Hill, 1964), p. 9.
3. Eucharistic Prayer IV.
4. *Tertio millennio adveniente*, ch. 2, 16 (Vatican City: Vatican Press, 1994), p. 21.

CHAPTER EIGHT: "REPENT, AND YOU WILL RECEIVE THE GIFT OF THE HOLY SPIRIT"

1. Saint Augustine, "Sermon 169," 11, in *Patrologia Latina* 38, p. 923. See Saint Augustine, "Sermon 169," in Rotelle, volume 5, p. 231.

CHAPTER NINE: WE WERE ALL MADE TO DRINK OF ONE SPIRIT

1. *Pesachim*, 10, p. 5. See Central Conference of American Rabbis, ed., *The Union Haggadah: Home Service for the Passover* (New York: CCAR, 1923), p. 38.
2. Saint Ambrose, "Commentary on the Psalms," 1, 33; in *Patrologia Latina*, 14, pp. 939–940.

3. See Hesychius, "On Watchfulness and Holiness: Written for Theodolus," in *The Philokalia*, volume 1 (London: Faber & Faber, 1979), pp. 162–198.

4. Saint John of the Cross, *Ascent of Mount Carmel* II, 5, 7, E. Allison Peers, trans. (New York: Image, 1958), p. 96.

5. Macarius of Egypt, "Love," in *The Philokalia*, p. 3.

6. Saint Ambrose, "Commentary on the Psalms" 35, 19.

7. *Lumen gentium*, 12, in Flannery, p. 363.

8 Yves Congar, *Actualité de la Pneumatologie*, in *Credo in Spiritum Sanctum* (Vatican City: Libreria Editrice Vaticana, 1983) 1, p. 18.

Index

Scripture Index

Pájara • A red sandstone doorway adorns the church in this picturesque village *(page 73)*

Costa Calma • Sweeps of white sand draw visitors to Fuerteventura's Sotavento beaches *(page 75)*

El Jable dunes • These great empty swathes of sand lie just outside lively Corralejo in northern Fuerteventura *(page 67)*

Fundación César Manrique • The former home of Lanzarote's iconic artist and architect *(page 41)*

Cueva de los Verdes • Take a trip through the dramatic lava-formed caves *(page 34)*

Puerto del Carmen • Lanzarote's biggest resort offers some of the island's best beaches *(page 49)*

CONTENTS

55

99

81

INTRODUCTION

Swept by trade winds and warmed by coastal currents, the islands of Lanzarote and Fuerteventura offer a consistently warm climate, with some 300 days of sunshine a year. They are part of the Canary Islands, which lie approximately 1,100km (690 miles) southwest of the Spanish mainland and, at the nearest point, 115km (70 miles) from the West African coast. Although part of Spain, in 1982 the islands became an autonomous province, divided in two: the eastern islands, which include Lanzarote and Fuerteventura, are governed by a Cabildo Insular (Island Council) from Las Palmas de Gran Canaria, the western islands from Santa Cruz de Tenerife.

Lanzarote is some 60km (38 miles) in length and 24km (15 miles) across at its widest point, with a population of about 116,000, of whom some 48,000 live in the capital, Arrecife. Fuerteventura is larger, at around 100km (60 miles) long and 30km (18 miles) wide, but sparsely populated – there are around 79,000 inhabitants, of whom about half live in Puerto del Rosario.

Landscape and Climate

The whole volcanic archipelago is barren, but Lanzarote and Fuerteventura are drier and more barren than the rest. Lanzarote's last volcanic explosion was in 1824, but the heat is still close to the surface, as you will find if you go to the Parque Nacional Timanfaya, and much of the island is still covered with cindery *malpaís* (badlands). Fuerteventura has seen no volcanic activity for some 5,000 years, but has less rain than any of the islands, and the landscape is coloured in shades of brown and khaki, with great expanses of dunes.

Sculpture outside the Fundación César Manrique

Camel trekking in the Parque Nacional Timanfaya

Lanzarote's highest point is Montaña Blanca, at 670 metres (2,198ft). The beaches around the major resorts, especially the famous ones at Puerto del Carmen, are covered with golden sands, as are the beautiful stretches close to Playa Blanca, while smaller, rockier coves retain their black volcanic sand. Of Fuerteventura's 152 beaches, some 50km (32 miles) consist of white sand, while about 25km (15 miles) are black volcanic shingle. The highest point on the island is Monte Jandía (807 metres/2,648ft).

The islands' average annual temperature is 20°C (68°F), soaring in high summer to 28–30°C (82–86°F). Fuerteventura is usually windy – one explanation for the island's name is that it comes from *viento fuerte* (strong wind). On both islands, early mornings can be cloudy before blue skies and sunshine take over. There is little rain – what there is falls mostly between October and January. In summer the islands sometimes suffer from what is known as *tiempo Africano*

(African weather), when the hot sirocco wind sweeps up from the Sahara, covering the landscape with reddish dust.

Vegetation and Farming

There are few trees, apart fom the Canary palms *(Phoenix Canariensis)* in the Haría Valley, and those planted along the roadsides of many towns and resorts. Parks, hotel grounds and botanical gardens are bright with exotic plants brought to the island from southern Africa, South America and elsewhere that flourish happily in the islands' subtropical climate. The Strelitzia (bird-of-paradise flower) is one of the most showy, but hibiscus, poinsettia and agave are also common, and vividly coloured bougainvillea rampages over the garden walls and facades of villas and hotels.

Various forms of *Euphorbia* (spurge) flourish on the scrubby soil, including the *Euphorbia Canariensis* (candelabra spurge) and the rare, cactus-like *cardón de Jandía (Euphorbia handiensis)*, found in the south of Fuerteventura.

A variety of prickly pear cactus cultivated mainly on Lanzarote is the nopal, on which the cochineal beetle feeds. When crushed, the beetle produces a red dye – cochineal. This is not the lucrative industry it was in the 19th century *(see page 16)*, but a recent resurgence of interest in natural products means cochineal is being produced in Lanzarote, but on a much smaller scale.

Another form of vegetation is that produced on the

Aloe vera

On both islands you will see aloe vera, another cactus-like plant that has become very popular for medicinal and cosmetic purposes – especially to soothe sunburn – and is being widely cultivated. The plant has long, greyish-green spiky leaves and spears of yellow flowers. You will find the products for sale in small shops, markets and supermarkets all over the islands.

Cacti flourish in the islands' dry, sandy soil

black lava called *picón*. This cinder, which collects and stores moisture from dew, is spread over arid soil and used for the cultivation of vines – especially in the La Geria region.

Wildlife

There is plenty for bird-watchers to spot on both islands in winter. Lanzarote's central plain is the best place to see Houbara bustards, kestrels, stone curlews and trumpeter finches – which are also found on Fuerteventura, along with the Fuerteventura chat. Berthelot's pipit can be seen all over the island, hoopoes are fairly common, and chiffchaffs and warblers are often found in urban settings. The Salinas de Janubio (salt pans) are a stopping-off place for many migratory birds, and numerous seabirds cluster on the offshore islands.

There are few mammals on either island: bats, rats, mice, squirrels, rabbits and hedgehogs are about the sum of it. There are reptiles, though: geckos and lizards. The water around the islands is home to dolphins, porpoises and whales, and is rich in fish, including *corvina* (a kind of sea bass), *cherne* (wreckfish or stone bass), *sama* (sea bream) and *vieja* (parrot fish), as well as more homely *sardinas* (sardines).

People and Language

The people of the Canary Islands have a strong sense of their identity as islanders and are keen to stress that they are *canarios* first and foremost. Spanish *(castellano)* is the language of the islands, but there are subtle differences from the peninsula, many of which reflect the two-way traffic between the Canaries and Latin America. Final consonants are swallowed and 'z' is pronounced 's', as in the Americas, rather than the lisped 'th' of mainland Spain. A number of Latino words have been borrowed, too: a bus is a *guagua* and potatoes are *papas*.

The Impact of Tourism

Traditionally, the islands' economy has been dependent on agriculture, but the principal source of revenue today comes from tourism. Lanzarote and Fuerteventura lack the loud nightlife and laddish culture that typifies parts of Tenerife and Gran Canaria. The strong winds and good waves attract surfing enthusiasts, but, apart from this, the equable climate means that the islands are all-round holiday destinations, with many older northern European visitors favouring the

Traditional costumes and music at a Lanzarote fiesta

cooler months as an escape from their own harsher winters, while families are in the majority during school holidays.

Obviously, the influx of tourists has had a major impact on the character of the islands, although Lanzarote has escaped the high-rise desecration that has spoiled parts of Tenerife and Gran Canaria. This is due in large part to the vision of artist César Manrique *(see page 25)*, who was influential in persuading the authorities to work with the island's landscape and natural features. Fuerteventura, which came later to tourism, has some rather characterless new resorts, but on the whole they are not badly done.

The resort of Caleta de Fuste on Fuerteventura

From volcanic landscapes to sandy beaches, the islands have much to offer, whether visitors are looking for watersports or family entertainment, or are keen to discover the island way of life. The islands are easy to get around on well-surfaced roads, and there are some pleasant walking routes to suit people of all ages. While most accommodation is in purpose-built complexes, *turismo rural* has gained a foothold, making it possible to stay in rural properties in beautiful surroundings *(see page 126)* and sample traditional food. All in all, enough to convince most people that the islands merit one of their early names – the Fortunate Isles.

A BRIEF HISTORY

The Canary Islands have been part of Spain since they were conquered in the late 15th century, but there was a flourishing culture here long before that, although no one is quite sure where the pre-Hispanic people came from. These early inhabitants are known collectively as the Guanches, although strictly speaking this was the name of a tribe that inhabited Tenerife. The people of Lanzarote and Fuerteventura prefer the name Majoreros, which is derived from Fuerteventura's indigenous name – Maxorata. Some historians think the original inhabitants were related to the Canarii people, who lived on the Saharan side of the Atlas Mountains. But as far as we know, the Guanches had no boats, so how they crossed from the African coast remains a mystery.

The Guanches were an agricultural people who mostly lived in groups of caves, but on the three eastern islands they also built houses. On Lanzarote and Fuerteventura their dwellings were grouped into hamlets around the edges of lava fields. Their society had a hierarchical structure, with kings – *guanartemes* – and priests – *faycans*. Lanzarote was a single kingdom, but on Fuerteventura there were two – Maxorata in the north and Jandía in the south, beyond La Pared, the wall that once stretched across the narrowest part of the island. These early people mummified their dead and buried them in caves or stone-lined graves, and it is evidence from mummies that has led scientists to place the islanders' ethnic origins in northwest Africa.

The Guanches did not have the wheel, they knew nothing of metalworking and did not use bows and arrows – their main weapons were wooden spears. Domestic implements were made from stone and bone or from obsidian, a black, volcanic glass. Porous lava was made into millstones and

Marital custom

Scientist and explorer Alexander von Humboldt, who visited Lanzarote in 1799 en route to South America, claimed the indigenous people had an unusual custom: 'A woman had several husbands, who each took it in turn to exercise the rights of the head of the family. Each husband was known as such during a lunar month; then another took his place while he returned to being a servant in the house.'

mortars. Their vessels and containers were made from pottery, wood, leather and woven cane. *Gofio*, toasted flour originally made from barley, was their staple food, but they also ate a variety of roots, wild fruits and berries. Pigs, sheep and goats provided meat as well as the materials for shelters, containers and clothes, and milk also came from sheep and goats. Fish formed a part of their diet, even when they had to travel some distance down to the coast to find it.

Arrival of the Europeans

The first documented account of a European expedition to the Canary Islands was in 1339, when the Genoese Lanzarotto Malocello discovered the island that was named after him. The first detailed description of the islands was written two years later by Genoese historian Nicoloso da Recco, who accompanied a slave-traders' voyage. He wrote: 'The natives of Fuerteventura are few in number and live on meat and milk, and are of great stature, and are very firm in their beliefs.' Various expeditions were mounted during the course of the century, but it was not until 1402 that the first conquerors arrived. Jean de Béthencourt and Gadifer de la Salle, Norman noblemen who had pledged allegiance to the king of Castile, claimed Lanzarote, Fuerteventura and El Hierro for their royal master, but failed to take Gran Canaria and Tenerife. Like most conquerors, they claimed the expedition was 'for the exaltation of the Christian faith', so they must have been delighted when the last king of Lanzarote, after several failed escape attempts, agreed to Christian baptism.

Many of the indigenous people were sold into slavery and many more died of European diseases, but those who survived intermarried with the colonisers, who settled down to a harsh life, making their living from the land and sea.

It was not until 1478 that another attempt was made to conquer the two larger islands, under the aegis of Ferdinand and Isabella – the so-called Catholic Monarchs of a newly united Spain. It took several years to subdue the indigenous people, but eventually all the Canary Islands became Spanish possessions.

Jean de Béthencourt

Because of their location, the islands were vital for Spanish colonisation in the Americas. This revolved around slavery and sugar cane, both of which were introduced to the Americas from the Canaries, but it was Gran Canaria and Tenerife that were the main beneficiaries. Of no interest to their Spanish masters and with little source of income, many inhabitants of Lanzarote and Fuerteventura turned to piracy during the 16th and early 17th centuries, a somewhat precarious way of earning a living, and one that laid them open to reciprocal attacks.

Explosive Events

During the mid-18th century, memories of pirate raids faded into insignificance when Lanzarote experienced a disastrous series of volcanic eruptions. In 1730, Volcán Timanfaya erupted, and continued to pour molten lava and black ash down its slopes for a further six years, until a third of the island had been devastated, many of its inhabitants had fled to Gran Canaria and some had set out on the long journey to Latin America. For almost a century the volcano appeared to sleep, but 1824 saw another series of eruptions, albeit smaller ones. Visitors to the dark, eerie landscape now protected as the Parque Nacional de Timanfaya may be able to visualise the devastation.

Although the eruptions overwhelmed the most fertile part of the island, the volcanic ash formed *picón*, dark cinders that collect and retain the dew, forming a natural irrigation system. On this the islanders were able to grow a variety of vegetables, and to profit from the cultivation of vines and the export of wine, ushering in a period of prosperity that lasted until the early years of the 19th century. This system, known as *enarenad*, was later practised in arid parts of the Spanish mainland, although silicon sand was used instead of cinder.

The next money-spinner was cochineal, a red dye created by crushing the beetle (*Dactylopius coccus costa*) that fed on the nopal cactus, and which was introduced to the islands in around 1825. For some 50 years the

Mountain of fire

The parish priest of Yaiza, Andrés Lorenzo Curbelo, described the 1730 eruption as 'an enormous mountain that rose out of the bosom of the earth. From its flat top flames belched out and continued burning for 19 days.' Several months later 'new eruptions came... [with] incandescent streams of lava, together with the densest smoke.'

Volcanic landscape formed by the eruptions of Timanfaya

industry flourished, before the creation of aniline dyes made it largely superfluous.

During the latter part of this period the larger, more powerful islands of Gran Canaria and Tenerife were flexing their muscles, demanding a degree of independence from Spain and vying with each other for supremacy at the same time. Tenerife, which had profited from the wine trade (Gran Canaria's soil was unsuitable for viniculture) and other long-distance commerce was by far the wealthier and had established a university in the town of La Laguna, which became an intellectual centre. Gran Canaria resented Tenerife's powerful position and, under the late 19th-century leadership of Fernando León y Castillo, foreign minister in the national government, made a bid for supremacy.

In 1903, emboldened by Cuba gaining freedom from Spain five years earlier, the Partido Local Canario was formed, with the aim of achieving some degree of independence and dividing the archipelago into two provinces. This was formalised in 1927, but brought little economic relief to the islands, whose trade had been badly hit by World War I and its economic aftermath. Lanzarote and Fuerteventura became part of the Eastern Province, governed, as they are today, from Las Palmas de Gran Canaria. The seat of island government (Cabildo Insular) alternates between Las Palmas and Santa Cruz de Tenerife every four years.

There had been a steady flow of people from the Canaries to the Americas since the late 16th century, but agricultural decline in the late 19th and early 20th centuries increased this traffic, as people went looking for a better way of life. Remittances were sent home, and many of those who made good returned to the islands and built homes or established small businesses, thus accentuating the ties with Latin America that are still apparent today. You can visit

Many *canarios* emigrated to the Americas

the Museo del Emigrante just outside Teguise (Lanzarote) to learn more about this *(see page 46)*.

Political Upheavals

In 1924, under the dictatorship of Miguel Primo de Rivera, Fuerteventura, the bleakest of the Canary Islands, was judged a suitable place to send political dissidents.

(see page 46).

> **Praise from Castro**
>
> Fidel Castro expressed his admiration for Canarian emigrants to Cuba, who 'helped forge the country with their proverbial hard work'. It was from them, he said, that 'our peasants inherited their seriousness, their decency, their sense of honour and also their rebelliousness.'

Writer and philosopher Miguel de Unamuno was the best known of these. He came to love the island, which he described as 'a rock thirsting in the sun, a treasure of health and honesty'. There is a monument to him in the north of the island.

In 1936, the three-year Spanish Civil War began, initiated by Francisco Franco, military governor of the Canary Islands. He spent the last night before launching his coup in the Hotel Madrid in Las Palmas.

After the bitter Civil War and World War II, the Canaries, like the rest of Spain, initially suffered from political isolation and economic hardship. Things improved a little in the 1950s, when Spain was once more recognised by the international community, but it was the advent of tourism in the following decade that really turned the tide.

Franco remained in power until his death in 1975, when his authoritarian regime was replaced by democratic government. The new Spanish Constitution of 1978 created the Autonomous Region of the Canary Islands – now one of 17 such regions. The archipelago is not completely separate from Spain, but the island government, known as the Cabildo Insular, does have a great deal of freedom.

A young islander looks to the future

In the national elections of 1996, the Coalición Canaria, a union of regional parties, took four seats in the Madrid parliament (this was reduced to three in the 2004 election, and to two in 2008). It now sees its role as working with the national government to win improvements for the islands, rather than looking for further independence. This is not to say that no resentment is felt towards Madrid, but resentment of central government is, perhaps, a fact of life wherever regional feelings are strong.

Many mainland Spaniards, particularly from the poorer regions – Andalusia and Galicia – are to be found working in the islands' service industries. They have integrated well into island life and, while there is some dissatisfaction expressed about them doing jobs that might be done by local people, there is relatively little ill-feeling.

The islands have enjoyed considerable commercial freedom and tax exemptions ever since the 19th century. When

Spain became a full member of the European Union, fiscal changes had to be introduced, but important tax privileges were negotiated. Motorists will be pleased to find that, in a period of rocketing fuel prices, the islands still have the cheapest petrol in Europe.

Tourism, Economy and Environment

Traditionally, the economy of the islands has been dependent on agriculture and fishing, but the principal source of employment and revenue today is in the service sector, of which tourism is a major part. Some 90 percent of Lanzarote's inhabitants work in the tourist industry and the infrastructure that supports it, and the percentage in Fuerteventura is similar. When Arrecife airport opened in the early 1960s (it was refurbished and extended in 1999 to cope with the large number of passengers), tourism started to take off. Fuerteventura's airport opened in 1969, and while the growth of the tourist industry was slower here than on the other islands, it has increased in recent years. Lanzarote now receives about 1.8 million visitors annually, Fuerteventura some 1.5 million, mainly English, Germans and Scandinavians, as well

Dangerous Journeys

Lanzarote and Fuerteventura have become the main route into Europe for illegal immigrants from Africa now that strict controls have made it more difficult for them to cross from northern Morocco to southern Spain. Desperate people, many from war-torn sub-Saharan regions, pay traffickers up to €1,200 (around £1,000) to reach the Moroccan coast, where they are loaded onboard small, ill-equipped boats to make the dangerous journey to these islands, which are the closest to the African coast. Many drown, or die of dehydration, during the course of their journey. Others reach the island shores to face an uncertain future.

as visitors from mainland Spain. There are believed to be around 50,000 foreign property owners on Lanzarote, and some have established bars, clubs and other small businesses. There are fewer home owners on Fuerteventura, but numbers are rising.

The eastern islands suffer from severe water shortage (they receive less rainfall than parts of the Sahara), a problem intensified by the strain that so many visitors place on the system. The creation of desalination plants has helped, but visitors should try to be frugal in their use of water, although in hot summer weather it can be rather difficult.

The islands utilise their strong winds, as they always have

The availability of work in the tourist industry has encouraged many young people to desert the land and the fishing industry (although Arrecife still has the biggest fishing fleet in the Canaries) in favour of higher wages and more fun in the resorts. But life for the islanders has rarely been easy, and it is understandable that the latest generation should look for alternatives. Most people believe that tourism has brought more advantages than disadvantages to the islands, and that the inhabitants' individuality and love of their lands will enable them to retain their special character, despite the many changes.

Historical Landmarks

c.2nd–1st centuries BC Settlements of Guanches – or Majoreros – in Canary Islands.

AD1339 Genoese Lanzarotto Malocello discovers Lanzarote.

1402 Jean de Béthencourt and Gadifer de la Salle invade and claim Lanzarote, Fuerteventura and El Hierro.

1478–83 Canary Islands brought under control of Spanish Crown.

16th–17th centuries Many inhabitants of impoverished Lanzarote and Fuerteventura turn to piracy.

1730–6 Continuous eruptions of Mount Timanfaya; a third of Lanzarote is devastated.

1730–1950 Poverty forces widespread emigration to Latin America.

1825–75 Economic boom follows the introduction of the cochineal beetle, but the industry is ruined by the invention of aniline dyes.

1852 Isabella II declares the Canary Islands a Free Trade Zone.

1911 Self-administration council – Cabildo Insular – introduced.

1927 Canary Islands are divided in two. Lanzarote and Fuerteventura become part of the Eastern Province, governed from Gran Canaria.

1936 Franco initiates the three-year Spanish Civil War.

1962 Lanzarote's Arrecife airport opens. Tourism rapidly develops into the most important industry.

1969 Fuerteventura airport opens. Tourism develops more slowly here.

1970s Influenced by artist and architect César Manrique, the Cabildo imposes strict building regulations on Lanzarote.

1978–82 Spanish Constitution joins the two island provinces to form the Autonomous Region of the Canary Islands.

1986 Spain joins the EU and negotiates special status for the Canaries.

1995 Islands integrated into the EU but retain important tax privileges.

2002 The euro becomes the national currency.

2005–6 Lanzarote receives about 1.8 million visitors annually, Fuerteventura some 1.5 million.

2008 In national elections, the Coalición Canaria wins two seats in the Madrid parliament (one fewer than in 2004).

LANZAROTE

Lanzarote is a small island, but it packs a lot of contrasts into a limited space. From the awesome, unearthly Montañas del Fuego in the Parque Nacional de Timanfaya to the verdant 'Valley of a Thousand Palms' around Haría; from the tranquillity of Isla Graciosa to the razzmatazz of Puerto del Carmen, there is always something to surprise the visitor. One thing is consistent, however: the building limits proposed by artist César Manrique and imposed by the island government have ensured that, with a few exceptions, the architecture consists of low white buildings with green, blue or brown balconies and shutters, which complement the indigenous architecture of the island.

Lanzarote is an easy place to get around. For the sake of simplicity this guide starts with the capital, Arrecife, then divides the island into three areas: north, south and centre. However, distances are so small that you may find yourself straying from one region to the other on a single trip. Just follow your own instincts and you won't go far wrong.

ARRECIFE

Arrecife lies 8km (5 miles) east of the airport, from where it is well served by inexpensive taxis. Buses *(guaguas)* run every 20 minutes to Costa Teguise and Puerto del Carmen, and taxi fares to both resorts are very reasonable. The town has a long history, as its two sturdy fortresses demonstrate. Castillo de San Gabriel was built in the second half of the 17th century to reinforce the town against attacks from the sea; it was the work of Genoese engineer Leonardo Torriani,

One of Playa Blanca's inviting beaches

who also built Teguise's Castillo de Santa Bárbara. The Castillo de San José dates from about a century later, when pirate attacks were still a problem. It was also a work-creation project, as the islanders were suffering great poverty following periods of drought and the eruption of Timanfaya, which had destroyed farmland in the most fertile part of the island. For a long time it was known as the Castillo del Hambre (Fortress of Hunger). In 1852, when piracy had ceased to be a threat, and links with Spain's American colonies meant that it made more sense to have a capital on the coast, Arrecife took over from Teguise as the capital of Lanzarote.

Arrecife is a down-to-earth, working city, home to almost half the island's population.

The Charco de San Ginés

It has few buildings of architectural interest and not a great deal in the way of culture, but it is well worth a visit to see a slice of island life, away from the resorts or the picture-postcard villages. It has a few decent tapas bars, an excellent restaurant in the Castillo de San José, food to be purchased in the market and local shops that is cheaper and more varied than in the resorts, and an excellent curved beach – Playa Reducto – with golden sands and calm, safe waters. If you want a quiet holiday there is a lot to be said for making a base here in one of the seafront hotels.

Exploring the Town

If you come to Arrecife by car, get off the *circunvalación* (ring road) at the west (airport) end of town, where you can park in a large car park at the end of the beach, opposite the smart new Cabildo Insular building, and thereby avoid the narrow streets and one-way system of the city. Looming at the other end of the beach is the

Kiosko de la Música

17-storey **Gran Hotel** (which has a large underground car park). This was the building that so upset Manrique when he returned from New York that he took steps to ensure that Lanzarote's skyline would not become disfigured by similar high-rises. The hotel was gutted by fire in 1994 and remained empty for years but has now reopened. Although it breaks all the rules, it is a sleek, well-designed building. Take the glass lift to the top, where a there's a restaurant and a café that offers views over the town and down to Puerto del Carmen – and good coffee and cake.

Newly planted gardens and a wooden walkway lead towards the town centre. On a corner, opposite an attractive Canarian-style building belonging to the Cabildo, old men sit in a little square playing dominoes. A broad promenade runs east from here. The statue at the beginning is of Blas Cabrera Felipe (1878–1945), an eminent scientist who was born in the town. There are seats in flower-decked bowers, and egrets squawk and flap in the palm trees. In the circular wooden **Kiosko de la Música**, where a band sometimes plays, you can pick up maps and leaflets giving tourist information. On the other side of the road (now the Avenida de

Guarding San Gabriel

la Marina, although some maps still show it as Avenida General Franco) is the post office and the Casa de Cultura Agustín de la Hoz, which houses a museum but has been closed for some time for renovation.

Cross a little bridge to the **Castillo de San Gabriel** (Tue–Fri 10am–1pm, 4–7pm, Sat 10am–1pm; free), with a rusty cannon standing outside. The little fortress houses a small exhibition on the Guanches, the island's original inhabitants, and outlines the history of piracy in a series of tiny, thick-walled rooms that will not detain you for long. You can cross back to the seafront via a parallel bridge, the **Puente de las Bolas**, named for the cannon balls atop its twin pillars. Follow the promenade (now called Avenida Coll) a short way to the right (towards the port), passing the Ayuntamiento (Town Hall), then cross the road to the **Charco de San Ginés**. This pretty little tidal lagoon, where boats bob serenely on the water, is surrounded by brightly shuttered buildings, several of which house restaurants. The only incongruous feature is a large, four-screen cinema – but local people are probably glad of the entertainment.

You can walk all the way round the lagoon then off into the town to the Plaza de las Palmas, and the parish church, the **Iglesia de San Ginés** (daily 9am–1pm, 4–7pm), with a distinctive white cupola topping its bell tower. It is dedicated to the town's patron saint, whose festival is celebrated here in August. There is a simple interior, with a good *mudéjar* ceiling of dark wood. If you find the church closed (the opening hours are not to be relied on), just sit on one of the benches in the shady square, listen to the drip of a central fountain and admire the exterior of the building.

Narrow lanes lead from the square into the centre of the town, focused on the pedestrianised shopping street, **Calle León y Castillo**, running back from the seafront. Here, branches of well-known stores such as Zara and Mango share space with the large HiperDino supermarket and a few delightfully old-fashioned shops such as the Almacenes Arencibia, with shirts and jerseys stacked neatly on glass-fronted wooden shelves.

Art in Arrecife

Go west, via the oblong Plaza de la Constitución – where there are a couple of tapas bars with seats outside in the square – towards Calle Betancort. Here (No. 33) you will find **El Almacén** (Mon–Fri 10am–2pm, 7pm–midnight; free), a cultural centre in an old store converted by César Manrique. The

León y Castillo

You may wonder why most towns and villages in Lanzarote have a street or square called León y Castillo. This has nothing to do with lions or castles, but pays homage to two brothers, Fernando and Juan, who were born in Telde, Gran Canaria, where there is now a museum devoted to them. Fernando, who became foreign minister in the Spanish government in 1881, implemented a programme of improvements to the port of Las Palmas, the plans for which were drawn up by his engineer brother Juan. This made it the major port in the archipelago and an important stop on the new steamship route to the West Indies, and changed the ailing fortunes of Gran Canaria and, by extension, of Lanzarote and Fuerteventura.

Castillo de San José

centre includes the Bar Picasso, where there is sometimes live music, two galleries with changing exhibitions and, on the top floor, the Cine Buñuel, which screens art house films.

Arrecife is a small town, and all of the above can easily be done on foot, but to visit the last place of interest you need to take a taxi. They are readily available, and it should cost no more than €4 from the centre to the **Castillo de San José**, which houses the **Museo Internacional de Arte Contemporáneo** (daily 11am–9pm; free). The fortress had fallen into disrepair by the 20th century, and in 1975 Manrique directed the renovation of the building and founded the Museum of Contemporary Art. In a series of cool rooms within the thick stone walls is a collection of paintings, sketches and sculpture by internationally known artists such as Antoni Tàpies, as well as Manrique himself and other renowned Canarian artists. Down a flight of stairs more paintings decorate the walls of a restaurant and bar (daily; restaurant 1–3.45pm, 7.30–11pm; bar 11am–midnight). From the floor-to-ceiling windows there is a view of the new Puerto de los Mármoles – not traditionally picturesque, but in this context the cranes, ships and containers have a sculptural beauty. You can eat very well here *(see page 134)*, or just enjoy the view from a low, comfy bar stool while you have a drink – and bar prices are surprisingly low for such a smart venue.

THE NORTH

The north of the island is a treasure trove of natural wonders and man-made attractions. Nature has given us the dramatic cliffs of Risco de Famara on the west coast, the *malpaís* (badlands) on the east, the fascinating Cueva de los Verdes and the tranquil island of Isla Graciosa, while man (or, to be specific, Manrique) has created the breathtaking Jameos del Agua, the Jardín de Cactus and the Mirador del Río.

Jardín de Cactus and Arrieta

From the *circunvalación* around Arrecife, take the LZ1 north towards **Guatiza** to visit the **Jardín de Cactus** (daily 10am–5.45pm; charge includes a drink in the café). As you enter Guatiza you pass fields of cultivated cactus, for this is the region where cochineal is still produced, albeit not in large quantities *(see page 16)*. Set in a volcanic crater, this Manrique-designed garden spirals in a circle of terraces up to a small windmill. There are cacti of all kinds: round and dumpy, tall and phallic, and some like little furry creatures snuggled in the volcanic soil. Manrique's designs on the external walls of the toilets are attractions in themselves.

Jardín de Cactus

A sad story

A strange house stands on one of Arrieta's jetties, pagoda-like in bright blue and brick-red. The building has a sad story to tell: in the 1920s a local man emigrated to Argentina, where he prospered, but his young daughter fell gravely ill and he was advised that the Atlantic winds would be good for her. He returned and built a house as exposed to the elements as possible in a style popular in Argentina at the time. Sadly, the daughter died, despite his care, and is buried in the local cemetery.

En route from Guatiza to the Jameos del Agua, you could make a brief detour to **Arrieta**. We are in Manrique country here, and one of his sculptures, like a giant wind chime, stands at a roundabout where a road leads the short distance to this tiny fishing village. To the right, before you enter the village, you could turn off to the pleasant **Playa de la Garita**. Arrieta is a sleepy place, although quite popular with divers, and it gets animated at weekend lunchtimes when several fish restaurants around the small harbour draw customers. Also worth a visit is the new **Aloe Vera House** (Mon–Sat 9am–6.30pm; free), which has lots of information on the production and uses of the plant.

Jameos del Agua and Cueva de los Verdes

Continue north for 3km (2 miles) to the well-signposted **Jameos del Agua** (daily 10am–6.30pm, Tue, Fri–Sat also 7.30pm–2am; bar 10am–6.30pm and 7pm–2am; restaurant 7.30–11.30pm; charge). You turn off onto a road that is in many places not wide enough for two-way traffic, but there are many passing places, and people are usually courteous about using them. This is one site that just about everybody comes to, so it can get busy – try to come fairly early, or at the end of the day – and it is like nothing else you will ever have seen. It is part of volcanic tunnel system that runs from

Montaña de Corona, which erupted about 4,000 years ago, out into the Atlantic. It was this eruption that created the *malpaís* (now a protected area) through which you will drive if you continue north. A *jameo* is the name for a cavity produced when the roof of a volcanic tunnel collapses.

Within this one, Manrique created an extraordinary underground world. You go down steps to the *jameo chico* (small cave) to a bar/restaurant, full of lush foliage and soft music, from where narrow paths lead to a saltwater lake of varying depth depending on the tide. The lake is home to a unique variety of crab *(Munidopsis polymorpha)*, white, blind and without shells – as they have no predators, they had no need to develop them. Notices around the lake (and on your ticket) tell you that it is forbidden to throw coins into the water, as their corrosion would endanger the crabs. At the other side of the lake, landscaped terraces lead up

Jameos del Agua

Cueva de los Verdes

to ground level. At the far side is a 600-seat auditorium, with splendid acoustics; closed for renovation for some years, it reopened for performances in 2008.

About 1km (½ mile) up a narrow road opposite lies the **Cueva de los Verdes** (daily 10am–5pm; guided tour; charge). *Verde* means green, but the name refers not to the colour of the rocks but to a family called Verde who used to keep their goats in the upper part of the cave. Over the years, these caverns served as a place of refuge for local people when pirates attacked the shores. The cave system is part of the same 'tube' that runs from Montaña de Corona to the sea.

You may have to wait a short while to go in as the numbers on each 50-minute tour are limited; however, they run very frequently. The temperature inside the caves remains at 18–20°C (64–68°F) throughout the year, which makes the visit a pleasant escape from summer heat. Claustrophobics should be all right, as, after an initial low, narrow stretch, the cave opens out into a vast cavern, and thereafter there are few places where you need to stoop. The tour does involve shuffling along rather slowly, however – how slowly depends on the composition of your group and how many people linger to take photos. It's worth the shuffle, though, as the shapes of the cave walls and ceilings, formed by the solidified lava and enhanced by discreet lighting, are extraordinary. Your guide will lead you into an auditorium, where concerts are sometimes held, as the acoustics are excellent. As the tour draws to an end, the guide will demand silence in order to introduce you to the 'secret of the caves' – it's an ingenious one, and we are not going to give the game away.

Mirador del Río and Parque Tropical

Continue north, through cindery *malpaís*, where only lichen-covered rocks and euphorbia bushes enliven the black terrain. After a while a few small vineyards appear, the vines planted in the traditional Lanzarote way, within a semicircle of rocks *(see page 49)*. On a hillside, a bodega offers tastings and sells wine. The road ends at the **Mirador del Río** (daily 10am–5.45pm; charge). You will not be surprised to learn that it was Manrique who transformed this disused gun emplacement into a lookout point and glass-fronted café. The views are stupendous, encompassing Isla Graciosa,

Looking out from the Mirador del Río

with the smaller islands of Montaña Clara and Alegranza in the distance. The stretch of water separating Graciosa from the mainland is called a *río* (river) but is, in fact, a narrow channel in the Atlantic.

A clifftop stretch of road leads along the Risco de Famara, then to lower ground. The views are wonderful, but don't stop to enjoy them until you find a suitable place, as the road is very narrow. You pass the oddly named village of Yé before reaching the **Parque Tropical** (daily 10am–5pm; charge) at **Guinate**. This is a great family outing, although, at €14 (€6 for children aged 4–13), it ought to be.

As well as clearly described subtropical plants and a big

Spick and span Haría

cactus garden, there is a vast number of exotic birds (the owners claim 1,300), plus a few monkeys rescued from illegal ownership, and the ever-popular meerkats. Those who object strongly to keeping birds in captivity will, of course, give it a miss, but the conditions are good. There is a large walk-through aviary, and the cages otherwise are huge and well furnished with plants, and appear to offer the birds all the freedom they need – except the freedom to fly away, of course. Parrot shows are held at intervals throughout the day, and there is a café with reasonably priced snacks and light meals.

Haría

Continuing south, you drop down into the greenest, most fertile part of the island, the valley of **Haría**, known as the 'Valley of a Thousand Palms'. This is an exaggeration, but there are quite a lot of them. As tour guides and brochures are keen to point out, the legend recounts that once upon a time a palm tree was planted for every girl born locally, and two for every boy. Haría is a nice little town (although a place of confusing road signs). Spick and span in white and green, it has attracted a number of artists and artisans in its time, and became Manrique's home during his later years. The church, **Nuestra Señora de la Encarnación**, is a modern copy of the 17th-century original which was damaged by a storm, then destroyed, in the 1950s. There's a good **craft market** in the square around the church (Plaza de León y Castillo) every Saturday. Much of the work on sale is made at the **Centro de Artesanía** (daily 10am–1.30pm, 4–7pm; free), a craft-workers' co-operative.

Orzola and Isla Graciosa

At the tip of the island, with its back to the badlands, lies the village of **Orzola**, jumping-off point for Isla Graciosa. There's not much to Orzola, apart from a number of good fish restaurants (see pages 136), from the terraces of which you can watch the comings and goings of boats to the island (see page 83 for details). The trip to **Isla Graciosa** takes about 20 minutes, but it leads you into another world. Part of the protected **Parque Natural del Archipélago Chinijo**, it has only one settlement, Caleta del Sebo, and a population of 630. There are no cars, except a

Parking in Orzola

There are car parks just inland from Orzola harbour; the bays directly in front of it only allow you to park for 2½ hours – no good if you're going to the island.

A daredevil goat at Las Pardelas

few Land Rovers and, apart from the *paseo* around the harbour, no paved roads. To get around, you have to walk, or hire a bike, which is easily done from a couple of outlets by the port. There are several fish restaurants around the harbour and in the streets behind it, but if you come on a weekday they may not all be open. Most people buy picnic supplies from one of three little supermarkets and head for the beaches. There's a small golden beach and protected waters right by the harbour where local children splash about, but the better beaches are a little way away. The currents are very strong, so swimming is not a good idea. Paddle instead, and explore the rock pools where tiny fish swim around your feet.

If you are back at the harbour around 3pm you'll see the fishing smacks come in, and you can watch as small fish are unloaded from the decks into wheelbarrows and taken a few yards away to be laid out on the jetty to dry in the sun. These are *pejines*; when dried, they are grilled and eaten as tapas.

Back on the mainland, going south from Orzola, the best route is along the coast, but there is a narrow lane out of the village that takes you back to the main Arrieta to Mirador del Río road, and a short way up the lane is **Las Pardelas** (daily 10am–6pm; charge). This friendly, family-run little ecological park with indigenous plants, domestic animals and donkey rides has a small restaurant, and makes a nice gentle stop if you are travelling with children.

THE CENTRE

The centre of the island is where you will find the airport, the capital, Arrecife, the two largest resorts, Puerto del Carmen and Costa de Teguise, the historic town of Teguise, a number of interesting rural museums, the wine-producing zone and the stunning Fundación César Manrique.

Costa Teguise

Costa Teguise is the only resort north of Arrecife. You enter on the Avenida del Mar (about 14km/8 miles from the airport, 6km/4 miles from the capital), a broad road lined with squat palm trees and flanked by hotels and apartment blocks. The main street, Avenida de las Islas Canarias, parallel to the coast, is lined with commercial centres, small supermarkets, several clinics and a plethora of car-hire outlets.

Playa de las Cucharas, Costa Teguise

Manrique designed the **Pueblo Marinero** at the southern end of the resort, and this is the most appealing part of the development. Low, whitewashed houses with blue or green balconies are clustered in narrow streets around a small square, and it does genuinely resemble a fishing village – which is what Pueblo Marinero means. Later construction, running down to the beach, was taken over by other, less purist hands. A clutch of restaurants and bars here offer fish and chips, hamburgers and pizza, and many have English names – including The Sunburnt Arms. Round the rocky headland there are more buildings going up, and there's a small beach, **Playa del Jablillo**, with a rather unlovely view of the desalination plant just outside Arrecife.

Running northwards, the **Playa de las Cucharas** and **Playa de los Charcos** merge. The former has the better beach, a long stretch of golden imported sand superimposed on the natural volcanic black, and a stretch that is popular with windsurfers, as the winds on this coast are often strong. There is sand on Playa de los Charcos, too, but here there are black rocks to clamber over between sand and sea.

A landscaped promenade runs the length of the beaches, with a scattering of cafés and restaurants, and passes the smart Hotel Meliá Salinas, designed by Manrique, which in the 1970s became the first to be built here. The early ambitions for Costa Teguise have not been realised; it lacks a real heart and is more downmarket than the other two major resorts. As a base for exploring the island, however, it has its advantages, as it is very convenient for visiting the cultural sites and villages in the north and centre of Lanzarote.

Fundación César Manrique

From the *circunvalación* around Arrecife the LZ1 leads some 5km (3 miles) to **Tahiche**, where, on the outskirts, you will find the **Fundación César Manrique** (July–Oct daily 10am–7pm; Nov–Jun Mon–Sat 10am–6pm, Sun 10am–3pm; charge). This was the artist's home, which he remodelled as a museum and gallery when creating the foundation in 1982. All is white: outside, paths and walls gleam like icing sugar on a cake; inside, the marble floors blend with the white walls. Huge windows give views over the surrounding landscape, where the coils of molten lava look as if they might still be liquid. The exhibition salons contain Manrique's own paintings, ceramics and sketches, as well as works by Picasso, Tàpies and Miró. Steps lead down to a series of volcanic bubbles, where trees reach up for the light. A subterranean garden has a pool and retains the atmosphere of a private

Manrique's abstract mural at the Fundación

home, with a huge barbecue and benches built into the walls. As you leave the building you pass through a small garden with a central pond and fountain, and a huge abstract mural that is one of Lanzarote's iconic sights.

Rural Heartland

About 8km (5 miles) west of the foundation you come to the sleepy little town of **San Bartolomé**. The parish church (often closed), the Teatro Municipal and the Ayuntamiento (Town Hall) form two sides of an attractive square with a colonnade, palm trees and a central fountain. Opposite, an open-ended plaza, planted with palms, cacti and oleanders, leads, via broad steps, down to the **Museo Tanit** (Mon–Fri 10am–5pm, Sat 10am–3pm; charge), an ethnographic museum that outlines the history of the island's earliest inhabitants and has displays on two centuries of island life.

A right turn from the outskirts of San Bartolomé takes you the short distance to **Mozaga** and the **Monumento del Campesino** (Monument to the Countryman), which is set in the exact centre of the island. Manrique's huge white sculpture depicts the *campesino*, surrounded, on the four compass points, by a camel, a donkey, a dog and a goat – although the abstract nature of the construction means that you need a bit of imagination to discern their figures.

Beside the monument a collection of attractive white buildings with green shutters comprise a bar and restaurant (daily noon–4.30pm) and the **Centro de Artesanía** (daily 10am–6pm; free). You can skirt the restaurant to reach the artisans' centre, but don't – if you enter via the huge, domed structure you go through a rocky tunnel and a cool grotto to reach your destination. On the ground floor around a square are workshops where demonstrations of weaving, leather-working and pottery take place. Upstairs a small museum displays models of Lanzarote's early *ermitas* (chapels) and some excellent Naïve ceramic works portraying primitive figures grinding and milling wheat.

The road leads north from the monument towards Tigua. On the far side of the village you reach a tiny white *ermita*, and a right turn leads to the **Museo Agrícola El Patio** (Mon–Fri 10am–5pm, Sat 10am–2.30pm; charge). A museum of agriculture might not be your first idea of fun, but this one is a delight. On a small estate, once a rural centre where corn was brought to be milled, a fascinating collection of agricultural and domestic objects (complete with some spooky figures, their faces made from gourds) has been gathered. Set in grounds where chicken scratch in the dust and a donkey, goat and camel keep the farmyard theme alive, the museum is housed in a *finca* (farmhouse) dating from 1840 and a large converted barn. Perhaps the most interesting of the displays are numerous old photos, dating from the early 20th

Remnants of a bygone age in El Patio Museum

century to the 1960s, depicting the hardships and the community spirit of rural life. Leaving the museum, you pass through the old bodega, where you will be offered a glass of local wine. A quotation on one of the museum walls by Tenerife-born writer Agustín Espinosa (1897–1939) reads: 'A land without traditions, without a poetic atmosphere, faces the threat of extinction.' This place is doing all it can to keep those traditions and atmosphere alive.

Teguise

Teguise was the first colonial capital of the island, built in the centre in the hope that it would be safe from pirate attacks. As you will learn if you visit the Castillo de Santa Bárbara *(see page 46)*, this was not the case, but 'the royal town', as it was known, remained the capital until 1852. It is an attractive place, a village more than a town, with cobbled streets and a number of well-restored colonial buildings with typical Canarian wooden balconies and pretty courtyards.

Sunday is **market day** in Teguise, and tourists from all over the island descend on the little town – coach tours run from all the resorts. If you come by car, a series of car parks on the approach to town make life easy; attendants collect a small fee. The market sprawls all over Teguise, and there's a lively atmosphere, although you won't find much that you couldn't get in tourist shops and markets in any resort in Europe. Even the food on sale in the stalls and kiosks tends towards hamburgers, doughnuts and pizza rather than anything local. There are several good restaurants, though, where you can find Canarian food *(see page 138)*, and a number of shops

Teguise carnival

Teguise has a very lively carnival in February or early March, in which characters dressed as devils and brandishing goatskin truncheons attempt to terrorise carnival revellers.

with more interesting goods: aloe vera products of all kinds are sold in several places, as are local cheeses, wine and jars of *mojo* sauce, and a few ceramics and woven goods, as well as an outlet of the Manrique Foundation. Around midday there is a 30-minute exhibition of *lucha canaria (see page 80)* in a domed structure in the village centre. Wine-and-cheese tasting are included in the ticket price.

The popular market at Teguise

There are three impressive churches in Teguise, two of them monastic, but, despite the information in some tourist-office leaflets, you may not find them open. The **Convento de Santo Domingo** (Sun–Fri 10am–3pm), founded by the Dominican Order in 1698, has now become an art centre, which holds regular exhibitions of contemporary work. The church itself is worth a look: it has two naves, and the chapel dedicated to the Virgen del Rosario is the only one in Lanzarote where the retrochoir (the area directly behind the altar) features painted murals.

The **Convento de San Francisco**, founded by Franciscans in the late 16th century, houses a museum of sacred art, but has been closed for some time. Enquire when you visit if it has reopened; otherwise you will have to be content with admiring the splendid main doorway. The **Iglesia de Nuestra Señora de Guadalupe** is an eclectic mixture of styles,

Convento de San Francisco

having been remodelled many times during its long history, following pirate attacks and fires. Again, you may not find it open, but do not despair – Teguise has some great domestic architecture, especially the **Casa-Museo Palacio Spínola** (Mon–Fri 10am–5pm, Sat–Sun 10am–4pm; charge), which is a delight. Built by an aristocratic family in the mid-18th century, it was restored in the 1970s, purchased by the local authorities and in 1989 became the official residence of the Canary Islands Autonomous Government. A series of beautifully furnished rooms, with wide, polished floorboards, beamed ceilings and lattice-work balconies and cupboards, is ranged around an internal patio, bright with bougainvillea, and an external one shaded by a huge fig tree.

The second of Teguise's palaces, now a small gallery for the works of local artists, is the **Palacio de Herrera y Rojas** (Mon–Sat 10am–1.30pm when there is an exhibition; charge). The third, the **Palacio del Marqués**, is now a restaurant and tapas bar, the Patio del Vino (see page 138), where, for the price of a drink (if you do not want a meal), you can admire the elegant dining room and shady patio.

A final place to visit lies just outside Teguise (take a right turn from the main road and drive up a steep but well-surfaced road). This is the **Castillo de Santa Bárbara y Museo del Emigrante** (winter Mon–Fri 10am–5pm, Sat–Sun 10am–4pm; summer Mon–Fri 10am–3pm, Sat–Sun 10am–2pm; charge), set on the top of the long-extinct Volcán de Guanapay. Built in the mid-16th century, this imposing building gave refuge to the people of Teguise and the surrounding countryside during repeated attacks by Turkish, French and English pirates. One particularly ferocious attack left the streets of Teguise running with blood, the island ransacked and the people starving. The castle is worth a visit to learn about local history and admire the far-reaching views, but the museum, devoted to Canarian emigration from the 16th to the early 20th century, is the most fascinating aspect. Documents, personal effects and early photographs tell the story of a poverty-stricken people who left for the Americas, either seeking a better life or, during a period in the 17th and 18th centuries, sent by the Spanish Crown to populate the colonies.

The Casa-Museo Palacio Spínola in Teguise

Tinajo

From Teguise a road leads 5km (3 miles) northwest to **Tinajo**. The **Iglesia de San Roque** has statues by José Luján Pérez (1756–1815), the renowned Canarian sculptor. However, you must take your chance on finding it open. Nearby, the village of **Mancha Blanca** is best known for the **Ermita de los Dolores**. Inside is a statue of Nuestra Señora de los Volcanes, who is credited with saving the village by halting the lava flow from a volcanic eruption in 1824. Even if the church is closed, the snowy-white exterior is very pretty. The peace of the village is only disturbed on 15 September when a pilgrimage (*romería*) brings people from all over the island, and a craft fair, the Feria Insular de Artesanía Tradicional, is held. From here it's a very short distance to the Timanfaya National Park Visitors' Centre, but this is best saved for a separate visit to the park (*see page 52*).

The Rocky Coast

Instead, go north to La Santa, a village on the rocky coast that has prospered because of the proximity of the **Club La Santa**. With facilities for 64 Olympic sports (as the *Guinness Book of Records* proclaims), the club has a vast stadium, an Olympic-sized pool, an artificial lake for windsurfing, and plenty of facilities for people of all abilities (or none), as well as those designed for training serious international sportspeople. If you want to visit the fishing village of **La Caleta de Famara**, the only other settlement on this coast, you must go back to Tiagua (about 12km/8 miles) and take another road north. There are a few good fish restaurants here and an excellent sandy beach, but strong winds make it unsafe for swimming.

Club La Santa

Back at the centre of the island (the Monumento del Campesino is an excellent marker), a road runs southwest through **La Geria** wine country. You could stop at the **Bodega El Grifo Museo del Vino** (daily 10.30am–6pm; charge). Set in an old bodega, the museum exhibits wine-making equipment and has a good display

Vines growing on *picón* soil in La Geria wine country

on barrel-making; and, of course, there's wine for sale. Next door to El Grifo is the **Bodega Barreto**, owned by the oldest wine-producing family on the island. There's no museum here, but you can sample and purchase their wine. Drive on through the landscape of coiled lava and vineyards, where the vines growing in the *picón* (cinders) are planted within semicircles of volcanic rocks to stop the soil blowing away in Lanzarote's strong winds. This road will take you to Uga and the Parque Nacional de Timanfaya *(see page 52)*.

Puerto del Carmen

Lying just 5km (3 miles) west of the airport, **Puerto del Carmen** is Lanzarote's biggest resort. Its splendid beaches, Playa Grande and Playa de los Pocillos, and the less popular Playa Matagorda (closest to the airport), extend eastwards for 6km (4 miles) from the little fishing harbour that was the heart of the original village.

Until the 1970s this was just a quiet fishing community, and the area around the pretty harbour retains its village atmosphere. There is a little church here, **Nuestra Señora del Carmen**, but you will only find the doors open for mass (Sat 8.30pm, Sun 11am and 7pm). There are numerous fish restaurants, too, mostly with excellent views. You can still see fish being unloaded from small fishing smacks by the jetty, but these vessels have been joined by leisure craft and excursion boats offering trips around the coast and across to Fuerteventura. The little rocky coves just east of the harbour, before the beaches begin, are popular with divers.

The golden sands of **Playa Grande**, lined with sunbeds (*hamacas*) and bright umbrellas for rent, offer all kinds of diversions – banana boats, pedalos in the shape of giant swans, beach cafés and, of couse, glorious waters. Parallel to the beach is the **Avenida de las Playas**. Along the sea-side

The inviting golden sands of Puerto del Carmen

runs an attractive promenade, planted with palms and flowering shrubs. Here you'll find a helpful little **tourist office** (Mon–Fri 10am–5pm), next door to a small gift shop belonging to the Fundación Manrique, as well as Lanzarote's only **casino**, a couple of nice restaurants, and a few little villa complexes. On the other side, the avenue resembles a vast amusement arcade, lined with cafés, bars and restaurants – mostly with Irish or English names, advertising Guinness, fish and chips and all-day English breakfasts, all at knockdown prices – along with tourist-oriented shops and kiosks offering tattos and hair-braiding. At intervals there are *centros comerciales*, with more shops and restaurants, and it is here that most of the late-night bars and clubs are found. Just past a rocky headland, the Punta de Barranquillo, these commercial outlets peter out, to be replaced with some smart little residential complexes. Then, where the **Playa de los Pocillos** commences, so do more shops and bars, but these are far more low-key than the earlier ones.

Puerto Calero is named after the developer José Calero, who initiated the construction of the marina in 1986. It lies about 4km (2½ miles) south of Puerto del Carmen and styles itself a *puerto deportivo* – a sports port. Its smart harbour is full of sleek yachts, its restaurants full of sleek people. You can charter a boat if you fancy a day's deep-sea fishing *(see page 82)*. If you're just dropping in for a look around, it's easiest to take a boat trip from Puerto del Carmen, so you don't have to worry about parking, which can be a problem.

THE SOUTH

The south of Lanzarote encompasses the extraordinary volcanic wilderness of the Parque Nacional de Timanfaya, the pretty, arty village of Yaiza, Playa Blanca with its splendid beaches, and the wild jagged coast to the west.

A camel ride around the volcanic slopes

Parque Nacional de Timanfaya

Going south from the airport, take the LZ2 motorway towards Tías, from where a straight (but non-motorway) stretch continues to Yaiza (about 18km/11 miles). Just before Yaiza lies the little village of **Uga**, looking like a Moorish settlement, with flat-roofed white houses surrounded by palms. About 3km (2 miles) further on a bypass encircles Yaiza. From a roundabout as you approach is a narrow road leading to the **Parque Nacional de Timanfaya** (daily 9am–5.45pm, last tour 5pm; charge). On the way up you pass the **Echadero de Camellos** (Camel Station) where visitors are taken for rides around the outer volcanic slopes on dromedaries. There's also a small museum of volcanic rocks here. The national park is one place that all visitors to Lanzarote include on their itineraries, and it's a place that few will ever forget. It is an experience that makes one aware of the awesome power of nature.

Bus tours around the **Montañas del Fuego** (Mountains of Fire) start from outside El Diablo restaurant and run throughout the day. There is a good recorded commentary in Spanish, English and German, giving background information about the park and about the volcanic eruptions that caused this once fertile area to be turned into a sea of lava. There are frequent photo stops at particularly dramatic points, but you are not allowed to get off the bus. Once the tour is over, most visitors stop for a while to watch park attendants throwing dried brush into a hole in the ground, whereupon flames roar upwards; or pouring buckets of water into a small crater, causing a cascade of boiling water to shoot into the air.

In the glass-sided restaurant, designed, of couse, by César Manrique, you can have a drink or snack, or eat meat that has been grilled over the natural heat emanating from just below the surface (you can watch chefs officiating over the barbecue at the back of the restaurant, so you know that they are not cheating).

Visiting Timanfaya National Park

At the entrance to the park, where Manrique's famous 'fire devil' sign stands, is a barrier, where you pay an entrance fee. You will probably have to join a queue while you wait for a space to become available in the car park, from where buses take visitors on a 40-minute tour of the Ruta de los Volcanes (included in the entrance price). At busy times – late morning seems to be prime time – the wait may be as long as an hour. Take drinking water and something to amuse children when they get bored. You are not allowed to walk, or drive, through the centre of the park, but you can drive around the periphery, and drop in at the Interpretation and Visitors' Centre at the Tinajo end. Any cars you see going straight ahead instead of waiting at the barrier are doing just that.

Yaiza

The visit over, return to the roundabout and take the road straight into **Yaiza**. This village relishes its reputation as the prettiest on Lanzarote – and it certainly is very picturesque. Some typically Canarian-style buildings survived the eruption that wiped out most of the village in the 1730s, and these have been complemented by later ones in the same style. Palms line the road as you approach, scarlet geraniums decorate green balconies and bougainvillea drips over snowy-white garden walls.

In the central square is the church of **Nuestra Señora de los Remedios**, which has columns of volcanic rock and a beautiful painted wooden ceiling; unlike many of the island churches, it is usually open. By contrast the **Galería Yaiza** (Mon–Sat 5–7pm; free), at the west end of the village, has good exhibitions of contemporary art, but the limited opening hours mean you have to make a special effort to see them.

Yaiza has several nice places to stay *(see page 131)* and a couple of good restaurants, although the famous **La Era**, set in an 18th-century farmhouse converted by Manrique, is currently closed and no reopening date is predicted.

Playa Blanca

The road from Yaiza leads south, through the bare, flat lands called El Rubicón, to **Playa Blanca**. This is Lanzarote's third resort, smaller, quieter and more upmarket than the other two. It used to be a flourishing fishing village, and retains something of that atmosphere, even as it has expanded.

The heart of the resort centres on the main street, Avenida de Papagayo, its pedestrianised extension, Calle Limones, and the Paseo Marítimo, a promenade lined with restaurants that runs parallel to the soft sands of **Playa Dorada** (Golden Beach) and **Playa Blanca** (White Beach) and leads to the port. West of the port, another tree-lined promenade runs

One of Playa Blanca's appealing seaside restaurants

round the Punta Limones headland to pretty little Playa Flamingo, backed by landscaped gardens, and with calm, safe waters. Across a narrow stretch of the Atlantic, the sands of Corralejo, on Fuerteventura, gleam in the sunlight.

Playa Blanca is big on watersports and all kinds of maritime excursions, whether you want to scuba dive, windsurf or simply take a trip in a glass-bottomed submarine (see pages 81 and 83).

How long Playa Blanca will retain its fishing-village atmosphere is hard to say. Already, *urbanizaciones* stretch to the left and right (where most of the big hotels and villa complexes are situated), and on the approach to the village new buildings are going up fast. The Cabildo Insular is worried that things are getting out of hand, and is trying to limit developments, going so far as to call on the district authorities to either reverse the many planning permissions they have granted in the area, or face legal proceedings. To the east of town, new roads lead to the **Marina Rubicón**, a brand new sports complex and 400-berth marina surrounded by apartments, a huge shopping and leisure centre and the five-star Gran Meliá Volcán Hotel *(see page 130)*. Not everyone is happy about this, either. On the wall of a row of neglected fishermen's cottages, where a few fish are pinned on a line to dry, and a tattered black flag flutters in the breeze, a sign in three languages reads 'There used to be a beach here'.

Further east, in a protected area known as **Los Ajaches**, lie Lanzarote's best beaches – **Playa de las Mujeres** and **Playa del Papagayo**. Be cautious about driving along the dirt road that gives access to them: insurance on hired cars does not cover you for 'off-road' driving, and the emergency services will not come and get you if you run into trouble. It's easier, and more pleasant, to take the *Princess Yaiza* Taxi Boat, which leaves four times a day from the harbour and the Marina Rubicón.

Salinas de Janubio and El Golfo

Parallel to the main road from Yaiza is another, the 701, which branches off westwards to the **Salinas de Janubio**. Salt production was one of the most important industries in

Particles of Peridot

The glimmers and glitters you will notice in the black-sand beach at El Golfo come from tiny particles of peridot, a semi-precious stone that is also called olivine, and ranges in colour from olive to lime-green. You will see peridot necklaces and bracelets for sale all over the island. It is the August birthstone and is believed to bring good luck. The stones used to be called evening emeralds, and it is said that the crusaders, who found them around the Red Sea, believed they *were* emeralds and brought them back home to adorn churches.

Lanzarote, but its main purpose was to preserve fish rather than for domestic use, and it is not needed in great quantities now that the catch can be refrigerated. These salt pans are the only ones still in use and they are an impressive sight, laid out like a patchwork quilt, the colour of each pan depending on the relative amount of water and salt it contains.

Los Hervideros

They are also an excellent spot for birdwatching, especially during the spring and autumn migratory periods.

A short way further up this rocky, deeply eroded coast is a spot known as **Los Hervideros** (The Boiling Pans). You will see coaches in the large car park, for this is a stopping point for tours coming from Timanfaya. It gained its name because the seething sea appears to boil in blowholes and underwater lava caves created by a volcanic tube emerging into the sea. Continue up the coast (where there are plenty of lay-bys to allow drivers to stop and admire the craggy coastline) and you soon arrive at **El Golfo**, a fishing village set between volcanic hills and pounding sea. It's just a collection of pretty cottages and fish restaurants, with outside tables by the sea. To the southern side of the village, the shell of a volcanic crater has been eroded into a jagged, richly coloured cliff. At its foot lie a small black beach and a vivid green **lagoon**, also called El Golfo. Park at the entrance to the village and follow a footpath in order to find it.

From El Golfo the 702 leads back to Yaiza, from where you pick up the main road back towards Arrecife and the airport. Your tour of this diverse island is over.

FUERTEVENTURA

On arriving at the coast of Fuerteventura in 1402, Jean de Béthencourt reputedly exclaimed '¡Que aventura más fuerte!' (What a great adventure!). That's one theory about the origin of the island's name. Others, more prosaically, believe it derives from *viento fuerte* – strong wind. Winds are certainly a feature of the island, and one that draws surfers, windsurfers, kitesurfers and parasailors to its gorgeous sandy beaches: the long stretches in the north, around El Cotillo and at Corralejo, now protected in a Parque Natural; and in the south, the sands stretch from Tarajalejo to Morro Jable and beyond. But there is more to Fuerteventura than beaches: the sleepy little towns in the interior are keepers of the island's history, places where life goes on pretty much as it has for centuries. We begin with the capital, then travel north before visiting the centre and south of the island.

THE NORTH

The north of the island is a diverse area that encompasses the capital, Puerto del Rosario; a number of inland towns and villages, set amid bare conical hills, where you can learn about the agricultural past; and the harbours, dunes and beaches of Corralejo to the east and El Cotillo in the west.

Puerto del Rosario

Puerto del Rosario lies about 7km (4 miles) north of the airport. The town was founded in 1795, called Puerto de Cabras (Goat Port), and became the island capital in 1860 (taking over the role from La Oliva). The name was changed

Getting an overview of Fuerteventura's desert landscape

Stone fisherman by the sea

in 1956, but the goat motif is evident in statuary and in a pastoral metallic mural. A small, busy port is used by ferries from Arrecife, container ships and, more recently, cruise liners. Puerto del Rosario is not a tourist-oriented town, but is worth a brief visit. The harbour front has been renovated in recent years and is a pleasant place to walk. Palms offer shade along the inland side, and the sea wall is lined with sinuous benches decorated with coloured tiles. An area designated the Parque de Mayores is a kind of outdoor gym for elderly people, with a variety of exercise machines (well used during the cooler hours) and notices warning of the dangers of over-exertion.

The town is known for its **street sculpture**, which ranges from a huge fountain on a roundabout on the Avenida Marítima, to an abstract metallic clock in the centre of town, to two naked dancing women in a square, and simple statues dotted all over the place – a fisherman stands on the sea wall, while an elderly man sits outside the church.

It was the church, dedicated to the **Virgen del Rosario**, that gave the town its new name. It's a simple grey-and-white building, somewhat neglected, standing in a tree-shaded square opposite the the island government offices. To the side of the square is the **Casa-Museo Unamuno** (Mon–Fri 9am–1pm, 5–7pm, Sat 10am–1pm; free), the house (then the Hotel Fuerteventura) where the Basque writer and philosopher Miguel de Unamuno (1864–1936) lived when he was exiled here in 1924, regarded as a thorn in the flesh of Miguel Primo de Rivera's dictatorship. Unamuno's time here was brief, but he quickly came to love the island and to appreciate the kindness shown to him by local people. They later reciprocated by erecting a huge statue of him on the lower flanks of Montaña Quemada (Burnt Mountain), just outside Tindaya. The rooms are furnished as they were in Unamuno's time, with portraits and memorabilia, and quotations from his writing are displayed on the walls.

At the roundabout where roads into Puerto del Rosario meet, you will find **Las Rotondas**, a huge new commercial centre that opened in 2006, adding greatly to the town's shopping opportunities with a range of internationally known stores.

Weaving at La Alcogida

Farms and Windmills

From Puerto del Rosario the FV10 runs northwest towards La Oliva. En route, a left turn is clearly signposted to **Tefia** and the **Ecomuseo La Alcogida** (Tue–Fri and Sun 9.30am–5.30pm; charge). This ingenious complex, which stretches out on either side of the road, is an abandoned farming settlement that has been restored as a museum, and allows visitors to see how rural life was lived, and what farming methods were used, during the last century. You can watch people demonstrating pulled-thread embroidery, basket-work, leather-work and weaving.

Just past the museum a road leads off to **Los Molinos** – passing, after a few hundred metres, a beautifully restored windmill, which is visible from La Alcogida. Los Molinos is a pretty little seaside village, with a couple of nice restaurants, about 8km (5 miles) west. The latter part of the road runs along the top of a gulley, the Barranco de los Molinos.

Returning to the main road and going north, you pass, on your left, **Montaña Quemada**, where Unamuno's statue blends with its craggy background; a little further on is the cheese-producing town of Tindaya and **Montaña Tindaya** (397 metres/1,303ft), which the island's indigenous people considered a sacred mountain (*see panel*).

La Oliva

You soon come to **La Oliva**. This sleepy little town was the seat of the Guanche king, Guixe, and briefly served as the colonial capital of the island in the early 18th century. Today, it's a workaday town, centred on a large church, **Nuestra Señora de Candelaria**, with buttressed walls and a square bell tower of volcanic stone, which makes it look as if it is

Chillida's Dream

In 1992 the Basque sculptor Eduardo Chillida put forward an ambitious proposal to create within Montaña Tindaya a vast open space. Nothing would be visible externally, but within the artist hoped to realise 'a utopia... where those who went inside would be able to see the light of the sun, the moon, to see the sea and the horizon...' The Cabildo Insular supported the plan, but there was a great deal of opposition from environmentalists. Whether or not the project would have gone ahead is unknown, as Chillida died in 2002.

Canarian Art Centre in La Oliva

growing out of the rocky landscape. The interior is quite plain, and the pulpit, decorated with pictures of the four Apostles, is supported on a slim, painted pedestal (€1 in a slot by the door gives five minutes' worth of illumination).

From the side of the Ayuntamiento, opposite the church, a straight, broad road leads to the **Casa de los Coroneles**. This grandiose and much-photographed building, with its many balconied windows, was the seat of the military rulers of the island in the early 18th century. After undergoing extensive restoration, the house was officially reopened by the king and queen of Spain in 2006. It is now a cultural centre where exhibitions and concerts are held.

En route to the colonels' headquarters you pass the **Centro de Arte Canario** (Mon–Sat 10am–6pm; charge) in the Casa Mané, a converted colonial house. The collection of works by contemporary Canarian, or Canary Island-based, artists is somewhat eclectic, and the sculpture in the extensive cactus garden even more so, ranging from innovative abstract pieces to leaping dolphins and even some (possibly ironic) gnomes. Don't miss the galleries situated down a flight of steps and through the shop (where there are some good posters and prints for sale), as this is where some of the best work is shown, in large, light rooms.

Villaverde and Lajares

From the centre of La Oliva the FV10 leads towards the northwest coast, but it may be worth taking the slightly longer way round (up the FV101 then turning onto the FV109), because you could then stop at **Villaverde**, where the **Cueva del Llano** (Tue–Sat 10.15am–12.45pm, 2.15–5.15pm; tours every 30 minutes; charge) was first opened to the public in 2006. This *jameo*, or lava tube, was discovered in 1979, and a new species of spider, *Arácnido triglobio*, was

La Rosita, for a glimpse of traditional rural life

found to be living here. A visitors' centre offers information about the *jameo*, which was formed by a lava stream from nearby Montaña Escanfraga. A few kilometres north is **La Rosita** (Mon–Sat 10am–6pm; charge), a farm that demonstrates traditional agricultural methods, including the use of camels on the land. Children especially enjoy contact with the farm animals.

Just before the FV109 joins the FV10 to El Cotillo, you reach **Lajares**, a village with a pair of well-restored windmills on the southern outskirts, and a stadium where *lucha canaria (see page 80)* is performed. In the main street is the **Escuela de Artesanía** (Tue–Sat 10am–1pm, 5–8pm, Mon 5–8pm; free). Although called a school, it is really more of a shop, where you can buy handmade products (not cheap) and watch local women embroidering table linen.

El Cotillo

The road continues about 8km (5 miles) to **El Cotillo**. Although you are greeted, on the outskirts, with a shop proclaiming that it sells 'best British products', closely followed by a fish-and-chip shop, do not be deterred. This village has a gloriously pretty little fishing harbour and a selection of good fish restaurants to go with it, plus beautiful, windswept dunes and beaches. Beside the harbour is the **Castillo de Tostón**, a sturdy fortress that houses a tourist information point (Mon–Fri 9am–4pm, Sat 9am–3pm) and a small gallery (same hours; free) with changing exhibitions of work by local artists. El Cotillo has a small but vibrant artistic community, with some French connections. From the fort's roof you get wonderful views down the coast. To the north, a narrow road runs through the dunes to the **Punta de Tostón**, where a lighthouse stands on a headland. A lot of construction work is going on in El Cotillo, and it is to be hoped that the character of the village won't be spoiled.

Corralejo

Return to the main FV101 and after about 6km (4 miles) you reach **Corralejo**. (You may, of course, have started here, having come, as many do, by boat from Playa Blanca in Lanzarote; *see page 115*). Corralejo is another tiny fishing village that has expanded to cope with the demand for tourist accommodation. The heart of the town, the area around the harbour, still has a character of its own. On **Muelle Chico** (Small Jetty) there's a **tourist information kiosk** (Mon–Fri 8am–3pm, Sat–Sun 9am–3pm) close to a bronze statue called the **Monumento Marinero**, showing a returned seaman embracing his wife and child; nearby, another woman looks out to sea, waiting for her husband's return. The narrow lanes that radiate from the harbour and the broad main street, Nuestra Señora del Carmen, filled with cafés, bars and shops, are reminiscent of an English seaside resort, and not just because most of the voices you hear are English. There's also something of a hippy-ish, beachcomber feel here, generated by the people who come in search of good waves and a laid-back lifestyle.

In Corralejo you can go diving and scuba diving, take a beach-buggy trip through the dunes to El Cotillo, hire a mountain bike, go on a dolphin-watching boat ride or, most popular of all, take a trip to **Isla de los Lobos** (Island of Wolves). The wolves in question were the sea lions that flourished here before they were devoured by Norman sailors who came to the island with Gadifer de la Salle's invasion force (*see page 14*). It's a peaceful, pretty place, uninhabited, although you'll have to share it with lots of other visitors, and it's small enough to walk around in about three hours. You can see seabirds – Cory's sheerwaters nest here – and a variety of vegetation in spring and early summer. The waters are sheltered and safe even for children to swim, so it is well worth bringing a picnic and spending a day here.

The Dunes

Drive out of town on the FV1, which runs parallel to the coast through great swathes of **El Jable dunes** that are now protected as the **Parque Natural de Corralejo**. Look out for goats, which sometimes wander in the road – perhaps hoping there is something more interesting than scrubby plants to eat on the other side. On the edge of, but just inside, the park looms the huge Riu Palace Tres Islas Hotel, built before strict planning controls made such construction illegal. Thereafter, there's little but sand and more sand, low brown hills to the right, and a gorgeous sweep of turquoise waters to your left, crashing against the 10km (6 miles) of beach that draw watersports enthusiasts in droves.

The road runs some 35km (22 miles) back to Puerto del Rosario, from where you can begin a tour of the centre and south of the island.

The sandy expanse of El Jable dunes

Antigua's windmill

THE CENTRE

Visiting the central part of the island offers the contrast of starting out on the coast at Caleta de Fuste, a smart, purpose-built holiday resort, then heading inland to Fuerteventura's first capital, Betancuria, and a number of other pretty towns and villages, set amid stunning mountain scenery and the occasional fertile valley.

Caleta de Fuste

Some 7km (4 miles) south of Puerto del Rosario and 9km (6 miles) south of the airport, on the FV2, lies **Caleta de Fuste**. This is a completely made-to-measure resort, clustered around a marina and the Castillo de Fuste, the 18th-century fortress from which it takes its name, and spreading inland and along the coast. Opinions are divided on Caleta de Fuste: on the one hand, it has the artificial feel of a resort created from scratch; on the other, it has been well designed, and there's a range of accommodation, good restaurants, and watersports and activities of all kinds, as well as a pleasant sandy beach. The Barceló Club El Castillo, in a prime site right by the beach, is a well-landscaped complex of attractive bungalows that resembles an entire village. To the north, a broad promenade leads along the rocky shore to Costa de Antigua; to the south, construction is going on apace up to and around the garish new Centro Atlántico, opposite which stands Fuerteventura's only McDonald's.

Follow the road a short way south to **Las Salinas** to visit the **Museo de la Sal** (Salt Museum; Tue–Fri and Sun 9.30am–5.30pm) and the surrounding salt pans, the **Salinas del Carmen**, and learn about the extraction of salt.

Antigua

The road turns inland from here, and after about 10km (6 miles) the FV50 leads off to **Antigua**, set in the very middle of the island. Antigua used to be an important commercial centre and was briefly the capital of Fuerteventura (1834–5). Today it's a quiet town, centred on its sturdy church, **Nuestra Señora de Antigua**, one of the oldest on the island. It stands in a huge paved square, to one side of which a smaller grassy area, the **Plaza de los Caídos**, features a large cross, commemorating those who died in the Civil War. The church has a wooden ceiling and a wide nave, and is largely unadorned apart from a brightly painted main altar.

On the town's northern outskirts is the **Molino de Antigua Centro de Artesanía** (Tue–Fri and Sun 9.30am–5.30pm; charge). This is a fascinating complex of buildings, set in pleasant gardens. There's a windmill, where you can see the machinery used to grind *gofio*, an archeological museum and an excellent collection of craft work. The granary has become a café/restaurant that serves typical Canarian dishes *(see page 141)* and is open even on days the museum is shut.

Stop for a view

Just past Antigua the FV416 goes off to the left towards Betancuria. En route, if you want a stunning view over the khaki-coloured landscape and undulating hills, stop at the Mirador Morro Velosa, where there is a recently restored restaurant and viewing area, designed by César Manrique.

Betancuria

Betancuria is a little jewel of a town, with scarcely a corner that is not picturesque, and it is well aware both of its prettiness and its historical importance. 'Six hundred years of history' announces a sign on the wall of the **Ayuntamiento** (town hall) – itself a delightful building with a courtyard you can pop into. This was Fuerteventura's first capital, founded in the early 15th century by Jean de Béthencourt when his original stronghold on the coast proved not strong enough to deter pirate attacks. You can still see the remains of the Franciscan Convento de San Buenaventura, which was established here so that the brothers who followed in the conqueror's wake could bring Christianity to the native people.

There are car parks at either end of the town, which you should use – you cannot drive into the village itself, although there is some roadside parking in the main street. Here you will

Iglesia de Santa María

find the **Museo Arqueológico** (Tue–Sat 11am–5pm, Sun 11am–2pm; charge), with displays ranging from bones, fossils and some prized fertility idols to Majorero ceramics and information on the first colonisers.

Walk through the cobbled streets to find the lovely **Iglesia de Santa María** (Tue–Sun 11am–4pm; small charge), which was consecrated in 1426, destroyed by pirates in 1593 and rebuilt a century later. Entrance to the

Museo de Artesanía

church and the **Museo de Arte Sacra** usually alternates every half-hour, a rather odd arrangement but one that seems to work.

The church has an intricately carved door, a splendid wooden ceiling and a most unusual floor – large square stones outlined with wooden boards. The ceiling in the sacristy is of *mudéjar* design, but decorated with a renaissance painting. There are some real treasures in both the church and the museum, including a lovely retable of La Inmaculada to the left of the high altar and numerous polychromatic wooden figures of saints, some of them salvaged from the convent. The oldest part of the church, the baptistery, has a Gothic ribbed vault.

Across the square from the church, attached to the Casa Santa María restaurant *(see page 141)*, is the **Museo de Artesanía** (Mon–Sat 11am–4pm; charge), arranged around a series of flower-filled courtyards. There are lots of domestic and agricultural implements, women in traditional costume demonstrating weaving, and lots of local produce for sale at very reasonable prices. Sometimes there are wine- and cheese-tastings included. Upstairs, you can watch a short film about the island.

La Vega del Río de las Palmas and Pájara

You drop down now to the 'Valley of Palms', a surprisingly green and fertile region of this dry island, where in mid-September the village of **La Vega del Río de las Palmas** hosts a festival to the Virgen de la Pena (Virgin of Sorrows), patron saint of the island. The rest of the year it's a very sleepy place, but in its main square stands an attractive sand-stone **church** (Tue–Sun 11am–1pm, 4–7pm), built in 1666 and dedicated to the Virgin. In the same square, which is lined with art deco-style wrought-iron benches, is an excellent restaurant, **Don Antonio** *(see page 141)*.

La Vega del Río de las Palmas

The road twists and turns on its way south, but it is well surfaced, and there's a protective barrier, and lots of lay-bys where you can stop to drink in the splendid views, take photographs, or just let an impatient driver pass you by.

When the road straightens out, you come to the pretty village of **Pájara**. Palms and oleanders line the main street leading to the church

A detail from the doorway of Nuestra Señora de la Regla

of **Nuestra Señora de la Regla** (daily 11am–1pm, 5–7pm), famous for its red sandstone doorway, carved with symbols that apear to be Aztec-influenced, including a figure with a plumed feather headdress. The church has two naves, each with a baroque high altar – put €1 in the box by the door to illuminate them.

Outside the church is a water pump with a long wooden 'arm' to which a camel used to be attached to do the heavy work of pulling up the water. To the side of the church, an attractive park, bright with bougainvillea in summer, lines a dry river bed. Leaving the village to the southeast, you pass a roundabout with a large sandstone statue depicting a farmer milking a goat.

Heading south now, the road rejoins the FV20 which will take you back to the capital or south to the beaches. Even if going south, you could, if you are interested in the island's famous windmills, make a slight detour to **Tiscamanita** where the **Centro de Interpretación Los Molinos** (Tue–Fri and Sun 9.30am–5.30pm; charge) demonstrates the history of milling.

THE SOUTH

It is the beauty of the southern beaches, and the activities they offer, that bring most visitors to Fuerteventura. The combination of barren, elephant-coloured hills, jagged cliffs and great sweeps of white sand is irresistible, and the reliably strong winds promise windsurf enthusiasts the time of their lives. There are also some sheltered coves, though, ideal for those who simply want to enjoy the almost perpetual sunshine. The Sotavento (Leeward) beaches on the east side of the Jandía Peninsula are the most popular; the Barlovento (Windward) beaches on the other side are only for the most hardy and experienced windsurfers. These, and the far tip of the peninsula, Punta de Jandía, are accessible only on tracks that most car-hire companies' insurance will not cover.

Gran Tarajal and Tarajalejo

Gran Tarajal, reached by a straight stretch of road off the FV2, is the island's second-largest port, and therefore has a character of its own that has not been subsumed by the tourist resort that has grown up around it. Narrow streets (where it's very hard to park) lead away from a black-sand beach and a broad promenade, planted with palms and lined with restaurants.

From **Tarajalejo**, a little further down the coast, the main road parallels the shore. Tarajalejo is a fishing village that has developed into a resort but, although expanding rapidly, it's still low-key and pleasant. It has a 1-km (½-mile) pebbly beach and a large main square. The village is popular with sailing enthusiasts and caters well for beginners.

About 5km (3 miles) down the coast, just before the Barranco de Tarajal, lies **La Lajita**, a nice little village with a harbour. On the main road you will find **La Lajita Oasis Park** (daily 9am–7.30pm; charge) with camel rides, giraffes, reptiles, sea lions, parrots and birds of prey, as well as an impressive botanical garden. It's quite expensive, but it makes an enjoyable family day out.

Playas de Sotavento

A little further down the coast a secondary road leads 5km (3 miles) across the narrow neck of the peninsula to the village and beach of **La Pared** (don't ever windsurf here alone – the currents are very dangerous). A wall *(pared)*, built by the Majoreros, stretched across here when the conquerors arrived, and now it roughly forms the boundary of the **Parque Natural de Jandía**, some 14,320 hectares (35,385 acres) in extent, which reaches down to the tip of the peninsula.

Next, you come to **Costa Calma** and the start of the long white beaches of Sotavento. Development at Costa Calma began in the 1970s and has expanded ever since,

One of the idyllic beaches of Costa Calma

encompassing a variety of accommodation, most of it block-booked by German tour companies, with the hotels providing most of the restaurants and entertainment their guests need.

A little further south, on the beautiful **Playa Barca**, the huge Hotel Meliá Gorriones *(see page 133)* commands a prime position. It is here that the world's largest windsurfing centre, the Pro Center René Egli, is located, and where the PWA/ISA Windsurfing and the PKRA Kiteboarding World Championships are held in late July–early August. You don't have to be a champion to windsurf here, but you do have to be careful.

Continuing down this overdeveloped coast, you will come to **Playa de Matorral** (confusingly also known as Playa de Jandía), where the long white beach has been subject to a rash of huge hotels, apartment blocks, shops and restaurants. A section of the Matorral area has now been designated a Site of Special Scientific Interest, in an attempt to preserve the vegetation and varied bird life of its salt marshes, and an EU project has been launched to raise awareness of the damage that is being done by uncontrolled development. On the **Punta de Matorral** stands a lighthouse, with a little café at its feet.

Playa de Matorral merges with **Morro del Jable**, the

Morro del Jable

southernmost resort on the peninsula – after this the concrete developments thin out. Morro del Jable is a proper town with a proper port, even though hotels and apartment blocks have stretched

Ferry crossings

From Morro del Jable Naviera Armas ferries run to Las Palmas de Gran Canaria seven times a week, taking about 2½–3 hours.

their tentacles up the hillsides behind it. There's an attractive seaside promenade, some good fish restaurants and opportunities for all kinds of watersports.

The North of the Peninsula

The roads beyond Morro del Jable down to Puerto de la Cruz and the Punta de Jandía, and round to Cofete on the northern side of the peninsula, are not to be recommended unless you have a four-wheel-drive vehicle, and even then you should check the details of your insurance cover. There is no road going across the peninsula, just a ridge of mountains cut through with *barrancos* (gullies) and dominated by **Montaña de Jandía**, the highest peak on the island at 807 metres (2,648ft). The most common form of vegetation here is the *cardón de Jandía (Euphorbia handiensis)*, the symbol of Fuerteventura, and in the most inaccessible regions the ö. The beaches at the peninsula's tip and the **Playa de Cofete** and **Playa de Barlovento** (both favoured by nudists) on the other side are largely deserted, undeniably beautiful, and swept by high winds. Rocks are sculpted into jagged forms, sea spurge survives on the dunes, and a few goats are the only sign of wildlife. The tiny hamlet of **Cofete** is known only for the Villa Winter, an abandoned house built by a Nazi sympathiser on land allegedly given to him by General Franco. All kinds of rumours have surrounded this villa over the years, but this untamed region is just the sort of place in which rumours flourish and myths are created.

WHAT TO DO

M ost of the things you can do in Lanzarote and Fuerteventura are done outdoors, many of them on or in the
water. Ideal winds and waves make windsurfing the most
popular activity, but there are many others – sailing, diving,
fishing, swimming and lots of boat trips. On land, there are
some good hiking trails, opportunities for horse riding and
exploring the rougher terrain by jeep, buggy or quad bike
safari, and plenty of activities for children.

SPORTS AND OUTDOOR ACTIVITIES

Windsurfing

On **Lanzarote** the Windsurfing Club Nathalie Simon, Calle
de las Olas 18, Playa de las Cucharas, Costa Teguise, tel: 928
590 731, www.sportaway-lanzarote.com, offers advanced,
beginners' and children's courses, plus other activities *(see
page 86)*. Windsurf Paradise, Calle la Corvina 8, Playa de las
Cucharas, Costa Teguise, tel: 928 346 022, www.windsurf
lanzarote.com, also offers lessons, from basic to advanced
levels, and surfing trips to other beaches on the island.

On **Fuerteventura** a selection of operators includes: The
Fanatic Fun Center, Costa Calma and Corralejo, tel: 928 535
999; www.fanatic-surf.com; Windsurf El Castillo, Caleta de
Fustes, tel: 928 163 100; Ventura Surf Center, Apartamentos Hoplaco, Correlejo, tel: 928 866 295, www.ventura-
surf.com; and *the* name in windsurfing, Pro Center René Egli
I, Hotel Meliá Gorriones, Playa la Barca, tel: 928 547 025,
www.rene-egli.com. There's a second centre, René Egli II,
3km (2 miles) further south, where winds are not as strong.

Windsurfing is popular on both islands

Kitesurfing

In **Fuerteventura** try the Fuerteventura Kiteboarding School, El Cotillo, tel: 928 538 504, www.ksfuerte.com, and Flag Beach Windsurf and Kitesurf Centre, tel: 928 826 389, www.flagbeach.com, in Corralejo.

Surfing

Lanzarote surf schools include Calima Surf, Caleta de Famara, tel: 626 913 369, www.calimasurf.com; Famara Surf, Avda El Marinero 39, Caleta de Famara, tel/fax: 928 528 676, www.famarasurf.com, for classes at all levels plus equipment; the Quiksilver Surf School, tel: 928 867 307, www.quiksilver-surfschool.com, for surfing (with or without accommodation) in Lanzarote and Fuerteventura; and Windsurf Paradise *(see page 79 for details)*.

There is less surfing in **Fuerteventura**, but Ineika Funcenter, Corralejo, tel/fax: 928 535 744, www.ineika.com,

Lucha Canaria

Lucha canaria is a popular sport that dates back to pre-Hispanic times. It is a form of wrestling in which members of two teams of 12 wrestlers take it in turns to throw an opponent to the ground. The bout *(brega)* is lost if any part of a wrestler's body (except his feet, of course) touches the ground. You are most likely to see the sport at village fiestas, and there is a demonstration in Teguise on Sunday market day, around noon. It also takes up hours of Saturday-night prime-time television on the regional channel, and generates strong feelings. Another traditional local sport is *juego del palo*, or stick-fighting. The object is to keep the body as still as possible, while fending off the blows from an opponent's stave – a stick about 1.8 metres (6ft) long. Again, you are most likely to see one of these bouts at a village festival; ask at a local tourist office.

caters for beginners and advanced surfers, and arranges transfers to the best surf spots on the island.

Diving

For diving in **Lanzarote**'s three main resorts, contact Calipso Diving, Pueblo Marinero, Costa Teguise, tel: 928 590 879, www.calipsodiving.com, which runs PADI/ BSAC courses, plus family

Snorkelling in clear waters

snorkelling excursions; Big Blue Sea Dive Center, Hotel de las Arenas, Playa de los Charcos, mobile: 616 215 734, www.lanzarotedive.de, for children's courses, beginners' PADI courses and advanced courses, scuba diving and wreck and cave diving; Manta Diving, Avda Juan Carlos I 6, Local 5, Puerto del Carmen, tel: 928 516 815, mobile: 649 121 142, www.manta-diving-lanzarote.com, also offers PADI courses and daily dives for groups and individuals, and specialises in 'Discover Scuba' shallow-water dives and snorkelling for children. In Playa Blanca the Rubicón Diving Center, Puerto Deportivo Marina Rubicón, tel: 928 349 346, www.rubicondiving.com, runs courses at various levels and takes Saturday trips to Isla de los Lobos (see page 66).

Diving opportunities are numerous on **Fuerteventura**, especially in Corralejo. Abyss Divers, Pro Centre, Corralejo, tel: 638 722 297 (mobile), www.abyss-fuerteventura. com, is Irish-owned and has a good reputation. Dive Center Corralejo, Nuestra Señora del Pino 22, Corralejo, tel: 928 535 906, www.divecentercorralejo.com, takes divers to more than 40 sites, runs classes at all levels and has an

indoor instruction pool. Punta Amanay Dive Center, Calle El Pulpo s/n, Edificio Dunas Club, Corralejo, tel: 928 535 357, www.punta-amanay.com, runs dives in El Cotillo, El Jablito, Caleta de Fuestes and Morro Jable, although based in Corralejo. In Jandía, there's the Club Aldiana, Ctra de Jandía s/n, tel: 928 541 447, and the long-established Hotel Robinson Club, Playa de Matorral, tel: 928 169 100, www.robinson-espana.es, for scuba diving and windsurfing.

Sport Fishing

Fishing can be social or solitary

The biggest operator in **Lanzarote** runs *Mizu I, Mizu II* and *Mizu III* from Puerto Calero marina, mobile: 609 886 980, www.sportfishinglanzarote.com, offering shark fishing, bottom fishing and trawling on well-equipped boats. Transport to and from your hotel and lunch are included in all-day trips. It also does private charters. *Ana Segundo*, tel: 928 514 322, www.anasegundo.com, runs big-game fishing trips from Puerto del Carmen. On **Fuerteventura**, there's *Barvik* on Corralejo's Muelle Deportivo, tel: 928 535 710, and *Pez Velero*, tel: 928 866 173.

Sailing

In **Lanzarote**, Active Adventures, based in Costa Teguise, offers sailing among its other activities, UK tel: 0871 231 1123, www.activeadventures.co.uk. The Cat Company, www.learn-catamaran-sailing.com, offers catamaran lessons on Top Cat catamarans in Tarajalejo and Las Playitas, **Fuerteventura**.

Boat Trips

Among many companies competing for business in **Lanzarote** are Líneas Marítimas Romero, Calle García Escámez 11, Isla Graciosa, tel: 902 401 666/928 842 055, www.lineas-romero.com, with trips from Orzola to Isla Graciosa five times a day in high summer; and Papagayo Sailing, Playa Blanca harbour, mobile: 610 693 644, where you can hire a yacht and its captain, Alex, for one-, four-or six-hour trips.

Princesa Ico, Puerto del Carmen, is a glass-bottomed catamaran that makes day-long trips to Corralejo, with dolphin-spotting en route. *Princess Yaiza*, Playa Blanca, is a glass-bottomed boat that makes trips from Playa Blanca harbour and Marina Rubicón to Playa de Papagayo four times a day (tel: 928 514 322 for both boats). Many boat trips can be pre-booked online at www.aquaticket.com, and most companies will pick you up from or near your hotel.

Rubicat, Marina Rubicón, Playa Blanca, tel: 928 519 012, is a 23m catamaran which makes all-day trips from the new marina to Playa Papagayo, with opportunities for jet-skiing and snorkelling. Submarine Safaris, Módulo C, Puerto Calero, tel: 928 512 898, www.submarine safaris.com, makes trips beneath the sea in a yellow (naturally) submarine.

The yellow submarine

A jeep safari kicking up dust

Most of **Fuerteventura**'s boat trips tend to be in the north of the island, where the winds and waves are not as strong as in the south. Catlanza, Puerto de Corralejo, mobile: 647 061 991, www.catlanza.com, organises catamaran trips to Isla de los Lobos, with snorkelling, lunch and jet-ski ride included (also trips from Puerto Calero, Lanzarote, to Corralejo, tel: 928 513 022); Excursiones Marítimas, Puerto de Corralejo (buy tickets at the harbour kiosk) run three trips a day to Isla de los Lobos, no frills, and much cheaper than the alternatives. In the south, Subcat, Avda de Saladar 1, Jandía, tel: 928 166 392, www.subcat-fuerteventura.com, takes you 30 metres (100ft) below the surface.

Jeep and Quad Bike Safaris

In **Lanzarote** there are various jeep and quad bike safaris organised by Biosphere Excursions, Costa Teguise, tel: 928 590 304; MegaFun Lanzarote, Puerto del Carmen, tel: 928

512 893, www.megafun-lanzarote.com, runs three-hour quad bike excursions; and Tamarán Jeep Safari, tel: 928 512 475, www.tamaran.com, offers extensive tours of the island from Tahiche to Playa Blanca and will arrange pick ups.

In **Fuerteventura** Tourventura, Caleta de Fuste, tel: 928 163 084, www.tourventura.info, runs buggy safaris, along with other activities; and Fuerte Trike, tel: 928 545 067, www.fuerte-trike.com, organises quad bike tours from various starting points.

Bike Hire and Tours

Road and mountain bikes are available for hire in all the resorts. On **Lanzarote** try Bike Station, Centro Comercial Las Maretas, Avda Isla de las Canarias, Costa Teguise, tel: 628 102 177; in Playa Blanca go to Electro Bike, Centro Comercial Punta Limones, tel: 652 200 570, www.electrobike-lanzarote.com; in Puerto del Carmen there's Renner Bike, Avda de las Playas, Centro Comercial Marítimo 25, tel: 928 510 612, www.mountainbike-lanzarote.com.

Fuerteventura has BikeCenter, Suite Hotel Atlanta Fuerteventura Resort, Calle Las Dunas s/n, Corralejo, tel: 928 535 362, www.mp-sports.de, for bike hire and excursions of varying levels; Backtrax at Hotel Elba Antigua Suites, Caleta de Fustes, tel: 928 160 206, www.backtrax1.com, does off-road motorbike tours; Rent A Bike, Avda Juan Carlos I, Corralejo, tel: 928 866 233, hires bikes and scooters; and Ventura Biking, Calle Gran Canaria 2, Corralejo, mobile: 626 098 459, www.ventura-biking.com, offers mountainbike tours.

Be prepared

Bike and buggy hire and excursions include insurance (check whether it is third-party or comprehensive) and provide helmets, but you must bring your driving licence and a credit card to acts as as a deposit.

Hiking

On **Lanzarote** Canary Trekking, Calle La Laguna 8, Costa Teguise, mobile: 609 537 684 or 696 900 929, www.canarytrekking.com, conducts guided walks in Timanfaya National Park, the Playa de Famara Natural Park, and the protected landscape of La Geria. Windsurfing Club Nathalie Simon *(see page 79)* also offers guided walks through volcanic landscapes. On **Fuerteventura** Caminata, Villa Volcana, Villaverde, tel: 928 535 010, organises a variety of treks on a network of hiking trails.

Horse and Camel Riding

Lanzarote a Caballo, Crta Arrecife–Yaiza, Km 17, Yaiza, tel: 928 830 038, www.lanzaroteacaballo.com, offers treks of varying lengths for beginners and experienced riders. Camel rides are also available.

Taking to the saddle at Lanzarote a Caballo

Golf

On **Lanzarote** Costa Teguise Golf Club, Avda del Golf s/n, Costa Teguise, tel: 928 590 512, www.lanzarote-golf.com, is an 18-hole course open to non-members that also offers lessons. On **Fuerteventura** there's the Fuerteventura Golf Resort, Ctra de Jandía, Km 11, Caleta de Fustes, tel: 928 160 005 or 902 182 282, www.fuerteventuragolfresort.com.

CHILDREN'S ACTIVITIES

There's lots for children to do on both islands, as well as play on the beach. Taking them out in the evening isn't a problem, either, as most restaurants welcome children. Many hotel complexes have entertainment geared to children between three and 10 years old. Most children, except the very young, will also enjoy the boat and submarine trips listed above and many of the activities detailed in the *Where to Go* chapter, such as the bus tour around the Ruta de Volcanos.

Water Parks

There is one on each island. On **Lanzarote** it is Aquapark, Avda de Teguise, Costa Teguise, tel: 928 592 128, with all the usual pools, chutes, slides and activities to suit kids of all ages (daily 10am–6pm). On **Fuerteventura** there is Baku Park, Corralejo, www.bakufuerteventura.com (daily mid-June–mid-Sept 10am–6pm; mid-Sept–Nov, Mar–May 10am–5pm), for all kinds of watery fun in a well-laid-out park.

Go-Karting

Go-Karting Club, Ctra Arrecife–Tias Km 7 (2km/1 mile from **Lanzarote** airport), mobile: 619 759 946, www.grankarting.com (daily 11am–9pm), offers tracks for children aged 16 and under, and 'senior tracks' for the parents; five-year-olds can learn on their own special track.

Animal Attractions

One of **Lanzarote**'s best-known attractions is Echadero de Camelos, Parque Nacional de Timanfaya (daily 9am–5.45pm), where children and adults alike find it hard to resist the fun of riding the camels. Lanzarote a Caballo (daily 10am–6pm; *see page 86*) is a good riding school for adults and children; they also do paintball sessions. Las Pardelas, Orzola, tel: 928 842 545 (daily 10am–6pm) is a family-run place with donkey rides and a playground. At Parque Tropical, Guinate (5km/3 miles north of Haría), tel: 928 835 500 (daily 10am–5pm), exotic birds, monkeys and meerkats are the highlights for children. Rancho Texas, Puerto del Carmen, tel: 928 841 286, www.ranchotexaslanzarote.com, puts on shows several times a day; there are crocodiles, parrots and birds of prey, plus canoes and pony rides (daily 9.30am–5.30pm; free transport from hotels in all resorts).

The reptile show at Fuerteventura's La Lajita Oasis Park

One of **Fuerteventura**'s big draws is Oceanarium Explorer, Puerto Castillo Yacht Harbour, Caleta de Fuste, tel: 928 163 514, with a glass-bottomed, non-diving submarine and a catamaran for dolphin-spotting trips. Also popular is La Lajita Oasis Park, Ctra General de Jandía s/n, La Lajita, tel: 902 400 434, www.lajitaoasispark.com (daily 9am–7.30pm), with camel rides, giraffes, reptiles, sea lions, parrots and birds of prey. At Zoo Safari, Ctra Majanicho, Lajares, tel: 928 868 006, there are camel safaris and a chance to explore the crater of Calderón Hondo (daily departures at noon), as well as shorter camel rides closer to the litttle camel farm.

SHOPPING

Shopping is not a major activity on either island, but there are some interesting items. Among them are consumables: *mojo* sauce can be bought in small jars in many places, as can cactus honey, wine from La Geria and the ubiquitous rum-and-honey liqueur called Ronmiel. Majorero cheese, made in Fuerteventura, can also be bought on both islands.

Aloe vera products of all kinds can be found everywhere. There are some specialist shops and stalls in markets, but products are also available in souvenir shops and supermarkets. Lanzaloe is an ecologically aware organisation based in Orzola that supplies large quantities of aloe vera to pharmaceutical and cosmetics companies. Other items include ceramics – nothing startlingly original, but you can find some good modern copies of traditional pottery – and peridot jewellery *(see page 56)*. There is also hand-embroidered table linen and basket work. The genuine articles are usually found in artisans' centres or museums; because it is such labour-intensive work, they are quite expensive.

Some places in **Lanzarote** worth checking out for comestibles are: Ahumaderia Uga, Ctra Arrecife–Yaiza, Uga, for excellent smoked salmon; El Gourmet Deli, Calle Canalejas 8, Arrecife, which has a good selection of delicatessen items – cheese, ham, *mojo* sauces and honey as well as local wine; and the Bodega El Grifo and Bodega Barreto, next door to each other on the main road at La Florida, which both sell their own wine. The white *malvasía* is best, whether you like it sweet, dry or medium. You can taste before you buy.

For craft work, there is the Centro Artesanía de Haría, Plaza de León y Castillo, Haría, a co-operative that sells pottery, basket work and embroidered items, which can also be found in Haría's Saturday market. A the Centro de Artesanía at the Monumento del Campesino, Mozaga, you can buy traditional-stye items made on the premises, as well as wine from nearby La Geria.

Traditional-style ceramics

The Fundación César Manrique in Tahiche has a good selection of items with the artist's designs, ranging from prints and ceramics to canvas bags, scarves and aprons – all very well-priced. The Fundación also has outlets in Teguise and in Puerto del Carmen (next to the tourist office).

Teguise market is the best-known and biggest on Lanzarote, but most of the goods are not local – a lot of them are made in the Far East. However, there are a number of shops in the town that are open on Sunday and sell better-quality stuff. These include: Casa Atrium in Calle Cruz, which stocks some attractive casual clothes and prints; Casa Kaos, Calle León y Castillo, with a good selection of jewellery and pottery; and Galería La Villa, Plaza Clavijo, a collection of shops selling ceramics, bags and scarves, plus a 'wellness centre' and massage services. Herbolaria Demeter, Calle León y Castillo, specialises in aloe vera products, health food and

Teguise market

candles; and the friendly Frutería La Villa, Calle José Antonio, is one of the few places that sells organic produce.

In **Fuerteventura** Majorero cheese is one of the best buys. Hijos de Vera Montelongo, Calle de la Casa Alta 15, Tindaya, is one of the island's best-known cheese makers, and sells direct from its production centre. La Casa de Ganadero, Calle Salamanca 12, Puerto del Rosario, is an outlet of the Hijos de Vera Montelongo company.

Craftwork on Fuerteventura can be found in the Casa Santa María Centro de Artesanía, Betancuria. Traditional woven and embroidered items and pottery are sold in the museum shop, along with *mojo* sauce, cactus honey, wine and liqueurs. At the Escuela de Artesanía Canaria, Plaza Santa María, Lajares, you can see women embroidering table linen by hand and buy the products.

The best range of contemporary posters, prints and ceramics can be found at the Centro de Arte Canario, Casa Mane, La Oliva, and they are very reasonably priced.

NIGHTLIFE AND FESTIVALS

Most of the the islands' nightlife is provided either in the resort hotels, which usually have middle-of-the-road live acts several times a week, or in the bars and discos of the commercial centres, which tend to have quite a high turnover rate. Temporary structures are often set up on or near the beaches for performances by rock and pop groups. Corralejo and El Cotillo, on Fuerteventura, have the best reputation for rock, pop and jazz – posters and flyers in the resorts will tell you what's on where. The Auditorio Insular in Puerto del Rosario, tel: 928 532 186, has occasional high-quality jazz performances. El Almacén, Calle Betancort, Arrecife, often has jazz, rock or guitar music on Friday nights (the Cabildo puts out a monthly leaflet, called *Cultura*, listing events here and in the theatres in San Bartolomé and Teguise). The centre also has a small cinema which shows art-house films, but these are all in Spanish, as are those in Arrecife's mainstream cinema (Charco de San Ginés).

In October, the Visual Music Festival of Lanzarote stages performances of contemporary music in interesting venues all over the island – chiefly the auditoriums in the Cueva de los Verdes and the Jameos del Agua, as well as the Convento de Santo Domingo in Teguise.

Making music in Corralejo

There is one casino, Gran Casino de Lanzarote, Avda de las Playas 12, Puerto del Carmen, tel: 928 515 000 (5pm–4am; restaurant 7pm–3am; dress smartly and take your passport).

Calendar of Events

6 January Cabalgata de Reyes (Procession of the Three Kings), Arrecife. The kings parade through the streets on camels, throwing sweets to children. Some processions in other towns on both islands.

February–early March Carnival. Celebrations, held in most towns and resorts on both islands, staggered so they do not clash with each other. Several days of flamboyant fun start with the *murgas*, a parade of costumed revellers accompanied by whistles and drums. Carnival ends with the *entierro de la sardina*, a strange ritual common to all Spanish carnival celebrations, in which a papier-mâché model of a sardine is burnt.

Late March–mid-April Semana Santa. The week preceeding Easter is a time of solemn processions.

Mid-June Corpus Christi. Intricately designed carpets of salt, dyed various colours, cover the roads around the Iglesia de San Ginés in Arrecife, where processions are held.

23 June San Juan. On the eve of the saint's day bonfires are lit in some town and village squares. The biggest celebration is in Haría.

14 July San Buenaventura. The island's patron saint is celebrated throughout Fuerteventura but especially in Betancuria.

16 July Nuestra Señora del Carmen. The patron saint of fishermen and sailors is celebrated in most coastal places with processions in the streets and sometimes in decorated boats. The biggest celebrations on Lanzarote are in Puerto del Carmen, Playa Blanca, Isla Graciosa and, although it is inland, Teguise. On Fuerteventura, Morro Jable and Corralejo stage the most colourful events.

25 August San Ginés celebrations, in honour of Arrecife's patron saint include processions and dancing, and last about a week.

Early September Nuestra Señora de los Volcanes. According to legend, the Virgin halted the flow of lava from a volcanic eruption in 1824 and saved the village of Mancha Blanca, Lanzarote. She is honoured with a pilgrimage, a folklore festival, an artisans' fair and bouts of *lucha canaria*.

Mid-November Kite Festival: Playa del Burro, Corralejo. Kite-flyers from all over the world come to this two-day event.

EATING OUT

Canary Islands food has much in common with that of mainland Spain, but with interesting regional differences. There are also dishes similar to those found in parts of Latin America – although whether these recipes were introduced to the New World by Canarian emigrants, or American inventions brought back by returnees, is debatable.

You will also find some restaurants where the cooking is described as *cocina vasca* (Basque), because a number of cooks from this northern region of Spain have come to work on the island or opened their own restaurants here. Their familiarity with Atlantic fish and seafood may help them feel at home. As the Basque region has a reputation for some of the best cooking in Spain, they are a welcome addition.

Where and When to Eat

When it comes to places to eat, the choices are between the fish restaurants that line the seafronts and harbours; the places serving typically Canarian food, which are found mainly in the towns and villages – although there are a few in the resorts; and the all-purpose pizza, pasta and burger joints. There are a few expensive venues, but most are very reasonably priced. You may see restaurants advertising *cocina casalinga* or *comidas caseras* – this simply means home cooking, and, while the quality may vary, it is a sign

Authentic offerings

In the resorts, you may have to bypass numerous restaurants offering burgers, chips, pasta and pizza, not to mention all-day English breakfasts, before you find ones serving genuinely Canarian – or even Spanish – food, but they do exist. And good fresh fish, simply cooked, can be found almost everywhere.

Lunch is served on Playa Blanca's marina

that you will be getting authentic, and inexpensive, island food. There are not many places that style themselves tapas bars, but in many middle-of-the-range and inexpensive restaurants there will be a variety of tapas on offer, and some of the portions are quite large – two or three would make a meal for most people. You will also see *raciones* (portions) advertised: these are larger than tapas, but not full meals.

Bars are generally places in which to drink, not eat, although many will serve sandwiches *(bocadillos)* or a limited range of tapas. A *piscolabis* is a bar serving a variety of little sandwiches and snacks. *(See pages 134–42 for a selection of recommended restaurants.)*

The islanders, like the people of mainland Spain, eat late. Between two and three o'clock is the time to sit down to lunch, and ten o'clock is not too late for dinner. Some restaurants may close between lunch and dinner, but many serve food all day. Those that cater mostly to foreign visitors, aware that habits are different, will have their lunch menus out by midday and serve dinner as early as you like.

Sunday lunch is a major event, and as this continues throughout the afternoon many restaurants are closed on Sunday evening. Some also close one evening during the week, and a number of places will close for a month in early summer to prepare themselves for their busy season in July and August.

Fish

The waters around the islands are rich in fish, which turn up on menus in the restaurants. Along with the ubiquitous *sardinas*, fresh from the ocean, the fish most commonly seen on menus are *corvina* (a kind of sea bass), *cherne* (wreckfish or stone bass), *sama* (sea bream) and *bacalao* (salt cod). You will also find *merluza* (hake), *atún* (tuna) and seafood such as *gambas* (prawns), *pulpo* (octopus), *calamares* (squid) and *almejas* (clams).

Cheese

Fuerteventura is known for its goat's cheese, Majorero, which has been awarded a *denominación de origen controlada* (doc) and is said to be one of the best of its kind in Spain. Goat's milk – which must be unpasteurised to make the cheese – has a high fat content and is very aromatic. The young, fresh cheese has a white rind and a crumbly texture; the matured version has a yellow rind, which may be rubbed with oil or paprika or, sometimes, *gofio*. You will find it on most menus in Fuerteventura, and quite a few on Lanzarote. You will also see cheeses from Gran Canaria: *queso de flor*, a soft cheese that is a mixture of sheep's and cow's milk curdled with the juice of flowers from the cardoon thistle; and *queso tierno de Valsequillo*, which ranges in flavour from mild to strong – the stronger it is the darker the colour.

Fish will often be served simply grilled along with salad, *mojo* sauce and *papas arrugadas (see page 98)*, but there are numerous other ways that it may appear on your table. *Sancocho canario* is a popular dish, a stew made with red grouper or sea bass, potatoes and yams, spiced up with a hot variety of *mojo* sauce. *Salpicón de pescado* is another dish you may see on menus; this is sea bass cooked, chopped and served cold with a mixture of onions, garlic, tomatoes and

Fresh fish can be found everywhere

peppers, topped with hard boiled egg and olives. A delicacy introduced from the Basque country is *calamares rellenos de bacalao* – small squid with a cod-based stuffing, sometimes served in a creamy sauce (a similar dish is made with stuffed peppers – *pimientos*).

Paella is not a Canary Island dish, but you can still find it, along with other rice and seafood dishes such as *arroz negra* (rice with squid and squid ink, which makes it black).

Meat

If you don't like fish, don't despair – there's plenty of meat to be found. *Cabrito* (kid) and *conejo* (rabbit) are most common, but pork *(cerdo)* and chicken *(pollo)* are popular, and there are some good steaks to be had as well. Goat and rabbit are often served *al salmorejo* (with green peppers, in a herb and garlic marinade). Chorizo – the red spicy sausage found all over Spain – also crops up in a variety of guises.

Soups

Most of the world's traditional dishes originated as a way of filling stomachs with what was available and inexpensive. In the Canary Islands, this meant a whole range of substantial soups and stews. *Ropa vieja* (literally, old clothes) may not sound very appetising, but it's a tasty mixture of meat, tomatoes and chickpeas; *puchero* includes meat, pumpkin and any vegetables available; while *rancho canario*, made with chicken, chorizo, bacon, chickpeas and various herbs, is the most elaborate and, some say, the best.

Vegetarians should be aware that even such innocent-sounding dishes as watercress soup *(potaje de berros)*, a staple found on many menus, has chunks of bacon in it, and celery soup *(potaje de apio)* may contain scraps of pork.

Vegetables

The vegetables you are offered will be those that are in season, and, because the island does not produce a great variety and imports are expensive, choice may be limited. Pulses such as lentils *(lentejas)* and chickpeas *(garbanzos)* are used a lot. Canary tomatoes are delicious – although most of those you get here will have been imported from Gran Canaria – and Lanzarote onions are far sweeter than those from mainland Spain. If you like garlic, ask for *tomates aliñados*, tomato salad smothered with olive oil and garlic. *Pimientos de padrón* – small green peppers cooked whole and covered with salt – originated in Galicia and are now found everywhere. Avocados (strictly speaking a fruit, not a vegetable) are served at a perfect stage of ripeness.

Most dishes contain or are accompanied by potatoes *(papas)*. You won't go far without encountering *papas arrugadas* (wrinkled potatoes), which are served with meat and fish or by themselves as tapas. They are small potatoes – the yellow-fleshed Tenerife variety are best – cooked in their skins in salted water, then left to dry over a low heat until their skins wrinkle and a salty crust forms. It is said that this dish originated with fishermen who used to boil the potatoes in sea water.

Mojo

Papas arrugadas, and many meat dishes, are usually accompanied by *mojo rojo*, a sauce whose basic ingredients are tomatoes, peppers and paprika. A spicier version *(mojo picón)* contains hot chilli pepper as well. *Mojo verde* is a green sauce made with oil, vinegar, garlic, coriander and/or parsley, usually served with fish. The sauces arrive at the table in small bowls, so you can use as much or as little as you like. Every restaurant – and probably every home – seems to have their own version, and entire *mojo* recipe books are published.

Papas arrugadas with peppers and *mojo rojo*

Gofio

Made of wheat, barley or a mixture of the two, *gofio* was the staple food of the Guanches and still forms an essential part of the diet today. The cereal is toasted before being ground into flour, and then has a multiplicity of uses. It is stirred into soups and into children's milk, used to thicken sauces, and mixed with oil, salt and sugar into a kind of bread, not unlike polenta. It is also blended with fish stock to make a thick soup called *gofio escaldado*.

Fruit and Desserts

There is not enough rain to grow much fruit in Lanzarote or Fuerteventura, but products imported from mainland Spain or the other islands are usually delicious when in season. On many menus desserts are limited to ice cream *(helado)*, flan (the ubiquitous caramel custard), fresh fruit, dried fruit and nuts, and the one you see everywhere, *bienmesabe*, which translates as 'tastes good to me' – and so it does. There are numerous recipes, but basically it is a mixture of crushed almonds, lemon, sugar (lots), cinnamon and egg yolks.

Dried fruit and nuts are often found on the dessert menu

What to Drink

The breakfast drink is coffee. *Café solo* is a small, strong black, like an espresso; a *cortado*, served in a glass, is a shot of coffee with a small amount of hot milk; *café con leche* is a large milky coffee. An *Americano* is a shot of coffee with added hot water. However, espresso and cappuccino are widely understood terms.

At bodegas you can try wine from the barrel before buying

Hot chocolate is sometimes available for breakfast, but if you ask for tea you will just get a teabag in a little pot.

You are advised not to drink tap water, but *agua mineral* is available everywhere – *con gas* is sparkling, *sin gas* is still. *Zumo de naranja*, freshly squeezed orange juice, is widely available, and in some bars you can get more exotic juices.

Wine is usually drunk with meals, most of it imported from the mainland; Rioja is one of the favourites. But Lanzarote does produce its own wine: *malvasía*, known in English as malmsey. Shakespeare alluded to malmsey several times, and the Duke of Clarence drowned in a vat of it in 1478. Although this is best known as a sweet wine, there are excellent dry and semi-dry varieties, and some reds, although the whites are better. The grapes are grown in the volcanic soil of the La Geria region, where you can visit bodegas, and in the far north of the island, near the Mirador del Río. El Grifo is regarded as the best, but Barreto is also a reputable producer. You will find local wines in many restaurants, usually quite reasonably priced. Neighbouring Gran Canaria has some 32 wineries, and a recently introduced *denominación de origen controlada* (DOC); Monte Lentiscal, which has its own DOC, is one to look out for. Tenerife is a bigger producer, but its wines are not regularly found in restaurants.

Rum, some of which is produced at Arucas, Gran Canaria, forms the basis of Ronmiel, in which the spirit is blended with honey and lemon in a pleasant, sweet liqueur. You may also find Guindilla, a cherry liqueur from Gran Canaria, and Manzana Verde, an apple-based schnapps that is actually made in Cataluña but is widely available here.

Beer is extremely popular. You will see familiar Spanish brands such as San Miguel, and imported German and English beers, along with the Canary Islands' own Tropical and Dorada. If you want a draught beer, ask for a *caña*.

Restaurants with terraces by the sea are always popular

To Help You Order...

Could we have a table?	**¿Nos puede dar una mesa?**
Do you have a set menu?	**¿Tiene un menú del día?**
I'd like…	**Quisiera…**

beer	**una cerveza**	milk	**leche**
bread	**pan**	mineral water	**agua mineral**
coffee	**un café**	potatoes	**patatas/papas**
dessert	**un postre**	rice	**arroz**
fish	**pescado**	salad	**una ensalada**
fruit	**fruta**	sandwich	**un bocadillo**
glass	**un vaso**	sugar	**azúcar**
ice cream	**un helado**	tea	**un té**
meat	**carne**	water (iced)	**agua (fresca)**
menu	**la carta**	wine	**vino**

…and Read the Menu

aceitunas	olives	**langosta**	spiny lobster
albóndigas	meatballs	**langostino**	large prawn
almejas	baby clams	**mariscos**	shellfish
anchoas	anchovies	**mejillones**	mussels
atún	tuna	**melocotón**	peach
bacalao	cod	**merluza**	hake
besugo	sea bream	**navajas**	razor clams
boquerones	fresh anchovies	**ostras**	oysters
calamares	squid	**pastel**	cake
caracoles	snails	**pollo**	chicken
cerdo	pork	**pulpitos**	baby octopus
chuletas	chops	**salsa**	sauce
cocido	stew	**sepia**	cuttlefish
cordero	lamb	**ternera**	veal
entremeses	hors-d'oeuvres	**tortilla**	omelette
gambas	prawns	**trucha**	trout
habas	broad beans	**uvas**	grapes

HANDY TRAVEL TIPS

An A–Z Summary of Practical Information

A

ACCOMMODATION *(Alojamiento)*

Most accommodation on Lanzarote is concentrated in the three major resorts: Puerto del Carmen, Costa Teguise and Playa Blanca. Self-catering apartments are far more common that hotel rooms, and are good value. Elsewhere, there is not a great deal of choice, although there are some very pleasant small hotels in the interior, and several very acceptable ones in Arrecife. You will not find budget accommodation in the resorts. Similarly in Fuerteventura, nearly all hotel and self-catering accommodation is in the main resorts *(see Recommended Hotels, pages 126–33).*

Hotels are rated from one-star to five-star Gran Lujo (GL). Prices within the categories may vary considerably. Prices must, by law, be displayed in hotel reception areas. Breakfast is usually included in the basic rate. Package holidays tend to be the most economical, offering accommodation in large, comfortable hotels and self-catering apartments, usually with pools. Some are known as Aparthotels. Even if you don't want to spend all your holiday in the resorts, they provide a convenient base. It is wise to book accommodation in advance, especially around Christmas, Easter and July to August.

In the interior of both islands there is a growing number of *casas rurales* – rural properties that have been converted into small hotels or renovated and rented as self-catering accommodation. For information, contact www.turismoruralcanarias.com.

I would like a single/ double room with/without bathroom and toilet/shower	**Quisiera una habitación sencilla/doble con/sin baño/ducha**
What's the rate per night?	**¿Cuál es el precio por noche?**
Is breakfast included?	**¿Está incluido el desayuno?**

AIRPORTS *(Aeropuerto)*

Lanzarote's Arrecife airport has two terminals. The new Terminal 1 services international flights. There is a good range of shops, car-hire desks, restaurants, exchange facilities and ATMs. Thursday is 'change over' day in Lanzarote's resorts, which means the departures section can be very busy and best avoided if possible. The airport is about 6km (4 miles) west of Arrecife. There is a bus service to Arrecife every half-hour (No. 22 or 23 at weekends; €1.20).

A taxi from the airport (the rank is next to the arrivals terminal) to Arrecife costs about €12, to Puerto del Carmen around €15, to Costa Teguise €20 and to Playa Blanca €28.

Arrecife airport information, tel: 928 846 000.

Taxi information, tel: 928 520 176.

Fuerteventura's airport is modern and efficient. It is situated about 7km (4 miles) south of Puerto del Rosario and about 9 km (6 miles) north of Caleta de Fuste. Buses run to Puerto del Rosario and Caleta de Fuste every half-hour (€1.80 to Puerto del Rosario, €2.20 to Caleta de Fuste). A taxi from the airport to the capital costs about €12, to Caleta de Fuste about €15 (all rates valid as of 2008).

Fuerteventura airport information, tel: 928 860 600.

Taxi service, tel: 928 855 432/850 216.

B

BICYCLE HIRE *(Bicicletas de alquiler)*

Road bikes, mountain bikes and scooters can be hired in most of the resorts *(see What to Do, page 85).*

BUDGETING FOR YOUR TRIP

Lanzarote and Fuerteventura are relatively inexpensive compared to many European destinations. To give you an idea of what to expect, here's a list of some average prices in euros. A euro was worth approximately £0.80 and US$1.45 at the time of going to press.

Accommodation: Rates for two sharing a double room in high season can range from as low as €60 in a basic apartment or at a *pensión* or hostel (although there aren't many of these) to as much as €400 at a top-of-the-range five-star hotel. A pleasant three-star hotel, which is where you will find the majority of accommodation, will cost in the range of €100–€120. Rates drop considerably out of season, except at Christmas and Easter – although for some reason October is expensive in some hotels. Bear in mind that rates quoted on websites do not bear much relation to what you will have to pay. Most people go to these islands on deals that include flights and accommodation, which usually means that room rates are lower than they first appear.

Attractions: The major attractions such as the Manrique sites and Cueva de los Verdes charge around €7–8; smaller museums around €4–5. More expensive are the family attractions such as the Jardín Tropical and the Aquapark, but these are places where you can easily spend half a day, and there are reductions for children.

Bike hire: between €10 and €12 a day, depending on the bike and the number of days for which it is hired.

Buses: inexpensive. For example, you can go from Arrecife to Puerto del Carmen or Costa Teguise for €1.20.

Car hire: Including comprehensive insurance and tax, rates are around €30–40 a day from the big international companies; you get a better deal if you book for a week and if you book in advance. There are many competing firms in the resorts that will offer lower rates; cars booked in advance via the internet may also be considerably cheaper *(see page 109)*.

Getting there: Air fares vary enormously, with those from the UK to Lanzarote ranging between £100 in November to £400 in August (€145–€585), with spring and early-summer flights somewhere in between; budget airlines, which offer the majority of flights, are, of course, cheaper. From the US, flights cost around $900–1,000. To Fuerteventura they range between £100 in November to around

£280 (€145–210) in August – the lower summer price compared to Lanzarote due to the fact that there are *only* budget flights to Fuerteventura. Cheapest flights are available via the internet, and booked well in advance, or by taking a chance on a last-minute offer.

Meals and drinks: The cheap, three-course set meal called the *menú del día* is found less on these two islands than it is in most other parts of Spain. The average price of a three-course à la carte meal, including house wine, will be about €30 per person, but you can pay a lot less. At the top restaurants you may pay nearly twice that, but there are very few of these.

Petrol: still cheap by UK standards – around €1 a litre.

Taxis: Prices are controlled, and reasonable. From Lanzarote airport to Puerto del Carmen the fare is around €15.

I want to change some pounds/dollars	**Quiero cambiar libras/dólares**
Do you accept travellers' cheques?	**¿Acepta usted cheques de viajero?**
Can I pay with this credit card?	**¿Puedo pagar con esta tarjeta de crédito?**

C

CAMPING

There are three official campsites on Lanzarote (all June–Sept only), but they do not offer much in the way of space or facilities:

• Camping El Salao, Isla Graciosa, tel: 928 845 985 (temporarily closed; call ahead for reopening date)

• Camping San Juan, Famara, tel: 928 845 985

• Camping de Papagayo, Papagayo, Playa Blanca, tel: 928 173 724

On Fuerteventura there are no official campsites, but rough camping is tolerated in some places; check with the local tourist office.

CAR HIRE (Coches de alquiler; see also DRIVING)

You must be over 21, sometimes 24, to hire a car, and to have held a valid driving licence for at least 12 months. You need your passport and a major credit card. It is not easy to find a vehicle with automatic transmission. There are dozens of local companies in the resorts, and these tend to be cheaper, but do check that the cars are reliable and make sure you know what insurance you're getting: comprehensive with full damage waiver (todo riesgo) is more expensive but can save you money, as a mere scrape in a car park can otherwise cost you quite a lot. It may also be cheaper to hire a car via the internet before you leave home. Cabrera Medina is the biggest and most respected of the local companies, with numerous outlets in the resorts and in Arrecife as well as at the airports. The big international companies (Avis, Europcar, Hertz) also have offices at both islands' airports and in the resorts.

- Avis, www.avis.com
- Cabrera Medina, www.cabreramedina.com
- Europcar, www.europcar.com
- Hertz, www.hertz.com

I'd like to rent a car for one day/week	**Quisiera alquilar un coche por un día/una semana**
Please include full insurance.	**Haga el favor de incluir el seguro a todo riesgo.**

CLIMATE

The islands have some 300 days of sunshine a year and an average annual temperature of 20°C (68°F), with midsummer temperatures soaring to 30°C (86°F). There is little rain – what there is mostly falls between October and January. The average sea temperature around the islands is 23°C (72–73°F) in high summer (July–September), and around 18°C (64°F) in winter.

CLOTHING

Light summer clothes, sandals and a swimsuit are all you need for much of the time, but bring a sweater or jacket for cooler evenings and windy boat rides, and strong shoes if you want to do any walking. A jacket for men and a smart dress for women is appreciated, although not obligatory, in the more expensive restaurants. Don't offend local sensibilities by wearing swimwear or very skimpy clothing in city streets, museums or churches, although you can get away with almost anything in the resorts.

CRIME AND SAFETY

Crime rates are not high, but there is some opportunistic bag-snatching and pickpocketing in tourist areas, especially in crowded places such as markets or at fiestas. Robberies from cars are probably the most prevalent, so never leave anything of value in a car. If you have one, use the safe deposit box in your room for valuables, including your passport (carrying a photocopy of your passport is a good idea). Burglaries of holiday apartments do occur, too, so keep doors and windows locked when you are out. You must report all thefts to the local police within 24 hours for your own insurance purposes.

> I want to report a theft.   **Quiero denunciar un robo.**

CUSTOMS AND ENTRY REQUIREMENTS *(Aduana)*

Most visitors, including citizens of all EU countries, the US, Canada, Ireland, Australia and New Zealand, need only a valid passport to enter Gran Canaria. No inoculations are required. Although the islands are part of the EU, there is a restriction on duty-free goods that can be brought back to the UK. The allowance is 200 cigarettes or 50 cigars or 250g tobacco; 1 litre spirits over 22 percent or 2 litres under 22 percent, and 2 litres of wine.

D

DRIVING

Driving conditions: The main roads are generally well surfaced and well signposted – although signage in the north of Lanzarote can be a bit arbitrary. There are lots of roundabouts, but no traffic lights outside Arrecife. The rules are the same as in continental Europe: drive on the right, pass on the left, yield right of way to vehicles coming from your left on roundabouts, but give way to vehicles coming from the right at junctions. Use your horn when approaching any sharp bends. In rural areas, be aware that you may come across a very slow tractor or a large pothole. In Fuerteventura goats may also stray into your path.

Speed limits: 100km/h (62mph) on dual carriageways/motorways, 90km/h (52mph) on primary roads, 50km/h (30mph) in built-up areas; 40km/h (25mph) in residential areas.

There are only a couple of stretches of motorway, around each of the capital cities and their airports, and they are toll-free.

Traffic and parking: In Arrecife traffic can be heavy, parking difficult and the one-way system confusing. Early afternoon (island lunchtime) is a good time to get in and out of town, and you are more likely to find a parking space. In Puerto del Rosario parking is rarely a problem. Elsewhere on the islands there are very few traffic jams or parking problems.

It is an offence to park facing the traffic. Don't park on white or yellow lines. Blue lines indicate pay-and-display parking areas.

Petrol: Petrol is much cheaper than in the UK and the rest of Europe. Unleaded petrol is *sin plomo*. A few of the larger petrol stations are open 24 hours, and most accept credit cards. In the interior of the north of Lanzarote and the interior of Fuerteventura there are fewer petrol stations (*gasolineras*), so don't run too low on fuel.

Rules and regulations: Always carry your driving licence with you. Seat belts are compulsory. Children under 10 must travel in the rear.

Don't use a mobile phone while driving. Obviously, you should never drink and drive.

Road signs: Apart from the standard pictographs you may encounter some of the wordings listed below.

Traffic police: Armed Civil Guards (Guardia Civil) patrol the roads on motorcycles. In towns the municipal police handle traffic control. If you are fined for a traffic offence, you may have to pay on the spot or take your fine to the local town hall.

aparcamiento	parking
desviación	detour
obras	roadworks
peatones	pedestrians
peligro	danger
salida de camiones	truck exit
senso único	one way

Useful expressions:

¿Se puede aparcar aquí?	Can I park here?
Llénelo, por favor.	Fill the tank please.
Ha habido un accidente.	There has been an accident.

E

ELECTRICITY (*Corriente eléctrica*)

220 volts is standard, with continental-style, two-pin sockets. Adaptors are available in UK shops and at airports. American 110V appliances will need a transformer.

EMBASSIES AND CONSULATES (*Embajadas y consulados*)

If you lose your passport, or run into trouble with the authorities or the police, contact your consulate for advice.

Ireland: Calle León y Castillo 195, Las Palmas, tel: 928 297 728.
South Africa: Honorary Consulate, c/o Calle Albareda 54, Las Palmas, tel: 928 265 452.
UK: Calle Luis Morote 6, Las Palmas, tel: 928 262 508.
US: Calle Martínez Escobar 3, Las Palmas, tel: 928 271 259.

Where is the American/British consulate?	¿Dónde está el consulado americano/británico?

EMERGENCIES *(Urgencias;* see also EMBASSIES, HEALTH, POLICE)

Here are a few important telephone numbers, which are common to all the islands:

General emergencies:	112
National police:	091
Local police:	092
Guardia Civil:	062
Traffic police:	928 315 575
Ambulance:	061
Fire brigade:	080

Police!	¡Policía!
Help!	¡Socorro!
Fire!	¡Fuego!
Stop!	¡Deténgase!

G

GAY AND LESBIAN TRAVELLERS

Friends of Dorothy Holidays, tel: 0870 609 9699, www.friendsof dot.com, cater to the interests of gay travellers of both sexes; for more information, visit www.gayinspain.com/canarias.

GETTING THERE

By air: There are numerous budget airline flights direct from most UK airports to **Lanzarote**. The flight time is about four hours. Iberia flies from London Heathrow but goes via Madrid and sometimes via Gran Canaria too, which makes it a long journey, www.iberiaairlines.co.uk.

There are not so many direct flight options to **Fuerteventura**, but Thomas Cook has a number of direct flights, www.flythomascook.com; flights operated by a number of other airlines can be found through www.flydeals.co.uk.

Check the web and advertisements in the travel sections of Sunday papers for good flight-only deals. Many people go to the Canaries on all-in package holidays, which can be the cheapest way.

At present there are no direct flights from the US, but several transatlantic carriers, such as American Airlines, Iberia and Air Europa, have flights via Madrid, although sometimes you also have to make a connection in Las Palmas; the overall flight time is about 12 hours. Connections can also be made via London airports; check with a travel agency, or visit www.opodo.com.

Inter-island flights are operated by Binter Airlines, tel: 902 391 392 or 928 579 433, www.bintercanarias.es, for information, or book through any travel agency. The flight from Las Palmas de Gran Canaria to Arrecife takes about 45 minutes.

By ship: The Trasmediterránea ferry company runs a weekly service from Cádiz to Las Palmas de Gran Canaria and from there there are regular services to Puerto del Rosario and Arrecife. For details, tel: 902 454 645 or check the website www.trasmediterranea.es. Naviera Armas (tel: 902 456 500 or 928 517 912 in Playa Blanca, www.naviera-armas.com) has services three times a week from Gran Canaria to Fuerteventura and to Lanzarote. Naviera Armas runs ferries from Playa Blanca, Lanzarote, to Corralejo, Fuerteventura, seven times daily; crossings take about 35 minutes. The Fred Olsen

Shipping Line, tel: 902 100 107 or 928 495 040, www.fredolsen.es, runs the *Bocayna Express* catamaran from Playa Blanca, Lanzarote, to Corralejo, Fuerteventura, six times a day; the journey time is about 20 minutes (both lines have only five sailings on Sunday). Although they are more expensive, the advantage of the Fred Olsen sailings, for anyone who is not staying in the south of the island, is that there is a free bus service from Arrecife and Puerto del Carmen, which also calls at the airport.

There is also a new service, run by Naviera Armas, from Puerto del Rosario to Tarfaya in Morocco, journey time about three hours. At the time of writing timetables and prices have not been released.

H

HEALTH AND MEDICAL CARE

Non-EU visitors should always have private medical insurance, and athough there are reciprocal arrangements between EU countries, it is advisable for UK citizens and other member nations to do the same, because the arrangements do not cover all eventualities. The European Health Insurance Card (EHIC) entitles UK citizens to reciprocal medical care. You can apply for one online (www.ehic.org.uk), by phone (tel: 0845 606 2030) or by picking up a form at a main post office. Only treatment provided under a state scheme is covered, so before being treated make sure the doctor or service is working within the Spanish Health Service. Leave a photocopy of the card with the hospital or doctor. Dental treatment is not available under this system. Hotel receptionists or private clinics should be able to recommend dentists.

Hospitals: The main hospital in Arrecife is Hospital Insular, Avda Olaf Palme (Puerto de Naos), tel: 928 810 500.

In Puerto del Rosario: Hospital General, Ctra General del Aeropuerto Km 1, tel: 928 862 000 or 920 531 799.

Red Cross (Cruz Roja), tel: 928 812 222.

Private clinics: In the resorts on both islands there are private clinics where you will have to pay for treatment on the spot and reclaim it on your medical insurance. Most have English-speaking staff.

Private clinics in Lanzarote:
Branches of Clínica Lanzarote offer 24-hour service. The 24-hour emergency number is tel: 900 444 999. Clinics are located at:
• Costa Teguise: Avda Islas Canarias, tel: 928 513 171.
• Puerto del Carmen: Avda de las Playas 5, tel: 928 513 171.
• Playa Blanca: Hotel Lanzarote Park, Limones, tel: 928 519 039.
  The Deutsch Britische Klinik medical centres (tel: 928 592 125) are highly visible in all the resorts, and are reliable.
  Hospiten Lanzarote, www.hospiten.com, Calle Lomo Gordo, Puerto del Carmen, provides 24-hour assistance, tel: 928 596 100.

Private clinics in Fuerteventura:
• Corralejo: Centro Médico Brisamar, Calle Nuestra Señora del Carmen, tel: 928 536 402.
• Caleta de Fuste: Salus, Centro Comercial el Castillo, Local 15, tel: 928 163 445.
• Costa Calma: Costa Calma Medical Centre, tel: 928 875 300.
• Morro Jable: Centro Médico Morro Jable, Edificio Don Carlos, Local A, Playa Matorral, tel: 928 540 333/928 541 543.

Farmacias: Most problems visitors experience are due to too much sun, too much alcohol, or food that they are unused to. These problems can often be dealt with by *farmacias* (chemists/drugstores). Spanish pharmacists are highly trained and can often dispense medicines over the counter that would need a prescription in the UK. They are open during normal shopping hours; after hours, at least one in each town remains open all night. Called the *farmacia de guardia*, its location is posted in the window of all other *farmacias* and in the local papers.

Where's the nearest (all-night) chemist?	¿Dónde está la farmacia (de guardia) más cercana?
I need a doctor/ dentist	Necesito un médico/ dentista
sunburn/ sunstroke	quemadura del sol/ una insolación
a fever	fiebre
an upset stomach	molestias de estómago

HOLIDAYS (Días festivos)

1 January	Año Nuevo	New Year's Day
6 January	Día de los Reyes	Epiphany
1 May	Día del Trabajo	Labour Day
30 May	Día de las Islas Canarias	Canary Islands' Day
16 July	Nuestra Señora del Carmen	Our Lady of Carmen
25 July	Santiago Apóstol	St James' Day
15 August	Asunción	Assumption Day
12 October	Día de la Hispanidad	National Day
1 November	Todos los Santos	All Saints' Day
6 December	Día de la Constitución	Constitution Day
8 December	Inmaculada Concepción	Immaculate Conception
25 December	Navidad	Christmas Day

Movable dates:

Carnaval	February or March. Later than on Tenerife and Gran Canaria so dates do not clash; different towns celebrate on different dates for the same reason.
Jueves Santo	Maundy Thursday
Viernes Santo	Good Friday
Corpus Christi	Corpus Christi (mid-June)

L

LANGUAGE *(Idioma, lenguaje)*

The Spanish spoken in the Canary Islands is slightly different from that of the mainland. For instance, islanders don't lisp when they pronounce the letters c or z. A number of Latin American words and expressions are used. The most common are *guagua* (pronounced *wah-wah*), meaning bus, and *papa* (potato). In tourist areas basic English, German and some French is spoken, or at least understood.

The *Berlitz Spanish Phrasebook & Dictionary* covers most of the situations you may encounter during your travels in Spain and the Canary Islands.

Do you speak English?	**¿Habla usted inglés?**
I don't speak Spanish.	**No hablo español.**

M

MAPS *(Planos)*

Most tourist offices will give you free maps, which should be sufficient. If you want something more detailed, you can find road maps in most gift/souvenir shops and supermarkets for around €3.

Do you have a map of the city/island?	**¿Tiene un plano de la ciudad/isla?**

MEDIA

Radio and television *(radio; televisión)*: Many hotels have satellite TV with several stations in various languages, including CNN. TV Canarias is a local station which includes some English-language news and tourist information in its programming. English-language radio stations include Radio FM 95.3 Mhz, Power FM 91.2 Mhz and Waves FM 96.8 Mhz.

Newspapers and magazines *(periódicos; revistas)*: Major British and German tabloids are on sale in the resorts on the day of publication, but English broadsheet newspapers are a bit more scarce. British and German magazines are widely available. The English-language Island Connections (fortnightly), www.newscanarias.net, has island news and tourist information.

For anyone who speaks Spanish, the island newspapers are *Canarias7* and *La Provincia*. Both of these contain listings of events so they can be useful, even if your Spanish is very sketchy, but they do concentrate more on Gran Canaria and Tenerife.

Have you any English-language newspapers?	**¿Tienen periódicos en inglés?**

MONEY *(Dinero)*

Currency: The monetary unit in the Canary Islands, as throughout Spain, is the euro, abbreviated €. Banknotes are available in denominations of €500, 200, 100, 50, 20, 10 and 5. The euro is subdivided into 100 cents, and there are coins available for €1 and €2 and for 50, 20, 10, 5, 2 and 1 cent.

Currency exchange: Banks are the preferred place to exchange currency, but *casas de cambio* also change money, as do some travel agencies, and these stay open outside banking hours. The larger hotels may also change guests' money, but the rate is slightly less advantageous. Both banks and exchange offices pay less for cash than for travellers' cheques. Always take your passport when changing money.

Credit cards: Major international cards are widely recognised, although smaller businesses tend to prefer cash. Visa/Eurocard/

MasterCard are most generally accepted. Credit and debit cards, with a PIN number, are also useful for obtaining euros from ATMs, which are to be found in all towns and resorts. They offer the most convenient way of obtaining cash, and will usually give you the best exchange rate, sometimes indicating the current rate on the screen.

Travellers' cheques: Hotels, shops, restaurants and travel agencies all cash travellers' cheques, and so do banks, where you will probably get a better rate (you will need your passport). It is safest to cash small amounts at a time, thereby keeping some of your holiday funds in cheques, in the hotel safe.

Banking hours are usually Monday to Friday 9am–2pm; large ones may also open on Saturday.

Where's the nearest bank/ currency exchange office?	**¿Dónde está el banco más cercano/la casa de cambio más cercana?**
I want to change some dollars/pounds	**Quiero cambiar dólares/ libres esterlina**
Do you accept travellers' cheques?	**¿Acepta usted cheques de viajero?**
Can I pay with this credit card?	**¿Puedo pagar con esta tarjeta de crédito?**

O

OPENING TIMES (*Horario comercial*)

Shops and offices are usually open Monday to Saturday, 9am–1 or 1.30pm, 4–8pm (although some close on Saturday afternoon). Large supermarkets may stay open all day and until 10pm, as do many shops in the tourist resorts, and some also open on Sunday. Banks usually open Monday to Friday 9am–2pm; post offices Monday to Saturday 9am–2pm.

P

POLICE *(Policía)*

There are three police forces in Gran Canaria, as in the rest of Spain. The green-uniformed Guardia Civil (Civil Guard) is the main force. Each town also has its own Policía Municipal (municipal police), whose uniform can vary but is mostly blue and grey. The third force, the Cuerpo Nacional de Policía, is a national anti-crime unit that sports a light brown uniform. All police officers are armed. Spanish police are strict but courteous to foreign visitors.

National police:	091 or 928 812 350
Local police:	092 or 928 811 317
Guardia Civil:	062

Where's the nearest police station? **¿Dónde está la comisaría más cercana?**

POST OFFICES *(Correos)*

Post offices usually open Monday to Saturday 8.30am–2pm; some open in the afternoon 4–7pm, but it is better not to count on it. They are for mail, not telephone calls. The main post office in Arrecife is at Avda de la Marina 8. In Costa Teguise, it's in the Centro Comercial Maretas on Avda Islas Canarias, almost opposite the police station. In Puerto del Carmen, Avda Juan Carlos I s/n; in Playa Blanco, Avda El Correlillo s/n. In Fuerteventura, Puerto del Rosario's post office is at Avda Primero de Mayo 58; in Morro Jable, Calle

Where is the (nearest) post office? **¿Dónde está la oficina de correos (más cercana)?**
A stamp for this letter/postcard, please **Por favor, un sello para esta carta/tarjeta**

Buenavista s/n. Stamps *(sellos)* are also sold at any tobacconist *(estanco)* and by most shops selling postcards, including supermarkets in the resorts. Mailboxes are painted yellow. If one of the slots is marked *extranjero*, it is for letters abroad.

PUBLIC TRANSPORT *(Transporte público)*

There is no train service. The bus services are cheap and reliable but really only useful for getting from the island's capital cities to the main resorts; buses to other towns are infrequent. (For inter-island ferries and flights, *see page 114–5.*)

R

RELIGION *(Religión)*

The majority religion is Roman Catholic. Respect people's privacy when visiting churches.

T

TAXES *(Impuestos)*

The Impuesto Generalisado Indirecto Canario (IGIC) is levied on all bills at a rate of 5 percent. The tax is not usually included in the price you are quoted for hotel rooms.

TAXIS

The letters SP *(servicio público)* on the front and rear bumpers of a car indicate that it is a taxi. It may also have a green light in the front windscreen or a green sign indicating '*libre*' when it is free. There is no shortage of taxis in urban areas and resorts. Fares are metered, but for longer, out-of-town journeys you may feel happier

How much is it to the centre of town? **¿Cuánto es al centro?**

if you agree an approximate fare in advance. Taxis are good value: the fare from the airport to Arrecife is about €12, to Puerto del Carmen €15, to Costa Teguise about €20 and to Playa Blanca €28. On Fuerteventura, the fare from the airport to Puerto del Rosario is about €12, to Caleta de Fuste around €15.

TELEPHONE *(Teléfono)*

Phone booths *(kioskos)* accept coins and cards *(tarjetas telefónicas)*, available from tobacconists, hotels and machines that you will see in all the shopping centres – they come in denominations of €5 and €10. Instructions in English and area/country codes are displayed clearly in phone booths. International calls are expensive, so have a plentiful supply of coins or use a card. *Cabinas* or *locutorios* – cabins where you make a call and then pay at a desk afterwards – are a more convenient way of making long-distance calls.

Calling directly from your hotel room is expensive, as it is anywhere in the world.

For international calls, wait for the dial tone, then dial 00, wait for a second tone and dial the country code, area code (minus any initial zero) and the number. International Operator: 025.

Country codes: Australia 61, Ireland 353, New Zealand 64, UK 44, US and Canada 1.

Telephone codes for the Canary Islands (which must always be dialled as part of the number, even for local calls): Gran Canaria, Lanzarote and Fuerteventura 928; Tenerife, El Hierro, La Gomera and La Palma 922.

TIME ZONES

The time in the Canaries is the same as in the UK, Greenwich Mean Time, but one hour behind the rest of Europe, including Spain, and five hours ahead of New York. Like the rest of Europe, the islands adopt summer time (putting the clocks forward by an hour) from the end of March through to the end of September.

TIPPING *(Propinas)*

A service charge is sometimes included in restaurant bills (look for the words *servicio incluído*). If it is not included, then add around 10 percent, which is also the usual tip for taxi drivers and hairdressers. In bars, customers usually leave a few coins, rounding up the bill. A hotel porter will appreciate €1 for carrying heavy bags to your room; tip hotel maids acording to your length of stay.

TOILETS *(Servicios, baños)*

Public conveniences are rare. The proprietors of some bars and restaurants do not mind if you drop in to use their facilities, but others keep the key behind the bar to make sure their toilets are not used by the general public or, if they are, that users pay a small sum.

TOURIST INFORMATION OFFICES
(Oficinas de información turística)

Tourist offices abroad:

• Australia: dealt with by National Tourist Office of Spain, 541 Orchard Road, 09–04 Liat Towers, Singapore 238881, tel: 65-6737 3008, fax: 65-6737 3173, e-mail: singapore@tourspain.es.

• Canada: 2 Bloor Street West, Suite 3402, Toronto, Ontario M4W 3E2, tel: 1416-961 3131, email: toronto@tourspain.es.

• UK: Spanish National Tourist Office, 79 New Cavendish Street, London W1W 6XB (appointments only), tel: 020 7486 8077, fax: 020 7486 8034, brochure line, tel: 08459 400 180, e-mail: londres @tourspain.com.

• US: 666 Fifth Avenue, New York, NY 10103, tel: 212 265 8822, fax: 212 265 8864, email: nuevayork@tourspain.es.

Tourist offices on the islands: (open approx. 9.30am–1.30pm)

Lanzarote:

• Airport: tel: 928 846 073 or 928 820 704.

• Arrecife: Blas Cabrera Felipe s/n, tel: 928 811 762.

• Costa Teguise: Centro Comercial Los Charcos, tel: 928 827 130.

• Puerto del Carmen: Avda de las Playas s/n (next to the Fundación Manrique shop), tel: 928 515 337.
• Playa Blanca, El Varadero s/n, tel: 928 519 018.

Fuerteventura:
• Airport: tel: 928 860 604 and 928 866 235.
• Puerto del Rosario: Avda de la Constitución, tel: 928 530 844.
• Corralejo: Plaza Grande, tel: 928 866 235.
• Caleta de Fuste: Avda Juan Ramón Soto Morales 10, Centro Comercial Castillo, tel: 928 163 286.
• Morro Jable: Centro Comercial, Playa de Jandía, Local 88, tel: 928 540 776.

TRAVELLERS WITH DISABILITIES

Arrecife and Fuerteventura international airports and most modern hotels have wheelchair access and facilities for travellers with disabilities, but, generally speaking, facilities elsewhere are not good. Tourism for All is a UK-based organisation that provides information, tel: 0845 124 9971, www.tourismforall.org.uk.

W

WATER *(Agua)*

The islands suffer from water shortage, so try not to waste it. Don't drink tap water. Inexpensive bottled water is available everywhere. *Con gas* is sparkling, *sin gas* is still. If you are self-catering it's cheaper and easier to buy 5-litre bottles from supermarkets.

WEBSITES

www.ecoturismocanarias.com natural parks and rural tourism.
www.fuerteventura.com helpful site for general information.
www.gazettelanzarote.com helpful listings.
www.lanzaroteguidebook.com lots of general information.
www.turismolanzarote.com official Lanzarote tourism site.

Recommended Hotels

Most accommodation on both islands is concentrated in the resorts. Elsewhere, there is not a great deal of choice, although there are some delightful *casas rurales* (rural hotels) in the island interiors, and several very acceptable ones in Arrecife. You will find very little budget accommodation in the resorts. Self-catering apartments are good value and represent a large number of the beds available. Most are in holiday complexes, some called Aparthotels, and usually offer hotel facilities such as a pool, restaurant, etc. You can also rent an apartment on a bed-and-breakfast or half-board basis.

Prices are for two sharing a double room, or a one-bedroomed apartment, in high season. Breakfast is usually included in the rates. Tax (IGIC) is extra if you book independently, but included if you book as part of a package. Prices should be taken as approximate only, and bear in mind that if you take a package deal you will usually pay less than these rates.

€€€€	over €200
€€€	€120–200
€€	€70–120
€	below €70

LANZAROTE: ARRECIFE

Arrecife Gran Hotel €€–€€€ *Parque Islas Canarias, tel: 928 800 000, fax: 928 805 906, www.arrecifehoteles.com.* This 17-storey hotel, recently completely renovated, is smart and glossy, with a conference room, shops, a hairdressing salon, swimming pool, sauna and gym, underground parking and stunning views from the restaurant/bar on the top floor and from many of the well-furnished rooms and suites.

Lancelot €€ *Calle Mancomunidad 9, tel: 902 505 350, fax: 928 826 960, e-mail: info@netreservas.com.* A pleasant modern hotel right by the Reducto beach, with babysitting services, a pool and a restaurant with sea views. A convenient base for a short stay.

Miramar €€, *Avda Coll 2, tel: 928 812 600, fax: 928 801 533, www.hmiramar.com*. A functional-looking building, newly renovated and central, opposite the Puente de las Bolas. Rooms are comfortable, many have sea views, and there's a rooftop bar.

NORTHERN LANZAROTE

HARÍA

Casa Villa Lola y Juan €€ *Calle Fajardo 16, Haría, tel/fax: 928 835 256, mobile: 630 44 66 21, www.villalolayjuan.com*. In the greenest part of Lanzarote, this agreeable little hotel is surrounded by fruit trees and vines. It comprises one villa and two apartments, each with a large terrace. There's a pool and a solarium.

Finca La Corona €€–€€€ *Calle La Rosita, Yé (Haría), tel: 902 363 318, fax: 928 804 209*. Set beween Monte la Corona and the Mirador del Río, with fantastic views. There are six apartments in the main house and a converted stable block, all comfortably furnished in rustic style, with white walls and tiled floors. There's a heated pool, a children's pool, a sauna and jacuzzi and mountain bikes.

La Ermita €€ *Máguez (Haría), tel/fax: 928 842 535, mobile: 659 021 447, www.casalaermita.com*. Four simply furnished apartments, a communal patio and pool, in a small hotel conveniently situated for visiting the Manrique attractions in the north of the island, and about 10 minutes' drive from Playa la Garrita and Arrieta. There are bikes for hire.

ISLA GRACIOSA

Apartamentos El Sombrerito € *Calle Sirena 71, Caleta del Sebo, Isla Graciosa, mobile: 696 942 874, www.elsombrerito.com*. Seven simple apartments a stone's throw from the harbour. Perfect peace.

Pension Girasole € *Calle García Escámez 1, Caleta del Sebo, tel: 928 842 118*. Right by the harbour, there are eight double rooms to rent in this family-run pension and restaurant.

COSTA TEGUISE

Apartamentos Celeste € *Avda de las Islas Canarias 21–25, tel: 928 591 720, fax: 928 592 482, www.apartmentsceleste.com.* Simple, pleasant apartments in an attractive building that is part of the pretty Pueblo Marinero, the nicest area in the resort. Very close to the beach.

Barceló La Galea €€€ *Paseo Marítimo s/n, tel: 928 590 551, fax: 928 590 530, www.barcelo.com.* Comfortable, well-equipped studios and apartments arranged around a pool in an attractive low-rise complex, built in traditional, Manrique-approved style by the beach at the west end of Playa de las Cucharas. All-inclusive packages are available.

Gran Meliá Salinas €€€€ *Avda de las Islas Canarias s/n, tel: 928 590 040, from the UK: 0808 234 1953, fax: 928 590 390, www.solmelia.com.* Right on the beach, this hotel has luxurious rooms, faultless service, and a wonderful lobby and atrium created by Manrique, with pools, tropical foliage and statuary. Hibiscus flowers are scattered everywhere, even in the marble-walled toilets. Such pleasures do not come cheap.

Lanzarote Gardens €€–€€€ *Avda de las Islas Canarias 13, tel: 928 590 100, fax: 928 591 784, www.h10.es.* One- and two-bedroomed fully serviced apartments in attractive gardens grouped around two swimming pools, just back from Playa de las Cucharas. All rooms have balconies. Restaurant, poolside bar. Children's entertainment every evening, and a small playground and children's pool area. Efficient, multilingual staff. Also offers full-board packages.

MOZAGA/SAN BARTOLOMÉ

Caserio de Mozaga €€ *Mozaga, tel: 928 520 060, fax: 928 522 029, www.caseriodemozaga.com.* An 18th-century farmhouse with a flower-filled courtyard and eight double rooms with tiled floors, wood-beamed ceilings and traditional furniture. Tradition is complemented with modernity: air-conditioning and internet access in the rooms. Great breakfasts and an excellent restaurant, open to the public *(see page 137)*.

Finca de la Florida €€ *El Islote 90, San Bartolomé, tel: 928 521 124, fax: 928 520 311, www.hotelfincadelaflorida.com*. In the wine-producing area of La Geria, about 2km (1 mile) from the Monumento del Campesino, this attractive blue-and-white hotel offers 15 comfortably furnished double rooms and one suite. Gym, sauna, pool, jacuzzi, and tennis and mountain bikes are available.

PUERTO DEL CARMEN

Balcón del Mar € *Calle Reina Sofía 23, tel: 928 513 725/928 510 726, fax: 928 511 117, www.balcondelmar.com*. These pleasant apartments and bungalows are up a hill from the beach and harbour. It's a bit of a hike, but it's right by a bus stop and set among gardens, with two swimming pools, splendid views and easy parking.

La Geria €€–€€€ *Calle Jupiter 5, Playa de los Pocillos, tel: 928 510 441, fax: 928 511 919*. Pleasant four-storey hotel at the quieter end of the resort. Rooms have sea views to the side, or garden/pool views. There's a landscaped pool area.

Los Cocoteros €€ *Avda de las Playas 17, tel: 928 510 361, fax: 928 510 872, www.sunlighthoteles.com*. Pleasant white block with Gaudí-esque chimneys. Well-equipped serviced apartments with patios. Most have sea views.

Los Fariones €€€€ *Calle Roque del Este 1, tel: 928 510 175, fax: 928 510 202*. This huge, comfortable 1960s hotel is right by the beach at the harbour end, set in lush gardens. Pool and tennis court. Opposite is the even smarter Fariones Suites Hotel.

Los Jameos Playa €€€ *Playa de los Pocillos s/n, tel: 928 511 717, fax: 928 514 219, www.los-jameos-playa.es*. A large, light hotel with Canarian-style balconies in the spacious reception area. Rooms built around a series of airy white-painted courtyards.

San Antonio €€€ *Avda de las Playas 84, tel: 928 514 200, fax: 928 513 080, www.hotelsanantonio.com.* At the point between Playa Grande and Playa de los Pocillos, where the road becomes quieter and more residential. Looks rather clinical from outside, but is extremely comfortable and well run. Most rooms have sea views.

SOUTHERN LANZAROTE

PLAYA BLANCA

Casa del Embajador €€€ *Calle La Tegala 30, tel: 928 519 191, fax: 928 519 192.* Unusual in Playa Blanca, this is a family-run hotel in an old house that once belonged to a diplomat (hence the name). Right by the beach, it has just 12 rooms and one suite, all well furnished and decorated. There's lots of atmosphere and wonderful views across to Fuerteventura.

Gran Meliá Volcán €€€€ *Urbanización Castillo de Águila s/n, tel: 928 519 185, from UK: 0808 234 1953, fax: 928 519 132, www. solmelia.com.* Spacious and luxurious, this new hotel, which overlooks the Marina Rubicón yacht harbour, has 255 rooms, all with terrraces or balconies, located in 20 separate buildings. There are three conference rooms, five restaurants, several bars, four pools, a gym and spa. Caters to businesspeople and holidaymakers.

Lanzarote Princess €€€ *Calle Maciot s/n, tel: 928 517 108, fax: 928 517 011, www.h10hotels.com.* Part of the reliable H10 chain, this hotel is set back a couple of hundred metres from Playa Dorada beach. The air-conditioned rooms all have terraces or balconies. There are three restaurants, two pools, tennis court, volleyball, children's facilities and entertainment.

Princess Yaiza €€€€ *Avda Papagayo s/n, tel: 928 519 222, fax: 928 519 179.* Right on the beach, this smart hotel has a strong Hispano-Arabic theme to the architecture. Five restaurants offer Japanese,

Italian and Mexican food, among other styles. There's a spa, gym, pools, squash, tennis, and Kikoland, a children's playground.

Timanfaya Palace €€–€€€ *Urbanización Montaña Roja s/n, tel: 928 517 676 fax: 928 517 035, www.h10hotels.com.* Another in the H10 chain, this hotel on Playa Flamingo has Arabic-style architecture, comfortable rooms, a pool, billiards and snooker, a gym and all-weather tennis court, plus babysitting services, a children's play area and free Wi-Fi in public areas.

UGA/YAIZA

Casa El Morro €€ *Uga, tel/fax: 928 830 392, www.casaelmorro lanzarote.com.* Perched on a hillside, this attractive complex offers modern conveniences and comfort in a traditional 18th-century building. Six individually decorated *casitas* surounded by palms and bougainvillea, ranged round a courtyard; small pool and views over the volcanic hills.

Casona de Yaiza €€€ *Calle El Rincón s/n, Yaiza, tel: 928 836 262, fax: 928 836 263, www.casonadeyaiza.com.* Eight attractively furnished rooms, heated pool and jacuzzi, good restaurant in the old wine cellar, gardens full of palms and cacti. The underground cisterns – *aljibes* – have become a small art gallery.

Finca de las Salinas €€€ (**€€€€** at Christmas/New Year) *Yaiza, tel: 928 830 325, fax: 928 830 329, www.fincasalinas.com.* A pink-washed country house, set in attactive gardens, on the road as you drive into Yaiza from the airport. There are 19 rooms, in buildings that used to be stables, decorated in earth shades and furnished with antiques. Pool, jacuzzi and sauna, views over Timanfaya Park.

FUERTEVENTURA: PUERTO DEL ROSARIO

Hotel Fuerteventura Playa Blanca €€ *Playa Blanca, tel: 928 851 150, fax: 928 851 158.* This former parador stands alone, right on the beach between the capital and the airport. In a distinctive – if not beautiful – building, it offers excellent service and ocean views.

Puerto Rosario JM Palace €€ *Avda Marítima 9, tel: 928 859 464, www.jmhoteles.com.* Opposite the port, this modern hotel has comfortable, air-conditioned rooms and friendly, obliging staff.

NORTHERN FUERTEVENTURA

CORRALEJO

Corralejo Beach Aparthotel € *Calle Nuestra Señora del Carmen 3, tel: 928 866 315.* Pleasant, functional apartments in the main shopping street, close to the beach.

Riu Palace Tres Islas €€€ *Avda Grandes Playas, tel: 928 535 700, fax: 928 535 858, www.riu.com.* Huge hotel, renovated in 2007, on the edge of the dunes, 5km (3 miles) from the town centre, with gym, tennis and all the facilities and comforts you would expect, indoors and out. Piano bar and children's daytime entertainment.

EL COTILLO/VILLAVERDE

Apartamentos La Gaviota € *Calle Fuerteventura, tel: 928 538 567.* This large white building sits in a garden close by the harbour and offers basic but comfortable accommodation in six apartments.

Hotel Rural Mahoh €–€€ *Sitio Juan Bello s/n, Villaverde, La Oliva, tel: 928 868 050.* Early 19th-century house built of volcanic stone, with gardens, pool and multi-purpose sports pitch. Bedrooms furnished in traditional style. Environmentally-aware owners. Only about 10 minutes' drive from beaches of El Cotillo and Corralejo.

CENTRAL FUERTEVENTURA

CALETA DE FUSTE

Barceló Club El Castillo €€ *Avda El Castillo, tel: 928 163 101 (from UK: 0845 090 3071), www.barcelo.com.* This beachside complex resembles a well-designed village, with pretty bungalows set in gardens; pools for adults and children, children's playground and several restaurants. Self-catering, B&B, half-board or all-inclusive.

Casa Isaítas €€ *Calle Guize 7, Pájara, tel: 928 161 402, fax: 928 161 482, www.casaisaitas.com*. A delightful place, white-walled with Canarian balconies and a pretty courtyard.

Casa de Los Rugama €–€€ *Ctra Puerto del Rosario–Antigua Km 10, Casillas del Angel, tel: 928 538 224, fax: 928 538 881*. An attractive country house in the centre of the island, with lush gardens and a small pool. Seven of the 13 rooms are in the main house, the others in the converted outbuildings.

Castillo San Jorge €€ *Calle Franch y Roca s/n, tel: 928 163 500, fax: 928 163 501, www.hoteleselba.com*. About 500m from the beach and the same distance from the town centre, this Aparthotel offers comfortable accommodation, in a complex with pools, sauna, restaurants, bars, etc.

SOUTHERN FUERTEVENTURA

JANDÍA PLAYA

Barceló Jandía Playa €€€ *central reservations tel: 902 101 001 (from UK: 0845 090 3071), www.barcelojandiaplaya.com*. Large hotel complex a few minutes from Morro Jable. All modern comforts in an attractive setting, plus four pools, a gym, solarium and restaurants.

Hotel Meliá Gorriones €€–€€€ *Playa la Barca, tel: 928 547 025, fax: 928 547 000, www.solmelia.com*. In a quiet spot at the start of the Jandía Peninsula, this large hotel offers everything you need for a relaxed and comfortable beach holiday, and is the base for the René Egli Windsurf School.

Iberostar Playa Gaviotas Hotel €€€ *Pasaje Playa 2, Jandía, tel: 928 166 197, fax: 928 166 110, www.iberostar.com*. Pleasant all-inclusive hotel right on the beach; air-conditioned rooms with terraces, restaurant, cocktail bar, sauna, two pools and children's pool.

Recommended Restaurants

Fish restaurants, serving fresh seafood of all kinds, line the seafronts and harbours in the resorts and coastal villages. Places serving typical Canarian food are found mainly in inland towns and villages, but there are a few in the resorts. Restaurants advertising *cocina casalinga* or *comidas caseras* serve home cooking – authentic island food. There are a few expensive venues on both islands, but most are very reasonably, and similarly, priced.

Local people eat late – lunch is at 2–3pm, dinner around 10pm – but as restaurants cater mostly to foreign visitors, they serve lunch from around midday and dinner as early as you like, and some serve food all day.

The following price guide (which is only approximate) is for a three-course meal for one with house wine.

€€€   €40–60
€€   €30–40
€   below €30

LANZAROTE: ARRECIFE

Arrecife Gran Hotel €€–€€€ *Parque Islas Canarias, tel: 928 800 000.* On the 17th floor of the island's only high-rise building *(see page 27).* The international-style food is well cooked and well presented – and the views are great.

Casa Ginory €–€€ *Calle Juan de Quesada 7, tel: 928 804 046.* In a narrow street leading from the Charco de Ginés, this small and friendly place serves good seafood and local products such as *setas* (wild mushrooms).

Castillo de San José €€–€€€ *Puerto de Naos, tel: 928 812 321.* Excellent Canarian and international food, including imaginative puddings, in the cool comfort of this Manrique-designed restaurant, with floor-to-ceiling windows giving views over the harbour. Smooth, efficient service – and less expensive than you might think.

ARRIETA

El Amanecer €€ *Calle La Garita 44, Playa Honda, no bookings*. A popular and highly recommended harbourside fish restaurant, open noon–8pm. Arrive before 1pm for lunch if you don't want to queue for a table.

El Charcón €–€€ *Calle de Nuria s/n, tel: 928 835 230/928 848 110*. An attractive little place, right by the quay, with lots of outside tables. Reliably good fish dishes.

HARÍA

Dos Hermanos €€ *Plaza León y Castillo, tel: 928 835 409*. In the middle of town, this busy place serves Canarian specialities such as goat *(cabra)* and rabbit *(conejo)*, as well as seafood. Always busy and bustling at Sunday lunchtime.

El Cortijo €€ *LZ10 on the southern (Teguise) exit from Haría, tel: 928 835 006*. Canarian country food, including rabbit dishes, served in an old farmhouse restaurant.

Restaurant Mirador del Valle €€ *Los Valles (LZ10 between Teguise and Haría), tel: 928 528 036*. Well-cooked local dishes are served at this *mirador* restaurant with stunning views over the surrounding countryside.

ISLA GRACIOSA

Girasol € *Calle García Escámez 1, Caleta del Sebo, tel: 928 842 118*. Close to the harbour, with a terrace and cool dining room. Garlic prawns come in bubbling hot oil, straight fom the oven.

Restaurant/Pensión Enriqueta €–€€ *Calle de la Mar Barloveto 6, Caleta del Sebo, tel: 928 842 051*. Back from the harbour, and easily recognisable by an ancient car and model ship balanced on a first-floor terrace. Reliably good fish. Also rents rooms and hires mountain bikes.

ORZOLA

Perla del Atlántico €€ *Avda Marítima 1, tel: 928 842 525/928 842 589*. Set on a little rocky headland, the Perla commands the bay and serves excellent fresh fish in all the usual ways – grilled *(a la plancha)* is simple and especially good. Watch the boats to Isla Graciosa come and go while you eat. Open daily but 10am–6pm only.

Punta Fariones €€ *Calle de la Quemadita, tel: 928 842 558*. Harbourside restaurant; fish is the speciality, but there are meat dishes as well, mostly grilled, some with *mojo* sauces.

CENTRAL LANZAROTE

COSTA TEGUISE

El Patio €€ *Plaza del Pueblo Marinero, tel: 928 581 102*. Italian restaurant that does a good carpaccio of salmon and interesting meat dishes. Also a full range of pizzas (from a wood-fired oven) and pastas which puts it in the **€** bracket. There are wooden tables set out on a green terrace in the square.

La Graciosa €€€ *Hotel Meliá Salinas, Avda de las Islas Canarias, tel: 928 590 040*. If you want to dress up and really treat yourself, this is the place to come. Elegant surroundings, attentive service and excellent, international menu with wines to match. It's advisable, although not essential, to book. And don't even think about wearing shorts and a T-shirt.

La Ola €€ *Playa de las Cucharas, tel: 928 581 634*. Right on the beach, this open-fronted restaurant with cool blue-and-white decor has the usual offerings on the menu, but also specialises in Basque-style cooking, which means tasty and interesting. It's part of the Lani chain, which has numerous restaurants in Lanzarote, all of a good standard.

Patio Canario €€ *Pueblo Marinero, tel: 928 346 234.* One of the few places in this resort serving genuine Canarian food. There's a wide selection, including *pimientos rellenos de bacalao* (small peppers stuffed with cod, in a creamy sauce). Large, wood-panelled dining room and tables outside in a quiet, shady square.

MOZAGA/SAN BARTOLOMÉ

Caserio de Mozaga €€–€€€ *Mozaga, tel: 928 520 060.* The restaurant in this *casa rural* is known as one of the best places to eat on the island (no lunch on Mon or Tue). Excellent fresh ingredients and some wonderful puddings served in the attractive setting of a converted barn.

Centro de Artesanía €€ *Monumento al Campesino, San Bartolomé, tel: 928 520 136.* Authentic Canarian food: *ropa vieja* (meat, tomatoes and chickpeas), *cabra* (goat) and *conejo* (rabbit) as well as fish, in this intriguing place. You can have tapas at the bar or at outside tables, or sit in the huge, palm-decked, domed restaurant for a full meal. Lunch only. Popular with local people on Sunday, when nobody is in a hurry to leave.

PUERTO DEL CARMEN

El Sardinero € *Corner Calle Nuestra Señora del Carmen and Avda Varadero, tel: 928 511 933.* Cosy little fish restaurant overlooking the harbour, highly regarded by local people.

La Lonja de Fondeadero €€–€€€ *Plaza El Varadero s/n, tel: 928 511 377.* This is *the* place to eat fish. A large, two-storey dining room and a long wooden counter displaying tempting dishes. No outside tables, but it's right by the harbour, and they have their own excellent fish shop next door. Does a great *parillada de mariscos* (grilled mixed seafood).

La Ola €€–€€€ *Avda de las Playas 35, tel: 928 515 081.* Painted pale blue and white (like its cousin in Costa Teguise), with crisp tablecloths and an international menu. There is also the **Asian**

Restaurant on the same site, with vivid, silky cushions and low tables, serving Thai and Indonesian food. Café La Ola has comfy white sofas and sunbeds set around a small pool by the sea, and serves good coffee and cake.

Puerto Bahía €€ *Avda del Varadero 5, tel: 928 513 793*. Another harbourside restaurant with excellent seafood and obliging staff.

Puerto Viejo €€ *Avda del Varadero s/n, tel: 928 515 265*. Excellent fish cooked by a chef known for his creativity. Frequented by local people, which is always a good sign. **El Bodegón** is a tapas bar under the same management.

TEGUISE

El Ryad €–€€ *Casa León, Calle León y Castillo 3, tel: 928 845 931*. Strong Middle Eastern influence, as the name suggests: kebabs, taboule, tajine chicken, etc. in an attractive old house with a patio. The adjoining café does coffee and cake as well as wine by the glass and plates of olives.

Ikarus € *Plaza 18 de Julio, tel: 928 845 332*. Cosy, red-walled rooms. Local fish and meat dishes and lots of different varieties of pasta in this long-established venue.

La Cantina €–€€ *Calle León y Castillo 8, tel: 928 845 109*. A series of small rooms and a patio to choose from in this old house. They specialise in *cherne* (stone bass), *corvina* (sea bass) and other local fish. Very busy at Sunday lunchtime, when everyone's in town for the market.

Patio del Vino €€ *Palacio del Marqués, Calle Herrera y Rojas 9, tel: 928 845 773*. There's a small, elegant dining room and tables in a courtyard under trailing bougainvillea. They serve typical Canarian food and specialise in local cheese, ham and Lanzarote wine. Closes at 8pm, so it's a lunch, tapas or early supper venue and certainly worth popping in for a glass of wine and a snack when you've finished touring the market.

EL GOLFO

El Golfo €–€€ *Avda del Golfo s/n, tel: 928 173 147*. Dining areas upstairs and down, inside and out. Good paella and other rice dishes, including *arroz negra* (black rice).

Mar Azul €–€€ *Avda del Golfo 42, tel: 928 173 132*. Pretty blue-and-white restaurant with tables set right by the sea. Specialises, naturally, in seafood, fresh from the sea and prepared with care.

PLAYA BLANCA

Brisa Marina €€ *Paseo Marítimo 10, tel: 928 517 006/928 517 206*. Green-shuttered seafront restaurant. Lots of fish, simply grilled with *mojo* sauces; efficient service.

El Almacén de la Sal €€ *Paseo Marítimo 12, tel: 928 517 885*. Good fresh seafood and meat dishes served in the pleasant surroundings of a converted salt warehouse by the sea.

L'Artista €€ *Calle La Tegala 18–20, tel: 928 517 578*. Just one street back from the beach, but with sea views, this attractive, green-balconied restaurant serves good Italian food, from *mare e monti* to pizzas and *tiramisú*. There's a good ambience, too.

YAIZA/TIMANFAYA

El Diablo €€ *Islote del Hilario, Parque Nacional de Timanfaya, tel: 928 840 057*. Meat is barbecued over natural heat from the volcano in a large Manrique-designed restaurant with wrap-around views.

La Casona €€€ *Calle El Rincón 11, Yaiza, tel: 928 836 262*. This attractive restaurant is set in an old winery in a *casa rural*, but is open to non-residents. It specialises in dishes made, as far as possible, from fresh local ingredients. Dinner only, except Monday when lunch is served. Closed Thursday.

La Marquesina Puerto €€ *Calle Pisarro 6, tel: 928 530 030*. Specialities include *pimientos rellenos* (stuffed peppers) and *sama sancochada* (sea bream in a spicy stew).

CORRALEJO

Cofradía de Pescadores €€ *Muello Chico 5, tel: 928 867 773*. Excellent fish, as you would expect at the fishermen's co-operative. *Lubina* (bass) baked in salt may be on the menu.

Cordón Blue €€ *Paseo Atlántico, tel: 928 535 554*. Small, simple place by the harbour that serves excellent grilled meat, as well as fish and salads. Friendly, prompt service.

El Rincón de Périco €€ *Calle General Linares 40, tel: 928 535 722*. It's a few metres back from the harbour, so no sea views, but the food is good. There's a *menú casero* that includes typical dishes such as *ropa vieja* and *salpicón de pescado (see page 97)*.

La Marquesina €€ *Calle El Muelle, tel: 928 535 435*. By the fisherman's statue on the harbour, this friendly restaurant is always busy with customers enjoying the fresh fish.

EL COTILLO

El Roque de los Pescadores €€ *Calle de la Caleta, tel: 928 538 713*. Tables set out by the lovely harbour where you can eat plates piled high with locally caught fish – even limpets, if they take your fancy.

Marea Alta €€ *Calle 3 de Abril 1979 25, tel: 928 538 687*. Attractive place on the road to the port, serves 'cocina creativa', including *lubina en papillote* (sea bass baked with tomato and garlic), and a good salad with mussels. Dinner only.

BETANCURIA/ANTIGUA/PÁJARA

Casa de Los Rugama €€ *Ctra Puerto del Rosario–Antigua Km 10, Casillas del Angel, tel: 928 538 224.* The atmospheric, stone-walled restaurant with an outside terrace in this *casa rural* is open to non-residents and has a well-deserved reputation for its Canarian and Spanish dishes.

Casa Princess Arminda €–€€ *Calle Juan de Betancort 2, Betancuria, tel: 928 878 979.* This bar and restaurant opened in 2006 in a house restored by the family who have owned it for 500 years – it's said to be one of the oldest on the island. Shady bar, dining room and pretty courtyard, serving locally produced meat dishes as well as some fish and good puddings.

Casa Santa María €€ *Plaza Santa María, Betancuria, tel: 928 878 282.* In a lovingly restored 16th-century farmhouse close to the church, you can eat roast lamb *(cordero asado)*, kid *(cabrito)* and much more besides. There's also a cafeteria, serving tapas and light meals, on the other side of the road.

Don Antonio €€€ *La Vega del Río de las Palmas (Betancuria), tel: 928 878 757.* One of the best restaurants on the island, serving original dishes made with locally sourced ingredients in a 17th-century country-house setting. Open 10am–5pm, except Monday.

El Molino de Antigua € *Ctra del Sur Km 19, Antigua, tel: 928 878 220.* The restaurant (also open Sun–Mon when the museum is closed) serves traditional island food: *rancho canario* (an elaborate stew), stewed or roast goat, cheese, ham and *corvina* (bass) are usually on the menu.

La Fonda €€ *Calle Nuestra Señora de la Regla, Pájara, tel: 928 161 625.* Opposite the church, La Fonda serves good island food – grilled rabbit and kid *al salmorejo* (with green peppers, in a herb and garlic marinade) and other dishes with *mojo* sauces.

CALETA DE FUSTE

El Camarote €€ *Avda El Castillo, tel: 928 859 070/928 869 073.* A pleasant place to sit and watch the world go by. The menu includes a range of local and international dishes served by helpful waiters.

La Paella, Barceló Club El Castillo €€ *Avda El Castillo, tel: 928 163 100.* Has a terrace right on the seafront. Lots of excellent fish and, of course, paella.

SOUTHERN FUERTEVENTURA

LA PARED

Bahía La Pared €€ *Playa de La Pared, tel: 928 549 030.* Great place, right on the beach with panoramic views from the terrace. The food's good, too.

MORRO JABLE/COSTA CALMA

Cofradía de Pescadores €–€€ *El Muelle, tel: 928 541 909.* Fish straight from the sea, along with *papas arrugadas* and other local dishes in this busy fishermen's bar/restaurant.

Don Quixote €€ *Apartamentos Santa Úrsula, Costa Calma, tel: 928 875 158.* International dishes and local specialities, all well presented.

Restaurant La Laja €€ *Avda del Mar, Morro Jable, tel: 928 542 054.* Great fish stews such as *sancocho canario*, grilled mussels with garlic, and other seafood in a beachside restaurant with a laid-back atmosphere. The service is quite laid-back, too, but no one seems to mind.

Saavedra €€ *Plazoleto Cirilo López 5, Morro Jable, tel: 928 541 056.* A long established place, with good fish, good atmosphere and good prices.

INDEX

Berlitz pocket guide

Lanzarote & Fuerteventura

Second Edition 2009

Written by Pam Barrett
Edited by Alex Knights
Series Editor: Tony Halliday

Photography credits
All photography by Neil Buchan-Grant/Apa
except Andrew Eames 15, Fonnollosa/Prisma
Archivo Fotográfico 18, Eric Roberts 33, Glyn
Genin 97, Profimedia International s.r.o./Alamy
99, Chris Coe 100

Cover picture: 4Corners Images

Printed in Singapore by Insight Print
Services (Pte) Ltd, 38 Joo Koon Road,
Singapore 628990. Tel: (65) 6865-1600.
Fax: (65) 6861-6438

Every effort has been made to provide
accurate information in this publication,
but changes are inevitable. The publisher
cannot be responsible for any resulting
loss, inconvenience or injury.

Contact us

At Berlitz we strive to keep our guides as
accurate and up to date as possible, but if you
find anything that has changed, or if you have
any suggestions on ways to improve this guide,
then we would be delighted to hear from you.

Berlitz Publishing, PO Box 7910,
London SE1 1WE, England.
fax: (44) 20 7403 0290
email: berlitz@apaguide.co.uk
www.berlitzpublishing.com